CHU

NOBO

TIME ON THE GROUND
OR SEEMS TO HAVE AS
MUCH FUN AS YOU --
A GREAT PLEASURE TO
COACH!

Bob Halloran

Destiny Derailed

Millennial Mind Publishing
An imprint of American Book Publishing
American Book Publishing
P.O. Box 65624
Salt Lake City, UT 84165
www.american-book.com
Printed in the United States of America on acid-free paper.

Destiny Derailed

Designed by George Shewchuk, design@american-book.com

Publisher's Note: *This publication is designed to provide accurate and authoritative information in regard to the subject matter covered. It is sold or distributed with the understanding that the publisher and author is not engaged in rendering legal, accounting, or other professional service. If legal advice or other expert assistance is required, the services of a competent professional person in a consultation capacity should be sought.*

ISBN 1-58982-259-5

Halloran, Bob, Destiny Derailed

Special Sales

These books are available at special discounts for bulk purchases. Special editions, including personalized covers, excerpts of existing books, and corporate imprints, can be created in large quantities for special needs. For more information e-mail orders@american-book.com, 801-486-8639.

Destiny Derailed

By Bob Halloran

For Richard

Always Loved, Never Forgotten

Foreword

By Karl Ravech
ESPN SportsCenter Anchor

The current commissioner of Major League Baseball, Bud Selig, has always maintained that for the sport to be healthy, fans of each and every team need to have both hope and faith when spring training begins—hope and faith that their team has a chance to play for a World Series championship. Boys and girls who grow up in New England have been lucky enough to have had both hope and faith nearly every spring when their beloved Red Sox first get together in Florida. Those same boys and girls become grandfathers and grandmothers and, sadly, each year—as reliable as snow in December—hope and faith turn to disappointment and despair. The 2003 season was destined to be different.

As a little boy growing up in Needham, Massachusetts, I had no choice but to be a Red Sox fan. Through my childhood years I had heard about 1918, the year the Red Sox last won a World Series. I knew Babe Ruth once played for Boston and was told about the exploits of the "greatest hitter who ever lived," Ted Williams. My generation was raised on the "Rooster," Rick Burleson, Rico Petrocelli, and Yaz. They gave way to guys named Fred Lynn and Jim Rice, El Tiante and Oil Can Boyd, the Eck and Wade Boggs. Each one of the teams these guys played for always had me believing that this was going to be the year. And when the season ended in disappointment, right away the refrain was "wait till next year."

The winters in New England can be painfully long. Cold mornings and even colder nights. The extra blanket becomes your best friend and your dreams take you to warmer places, like Fenway Park and Yankee Stadium.

Dreams allow us to see things the way we want to see them. In dreams the Red Sox can win the World Series, Grady Little can take Pedro Martinez out before he allows the final nail to be driven into the coffin. Humans are capable of having hundreds of dreams a night but only certain ones do we remember. If only we could keep a diary of the nightly trips we take in our sleep.

What would we learn about ourselves? In New England, you're likely to realize how significant a role the Red Sox play in your life. We live and die with the hometown team and that's the beauty of dreams. As Heart sang in the song These Dreams, "it's funny how your feet in dreams never touch the earth." In dreams we don't die. Neither do baseball fans. We can get kicked and dragged and brought to the brink, but we keep coming back for more. There is always next year, and there is always 2003.

Preface

I've always known that God didn't bless me with extraordinary height, might, insight, or the ability to choose a first wife wisely. But in early February 2003 I was struck with an overwhelming feeling that had me believing that God had once again revealed the future to me.

I'm not a psychic or a member of the lunatic fringe. I've only had this feeling twice before. Each time, the future appeared in a kind of lucid dream—so real that I awoke certain the event had already happened. The first dream came true. The other remains a distinct possibility. And now I've had a third.

The first divination occurred when I was eleven years old. I dreamed that I had won my soccer league's Most Outstanding Player Award. This was odd for at least two reasons. First, I wasn't *that* good. And second, no such award existed. At least, I had never heard of it. It was always "Most Valuable," not "Most Outstanding."

Still, at an awards ceremony about a week later, the coach stood up to present a new award created in memory of a teammate who had died earlier that year. "And the award for the Most Outstanding Player goes to…" Yep, me. I was happy, excited, and totally freaked out. I was attending Catholic school and suddenly had proof that God was speaking directly to me. Try carrying that weight around with you when your private thoughts stray toward the slightly less moral. God was all over me—protecting, loving, judging. Let's just say it was a bit unsettling. So was the next premonition.

About five years later I had a dream in which I attended my own funeral. I thought I had had the dream because I'd been reading *Tom*

Sawyer. But there was so much detail, and the truth of it seemed so powerful, that I had to believe it when a man in the back of the church said, "And he was only forty-four-years old." Thankfully, I remain a cynic, and I don't put much stock in silly, little dreams, but I've always wondered what it's going to be like on my forty-fourth birthday. The dream didn't specify if I had just turned forty-four or if I was approaching forty-five, so I expect that whole year—assuming I get there—will be full of trepidation and anxiety. Will I fly on vacation? Exceed the speed limit? Exercise more? It's only four years away now. I've never had the dream again, but I've never forgotten it, nor have I forgotten the feeling that accompanied it. And here it is again.

I woke up one morning simultaneously exhausted and exhilarated. I had had another one of my "divine prophecies," and it took a few seconds to rub the clairvoyance from my eyes and accurately distinguish reality from virtual reality. But for those few fantastic moments, I believed the Boston Red Sox had won the World Series. The dream had that "soccer award, dead at forty-four" feeling all over it. Each year, I am among the more confident Red Sox fans coming out of spring training, but this time I feel I've got a higher power on my side. Of course, if I'm right, I'm also a dead man. But at least I'll die happy, having had four years to bask in the glow of a Red Sox championship. For now, I'm enjoying the feeling that this year I won't have to wait till next year. And I've decided to affirm my faith by keeping a *Diary of Destiny*. It will be an account of what history will remember, and what the future has already seen.

1

Spring Training

FEBRUARY 14

Happy Valentine's Day! There hasn't been too much to think about or react to other than the Red Sox endless pursuit of Kevin Millar. Today, Millar was returned to the Florida Marlins by the Chunichi Dragons, thus clearing a path for him to eventually join the Red Sox. Millar had signed a $6.2 million contract to play in Japan, but then decided he didn't want to play there. It took a lot of negotiating and apologizing for Millar to win his release from Chunichi, but he finally did. Now he's the property of the Marlins and likely to be traded or sold to the Red Sox. Ah, freedom! Thy fickle friend.

When I spoke to Red Sox general manager Theo Epstein about Millar a few weeks ago, I said, "This seems like a lot of time, effort, and expense for a guy who's probably going to be your fourth outfielder." And he scoffed. He was on the phone, but I could tell he was scoffing. Epstein went on to explain that Millar would be much more than a fourth outfielder. "He's one of the best kept secrets in baseball," Epstein said, adding that if Millar got over 500 at bats he might lead the league in doubles. That's when I scoffed. But then I looked it up, and sure enough "Stat Man Caruthers" was right. In just 438 at bats with the Tampa Bay Devil Rays last season, Millar cranked out 41 doubles. He also hit .306 and drove in 57 runs. The year before, he had 39 doubles and 85 RBI in 144 games. So, no doubt about it, Millar can hit. But the question remains:

how is he going to get 500 at bats? My guess is he'll do a lot of DHing while David Ortiz and Jeremy Giambi fight for time at first base.

FEBRUARY 15

Pedro Martinez came to camp—on time—and with an agenda. Once the cameras started rolling and the scribes had clicked their pens, readying themselves to jot down every word the Great One would say, Pedro issued an ultimatum. He informed everyone that if the Red Sox don't pick up the option on his contract by the end of spring training, he will walk at the end of the 2004 season. Pedro maintains it's a matter of respect, but I think he's running scared. The option is for $17.5 million, and he wants that money in his back pocket *now*, because he's afraid of getting hurt this season—in which case he may never see an annual salary that high again. When he signed the contract, he agreed the Red Sox would have until November to decide whether to extend his contract another year. Why is he changing the rules in the middle of the game? What's changed?

He says, "If they don't pick it up now, it means they don't trust how I feel." But in truth, it's Pedro who doesn't trust how he feels. If he did, he'd have the confidence that a certain series of events will take place. First, he'll have another Cy Young-caliber, injury-free season. Then, the Red Sox would pick up his option, he'd have another outstanding year in 2004, and somewhere along the line he'd receive another multiyear, mega-million dollar contract either from the Red Sox or from some other team. If he "trusts" how he feels, he'd also trust that his performance level would be high enough that money matters would take care of themselves—as they always do for healthy players who excel. Why the deadline, then? Because Pedro knows it's extremely unlikely that he'll be hurt during spring training, when everyone is monitored so closely and pampered so diligently. But Pedro knows that once the season starts and he lets it all hang out, he could run into the same arm problems he's had over the past couple of years. And if he does, he knows his chances of getting that $17.5 million go down with every missed start.

The best quote from Pedro during his media session was "Would you stay with a woman that tells you she doesn't love you?" He was intimating that if the Red Sox don't pick up his option, it would be tantamount to their saying they don't love him. But I think the better question is "Would you marry someone and give them the option of leaving you after five years?" That's what Pedro did. He jumped into a union with someone (the

Red Sox) and essentially signed a prenuptial agreement that guaranteed him a certain amount of money during the marriage, and a certain amount if the marriage fell apart. (Pedro gets $2 million if the Red Sox don't pick up his option.) It's dangerous to compare business relationships with marriages, especially in sports, because there's always the issue of trades.

Still, I hope the Red Sox and Pedro kiss and make up. Whenever there's a divorce, it's the children who suffer. In this case, the children are the fans, and it's no fun watching mommy and daddy fight—especially when Daddy has won two Cy Young Awards while going 87-24 over the past five years. Also, the worries about Pedro's injury problems seem to be blown way out of proportion. He's made at least 29 starts in seven of the last eight seasons. The only time he didn't was 2001 when he made only 18 starts. That was a troublesome year, but he bounced back in 2002 and won 20 games while leading the league with a 2.26 ERA and 232 strikeouts. Fans can worry about Pedro, because if he goes down, so do the Red Sox. But we have more reasons to expect him to be healthy this year than reasons to believe he'll be hurt.

Pedro also accused New York Yankees owner George Steinbrenner and Chicago White Sox owner Jerry Reinsdorf of pulling "a little trick" in order to keep 20-game winner Bartolo Colon away from the Red Sox. Colon, highly pursued by the Red Sox, ended up going from Montreal to Chicago in a three-team deal that involved the Yankees' sending the aging and recently injured Orlando Hernandez to the soon-to-be-defunct Montreal Expos. Red Sox president Larry Lucchino threw the first punch when he called the Yankees the "Evil Empire" during the winter, primarily because they outbid the Sox for Cuban pitcher Jose Contreras. Now, Pedro casts suspicion upon the Yankees. I don't like his stand regarding his contract, but I love the way he stands up to the Yankees. He really seems to hate them. And I love that about him. It should be a great season!

FEBRUARY 18

It's Nomar Garciaparra's turn to grab headlines by complaining about something. This was fun—coming just days after Pedro's power play. I don't think the Red Sox have had back-to-back, blockbuster stories like this since they hired Euclides Rojas as bullpen coach and Jerry Narron as bench coach on December 2 and 3. And you thought those were big!

Now Nomar is telling the *Boston Globe*'s Dan Shaughnessy that he doesn't "know how to act this year." Well, he could start by acting like a .320 hitter with 30 home run power. That's all anybody really wants from him anyway.

We all learned a long time ago that Nomar's not much of a "voice" in the clubhouse. He's not Mister Soundbite or much of a friend to the media. He leads by example. He's a star who doesn't ask or demand to be treated like one. He shows up early, works hard, plays hurt, and is responsive to and appreciative of the fans.

But he may be the least charismatic star Boston has ever seen, and as a result he is merely respected and not adored. Maybe that's starting to bother him a little bit. Either that or he is extremely thin skinned, because this is a guy who almost never gets criticized. In fact, there's very little to criticize him for other than the occasional errant throw. But throughout the off-season, Nomar apparently carried with him, and obsessed about, one nearly undetectable criticism from a local writer.

The *Boston Herald*'s Steve Buckley had written a column some six months ago in which he basically said that if Nomar's so unhappy in Boston, he should leave. Buckley also falsely accused Nomar of calling the official scorer to have an error against him changed to a hit. Nomar wasn't about to forgive Buckley, despite his repeated apologies. Plus, Nomar took offense to the accusation that he's not happy. "You ask my teammates and my coaches. Nobody says I'm unhappy," Nomar told the *Globe*. Well, on his first day in camp, he sure gave the impression that he's not particularly happy with *all* aspects of playing in Boston. He may like the organization. He may love the fans. But he made his distaste for the media very clear on day one. I don't expect to hear much more from Nomar this spring.

FEBRUARY 19

Heard more from Nomar today. It was all good. After hitting 24 homers and driving in 120 runs last season, Garciaparra says, "The wrist feels wonderful." That confidence wasn't there a year ago when he was still trying to come back from wrist surgery. I had almost forgotten that Nomar only played in 21 games in 2001, because he had had surgery on his right wrist on April 2 of that year. It's really been about 2 1/2 years since Nomar played at 100 percent. He's definitely a tough guy—playing in 156 games last year—but if he's truly healthy, he could start putting up some monster numbers. With the Red Sox boasting a lineup that includes Nomar, Manny Ramirez, Johnny Damon, Kevin Millar, and Jeremy Giambi, I think Damon was right when he said, "Teams should fear our offense." Regarding the Red Sox emphasis on on-base percentage, free-swinging shortstop Nomar said, "I'm still going to be swinging at the first pitch…still going to be doing everything I normally do."

That's good. But that means he'll still be fiddling with his batting gloves every single at bat—which is about as irritating as foot fungus.

FEBRUARY 20

In much the same way that Nomar still feels burned by Steve Buckley's column, Manny Ramirez is still stinging from the backlash of criticism he received after failing to run out a ground ball last September against Tampa Bay. For this reason, and probably a host of others, Ramirez is refusing to speak with the media. In fact, based on the unnecessary upheaval caused by Nomar and Pedro on their first days in camp, I don't think it's such a bad idea for Ramirez to become the "Quiet Man." I wouldn't mind at all if I never heard from him again. We often joke about athletes' clichés, such as taking "one game at a time" or "giving 110 percent," yet we continue to harbor an insatiable appetite for their vapid words. It's like Oliver Twist eating a horrible meal but then imploring the man in charge, "Please, sir, I want some more."

Can you imagine a world in which professional athletes didn't speak? Sounds peaceful, doesn't it? Sounds like a grammatically correct world with no bleep-filled soundbites, no overused clichés, and nobody talking in the third person. Too bad such a world is inconceivable.

Not even John Lennon could sell that idea. I believe in the original version of Lennon's optimistic plea to a violent and exclusionary world, he wrote:

> Imagine there's no heaven. It's easy if you try.
> No hell with athlete blather. Above us, only sky.

But he scratched that idea for something more plausible—like a world without countries—which is probably why "Imagine" never made it as the Olympic theme song.

You may say I'm a dreamer, but occasionally, by making an effort to shut up, athletes raise the possibility that such a world could exist.

Ramirez began his silence while immersed in a race for the batting title. When he won the title, he walked out of the Red Sox clubhouse on the last day of the season without a word. That was fine with me.

I say bring back Prohibition. Let's drink to the sounds of silence in the locker rooms! Close your eyes and imagine it. You've just watched a great game. The final out. The final whistle. It's a wonderful moment. And nothing needs to be said.

Now, where was I? Oh yeah, Manny Ramirez isn't talking. It's gonna be a great season!

FEBRUARY 21

Look who's talking. Ramirez won't, but Pedro will. He's volunteered to be Manny's go-between with the media this year. If you want to know how Manny's feeling, just ask Pedro.

But the real news of the day is Pedro's softening his contract demand. On sports talk radio WEEI's Dennis and Callahan morning show, Pedro said that it wasn't an absolute certainty that he'd leave at the end of the contract if the team waits until November to address the option.

"I'm not forcing them; I'm not saying they have to…I wouldn't guarantee I would walk. I'll have to see if it's going to be worked out," he said.

Later he told a group of reporters that he's done talking about his contract status in the press: "I'm going to shut my mouth and do what I have to do. Let it be a guess. Is it a bluff? Just wait. Is it not? Wait. I'll keep everybody guessing."

Great, it'll be like a game. Folks can put together an office pool: If you think Pedro's going to stay, you have to pick the date upon which he receives a new contract. And if you think he's going to walk, you have to pick the day the Red Sox announce they're not going to pick up his option. Who's in for five dollars?

More to the point, it would seem that Pedro miscalculated how his mandate would play in the press and among the fans. I suspect he was supremely confident that if he threatened to leave, there would be a hue and cry from the fans, demanding that the Red Sox submit to his wishes and ensure his long tenure in Boston. That didn't happen. Instead, he was criticized for not wanting to abide by the terms of his contract, for behaving in a self-serving manner on the first day of spring training, and for substituting the word "respect" for the word "money." Plus, there were countless references to his slight frame, and vocalized doubts that he would have more than a few more healthy or dominating seasons. It took about six days, but finally Pedro had had enough. So, he folded up his tent and gave up the fight—for now. Of course, he still has us all guessing.

Pedro says he's done talking about his contract, but if his option isn't picked up by the end of spring, somebody's bound to ask him about it. If I get a chance to do it, I think I'll phrase it like this, "Pedro, without getting into an area you'd like to avoid, let me just ask you for a simple 'yes' or 'no' answer. Do you still have an open mind about staying with the Red Sox past next year?"

That really seems innocuous enough. I'm sure he'd still get upset, though.

FEBRUARY 24

What a long, strange trip it's been. But Kevin Millar's journey from Tampa Bay to Japan to Boston has officially ended. He signed a two-year, $5.3 million contract with an option for $3.5 million in 2005. The option officially kicks in if Millar registers more than 800 at bats over the next two seasons. After all the Red Sox went through to get this guy, he'd better average 400 at bats.

At one point during what Millar called "a six-week battle," the Chunichi Dragons threatened to place Millar on the suspended list, which would have prevented him from playing in either Japan or the U.S. for the next two seasons. Fortunately, the Major League Baseball Players Association jumped in and threatened to cancel the season-opening visit to Tokyo by the Seattle Mariners and Oakland A's. Things got nasty, and it was beginning to verge on an international incident. The Red Sox must think Millar's worth it, though, and the only way for that to be true is if he's in the lineup just about every day, getting more than 500 at bats per season.

The first three at bats for Millar last season were rather interesting—he was using a bat he had sprayed with deer urine. As the story goes, Millar was hunting with some friends who told him the scent of deer urine attracts bucks. Millar told the *Miami Herald* that he wasn't aware he was only supposed to put a drop of the urine on his shoes.

Instead, Millar said that he had been "putting it on like Calvin Klein cologne."

For whatever reason, Millar promised to use the deer urine on his bat on opening day. But he abandoned the idea after going 0-3.

Quick questions: Where do you get deer urine? And *how*? Do you sneak up on a deer while it's sleeping and stick its hoof in warm water?

Oddly enough, that wasn't the only urine story this spring. Florida Marlins right-hander Josh Becket said that he received lots of home remedy ideas to help him with a recurring blister problem. One fan (or maybe not a fan) wrote him and suggested Becket dip his finger in—you guessed it—urine. Supposedly, the acid in the urine would work like pickle brine. But then, the question begs to be asked: if the urine works like pickle brine, why not just use—oh, I don't know—*pickle brine*!

FEBRUARY 26

Can the Red Sox win the World Series without having one true closer? The answer is "yes," because teams have done it before. Consider the 2000 Arizona Diamondbacks, who began the year with Matt Mantei as closer. When he got hurt, the bulk of the responsibility went to Byung-Hyun Kim, who finished with 19 saves, and Bret Prinz had nine saves.

The 1975 Cincinnati Reds got 22 saves from Rawly Eastwick, 15 from Will McEnaney, seven from Clay Carroll, and five from Pedro Borbon. Eastwick was the primary closer, with two wins and one save in the World Series against the Red Sox, but it was McEnaney who got the save in Game Seven.

Perhaps more than any other manager, Tony LaRussa is credited with the evolution of the closer, but even he spread the wealth on his way to leading the Oakland A's to a World Series championship in 1989. Dennis Eckersley was the main man with 33 saves, but LaRussa also had faith in Rick Honeycutt, who saved 12 games that year, and Todd Burns, who saved eight others.

But the best example of a successful committee is the 1990 Cincinnati Reds. Rob Dibble, Randy Myers, and Norm Charlton—known as the "Nasty Boys"—anchored their pen. Myers and Dibble were a righty-lefty combination similar to that of Roger McDowell and Jesse Orosco for the 1986 World Series champion New York Mets. McDowell had 22 saves. Orosco had 21.

But the Nasty Boys were a three-headed monster—powerful, intimidating, and extremely effective. And the other pens were nearly as deep, or else anchored by one of the best closers in the history of the game, Dennis Eckersley.

Nobody expects the Red Sox bullpen to be as good as those "committees," but fingers are crossed that the Red Sox have a team that could ultimately compare to the 1988 Los Angeles Dodgers. Jay Howell led the Dodgers in saves that year with 21, but he appeared in 50 games, which tells you he wasn't used exclusively as a closer. Alejandro Pena had 12 saves in 60 appearances, and Jesse Orosco added nine more saves in 55 games. Even Tim Belcher, who started 27 games, also made nine relief appearances, finishing the year with a 12-4 record and four saves. Dodgers manager Tommy Lasorda counted on his pitching staff to fulfill a variety of roles, and when called upon, his guys did the job. Red Sox manager Grady Little will be hoping for the same this year. We'll see.

FEBRUARY 27

"Fat, drunk and stupid is no way to go through life, son." Dean Farber's line from *Animal House* might have been a better title for David "Boomer" Wells's new book The Yankees portly lefthander ticked off several of his teammates by writing a book entitled, *Perfect I'm Not! Boomer on Beer, Brawls, Backaches and Baseball.* Undoubtedly, Boomer has now written exactly one more book than he's ever read.

Basically, Boomer has lowered the boom and thrown the book at baseball. "As of right now," Wells dictated to someone who can type (Chris Kreski, who also wrote *Growing Up Brady* with Barry Williams), "I'd estimate 25 to 40 percent of all major-leaguers are juiced. But that number's fast rising."

It's the same claim that Jose Canseco and Ken Caminiti made in 2002. It's really a shame we only get these stories from undependable and less reputable players. Canseco's been arrested several times and was in a South Florida jail when excerpts from Wells's book were released. Caminiti was in drug rehab. And of course, Wells is trying to sell his book.

Among other beauties in Wells's book is his claim that he pitched his 1998 perfect game "half drunk" after attending a cast party for *Saturday Night Live*. First of all, there's no way it's true. Secondly, he sounds like a college blowhard trying to impress some undiscerning fool by bragging about how hard he can party. And lastly, can you be half drunk? I think you're either drunk or you're not. It's kind of like being half pregnant. Judging by Wells's gut, I'd be more likely to believe he was half pregnant. That's not sweat you see on Wells's shirt when he's pitching. He's lactating!

Wells also got the Yankees' spring off on the right foot by criticizing teammates Andy Pettitte, Mike Mussina, and even Roger Clemens. The criticisms weren't especially harsh or revealing, but that's what makes them so unnecessarily stupid.

I did see a quote from Clemens in which he says he calls Wells "Ely," "because if a story lasts more than 30 seconds, he's lying." Very clever. Makes me certain that Clemens didn't come up with it himself.

FEBRUARY 28

Jose Contreras got lit up—five runs in two innings, including a grand slam to the Reds' Adam Dunn. Contreras was a very big deal during the off-season. He was the guy the Red Sox targeted more than any other player (not named Millar, that is). But the Yankees lured him away with a four-year, $32 million contract—a move that triggered Red Sox CEO Larry Lucchino's "Evil Empire" reference.

Anyway, it was nice to see Contreras do so poorly, even if it was only his first spring training outing. Contreras and Japanese slugger Hideki Matsui are prime examples of people (read: the media) believing that everything the Yankees do is right. The Yankees got 'em, so they must be great. I remember during the 2001 off-season when the Yankees got Jason Giambi, Rondell White, Robin Ventura, and John Vanderwahl, and everyone thought they'd go 162-0. But they lost Paul O'Neill, Chuck Knoblauch, Tino Martinez, and Scott Brosius. It was a lot of maneuvering, but I expected it to come out pretty even statistically. They also gave up several so-called character guys who had contributed to World Series championship teams and picked up a bunch of question marks. Meanwhile, the pitching staff was another year older. So, I wasn't convinced the Yankees had improved at all. Then they went out and won 103 games, so I felt like a fool. When they got bumped in the first round of the playoffs, I felt much, much better.

I've often said that one of the best things about being a Red Sox fan is that you have two things that can make you feel like you're sitting on top of the world. First, if the Red Sox win the World Series. And second, if the Yankees don't. Since the Red Sox haven't won it all since 1918, the best feeling I have every year comes on the day the Yankees get eliminated.

Some of that is jealousy, but most is because of the overhyped respect the Yankees get for spending their money wisely. What a load! It doesn't take a genius to know that the best pitcher on the free agent market is Mike Mussina, or that the following year the best free-agent hitter available is Jason Giambi. Then, if it looks like the Yankees haven't spent their money wisely enough already, they'll pick up a guy like Raul Mondesi for the stretch drive. If that doesn't work out—and it didn't—they'll go out and spend another $53 million on two guys who've never played Major League Baseball—Contreras and Matsui. The Yankees' actual payroll for 2003 is about $155 million, $24 million higher than last season's. Throw in a few luxury tax penalties, and the total jumps to $179 million. So, forgive me if I'm not impressed by how prudently the Yankees spend their money.

MARCH 1

I was reminded today that the order of finish in the American League East has been the same for the past five years—Yankees, Red Sox, Toronto Blue Jays, Baltimore Orioles, and Devil Rays. And it might very well happen again.

I could see the Red Sox and Yankees changing places, or the Blue Jays and Orioles switching places, but the last five years looks like a fairly sound prediction for this year as well.

MARCH 10

I'm not sure I get it. But I'm very happy about it. The Yankees have fined hefty lefty and author David Wells $100,000. Of course, he was paid $500,000 to write the book, so he's still way ahead of the game, but I don't understand why he was fined at all.

Seriously. The Yankees claim his comments were detrimental to the team and tarnished the Yankees' image. How? Let's break it down.

His comments about steroids and amphetamines being used in the major leagues were either false or they weren't. If they were lies, then prove it. If not, the truth should be his defense.

His comments about his teammates were unflattering but relatively innocuous. He said there was a time when Andy Pettitte was unhappy with his contract. He said he respects Mike Mussina but doesn't consider him a friend. And he criticized Roger Clemens for throwing a bat in the general direction of New York Mets catcher Mike Piazza during the 2000 World Series. None of that seems worthy of a $100,000 fine. And all of that sounds like something you might hear a player say in a postgame interview. Besides, if criticizing a teammate is a finable offense, how much is Clemens going to get for telling anyone who'll listen that Wells is a pathological liar?

Finally, Wells's comments about his having pitched a perfect game "half drunk" tarnished his own reputation more than it did the Yankees' image.

It seems like a lot of money for very little damage. Perhaps most surprising, instead of touting his right to free speech and defending himself as a righteous voice delivering the truth, a rather contrite Wells admitted that he deserves to be punished and added that he won't appeal the fine. That's a pretty quick about-face, I presume in an effort to save face.

By the way, the money will be split among three charities chosen by the team: the Boys and Girls Clubs of New York, the Baseball Assistance Team, and the Special Operations Warrior Foundation.

Almost secondary to the Yankees circus was Pedro Martinez's 54-pitch effort against the Cincinnati Reds. Pedro gave up a run on three hits in three innings. He struck out four and once again talked about how healthy he feels.

"I feel pretty much on target, especially healthwise," said Martinez. "The way I have responded so far is really encouraging."

The fact that he's healthy is reassuring to Red Sox Nation, but it sure seems like Pedro's still negotiating in the press, trying to convince everyone he's healthy and deserves whatever amount of money he wants.

MARCH 12

Sadly, there were reports today that Red Sox pitching coach Tony Cloninger has bladder cancer. Indications are that he'll be all right. Let's hope so, for his family's sake, of course, but also because he seems to do a very good job, and the Red Sox are going to need someone who can manage an extremely diverse pitching staff. Think about it. In the starting rotation the Red Sox have a hard-throwing ace (Martinez), a sinkerballer (Derek Lowe), a knuckleballer (Tim Wakefield), a junkballer (John Burkett), and a 25-year-old lefty (Casey Fossum) attempting to start about 30 games for the first time in his career.

Tony Cloninger's mission, because he has chosen to accept it, is to keep Pedro healthy, ensure that Lowe closely resembles the D-Lowe of last year, help Wakefield and Burkett find their rhythm and maintain their consistency for an entire season, and develop Fossum into a reliable fifth man. If Cloninger can do all that, this Red Sox team could be phenomenal.

Then there's the bullpen. To quote Butch Cassidy and the Sundance Kid when they were trying to shake the posse, "Who are those guys?"

MARCH 13

Three stories to file under "Loving This." First, Yankees catcher Jorge Posada was scratched today because of a paper cut he "suffered" on his right index finger. Somewhere a hockey player just threw up in his mouth.

Second, Yankees manager Joe Torre had to answer questions about whether Jose Contreras would start the season in the minor leagues. The $32 million man has given up 14 hits, four homers, and five walks in eight innings. But Torre says Contreras will stay with the big-league club. Torre says he's confident Contreras will eventually adjust to the big leagues, but reporters are saying that somewhere between Cuba and Tampa, Contreras has lost a few miles per hour on his fastball.

And third, Torre had this to say, "I have been such a (Ramiro) Mendoza fan forever. It's going to be a little strange to pull against him. But obviously, where he is sitting in that dirty, rotten uniform he is wearing, we are going to have to pull against him."

Torre's "dirty, rotten uniform" comment won't get nearly as much play as Larry Lucchino's "Evil Empire" did, because Torre was smiling like a wise old sage when he said it. He's intentionally, good-naturedly tweaking the rivalry. I like Joe. It's a shame he'll be fired at the end of the season because the Yankees failed to win a championship for a third straight year, and Steinbrenner won't be able to bear watching Lucchino's Red Sox take the title.

MARCH 26

Another peek at the Yankees shows us that stud closer Mariano Rivera may start the year on the disabled list. He tweaked a groin muscle in his right leg two nights ago, and the Yankees intend to proceed with extreme caution. Rivera agrees with the safe approach.

"The one thing I won't do is rush it," says Rivera. "We're starting the season, it's not like it's August or September. I don't want it to happen, but if it does, it's better early than late."

It's a popular, though utterly ridiculous, notion that games in April and May aren't as important as the ones in late summer. It's a 162-game schedule. When it's all over, you add up the total number of wins. The team with the most wins goes to the playoffs. So, a loss on opening day counts just as much as losing game 162. And right now, the Yankees are in a bit of trouble.

For the past six years, the Yankees have relied heavily on a bullpen that included Rivera, Mike Stanton, and Ramiro Mendoza. Now, with Steve Karsay already on the disabled list and Rivera likely to join him, the Yankees will start the season with Juan Acevedo, Antonio Osuna, and Chris Hammond anchoring their pen. It's a solid trio, but it's a notch or two below what the Yankees have depended on for years.

Acevedo will be given first crack at the fill-in closer's job. And this is a guy who generated so little interest as a free agent that he signed a minor-league contract during the winter. After saving 28 games for the Detroit Tigers in 2002, Acevedo had to pitch his way onto the Yankees this spring—which he did by striking out 16 hitters and allowing just two earned runs in more than 11 innings.

Still, it looks to me like the Yankees don't have any better idea who their closer will be at the start of the season than the Red Sox do.

2

'Tis the Season

MARCH 31: OPENING DAY

"It was the best of times. It was the worst of times." It was Opening Day with Pedro Martinez on the hill facing the Tampa Bay Devil Rays, a team that could rival the futility of the 1962 New York Mets. It was an automatic "W." It was the kind of game you bet the house on. But as it turned out, it was the kind of game you use to convince obsessive gamblers that there's no such thing as a sure thing.

The game began as one might expect. Tampa Bay made two errors in the first inning, which led to three unearned runs. Pedro started mowing down D-Rays hitters, allowing just three hits and one unearned run in seven innings. But it never really seemed like the Red Sox had this one under control. Instead of piling on a whole bunch of runs against Tampa's "ace," Joe Kennedy—who won all of eight games last year—the Red Sox could only manage one. Still, they had a 4-1 lead heading into the home half of the eighth inning.

Time to put that bullpen theory to good use. Grady Little opted for Ramiro Mendoza in the eighth. One-two-three, piece of cake. The Sox don't score, and we head into the ninth. Who will be the first man chosen to close? Answer: southpaw Alan Embree. The reason: three lefties were scheduled to come up. This was textbook managing. Little couldn't be second-guessed. Some would wonder why Mendoza didn't come out for the ninth since he looked so sharp in the eighth, but nobody in the bullpen had worked since Friday (Fossum had carried the final four innings on Saturday, and Sunday had been a day off). Therefore, all the arms were rested and ready to go, and if Mendoza went more than one inning, he wouldn't be available the next day. That could be a problem, since so many of the Sox relievers are one-inning guys—like Chad Fox, Bobby Howry, and even Embree.

Unfortunately, Embree didn't have it. He gave up a hit, a homer, and another hit. Just like that, it was 4-3 with the tying run on first. Now, the beauty of not having one "go-to" closer is that if the guy pitching in the ninth inning doesn't seem to have it, Little can yank him. Proven closers almost never get pulled, even when it's obvious they're not about to get the job done. So, Little pulls Embree and brings in Chad Fox. This is the guy I'd like to see as the most frequently used closer, in part because he's the best strikeout pitcher the Sox have in the bullpen.

Fox strikes out D-Rays catcher Toby Hall, who failed on a couple of bunt attempts. One down. Runner still on first. Next, Brent Abernathy rolls a ground ball up the middle. Nomar Garciaparra fields it directly over the bag. He steps on second for the out there, but as he transfers the ball from his glove to his throwing hand, he loses control of it, forcing him to double-clutch. His throw to first is late. What should have been a game-ending double play—wasn't.

Marlon Anderson walked, and then up stepped 21-year-old Carl Crawford, who had gone 0-for-4 up to that point. Fox got the count to 2-2 before Crawford fought off a couple of pitches. This is where being a Red Sox fan starts working against you. Memories of watching the Red Sox lose one of the greatest World Series ever played in 1975, of seeing the Yankees' Bucky "Bleeping" Dent hit his home run in the 1978 playoff game at Fenway Park, of agonizing as the ball rolled under Bill Buckner's legs in 1986—all conspire to make us believe the Red Sox will find a way to lose. Though there's a much greater chance that the next pitch will be a game-ending strike than a game-winning homer, a Red Sox fan expects the home run.

It was a home run. Crawford dropped his bat on a low inside breaking pitch, one Fox later said "was right where I wanted it to be," and dropped the ball in the right-center-field seats. Game over.

Just as the ball cleared the fence, I was hit by a white flash of light, as if a bolt of electricity had shot through me. I'm sure I was unconscious for several minutes, but time stood still during my epiphany. There could be no doubt. I had become a Yankees fan!

It suddenly dawned on me that I'd been missing out on a life of happiness, excitement, and the kind of confidence that borders on arrogance—or, more accurately, the kind of arrogance that borders on the insufferable.

I've always said I don't have a problem with the Yankees. Throughout my lifetime, they've usually had an amusing, even likeable, cast of characters—Reggie, Goose, Thurman, Donnie Baseball. And how can you not like these current Yankees? They're so sickeningly sweet they could play their games at the foot of Walton Mountain while the Osmond Family hands out fruit baskets in the bleachers.

No, I've never had a problem with the Yankees per se—it's the Yankees *fans* who have always driven me crazy! All Yankees fans should have bumper stickers that sum up their attitude: "My team is better than your team; therefore, *I am better than you!*"

Now, I'm one of them. The team that sold its soul to the devil a hundred years ago is now *my* favorite team. I've gone to the dark side, and I've never been happier.

As a Red Sox fan, I knew beyond a shadow of a doubt that Crawford was going to hit a home run. Sometimes I know with utter certainty that a Yankee is about to reach on a bloop single, an error, or the ever-popular swinging-strike-three wild pitch with a catcher's throwing error tossed in just for giggles. (Check out Game Five of the 2001 American League Division Series against the A's, third inning, Bernie Williams. It really happened.)

A Red Sox fan's power to predict the future is rather narrow in scope. It only works in Red Sox and Yankees games, but it remains eerily accurate. That's why when Crawford kept fouling balls off, every true Red Sox fan knew that the ensuing home run was a fait accompli. The foul balls were simply a precursor—warning shots. It was like Paul Revere leaving the light in North Church to let everyone know the British were coming. I saw the light.

Years of training have prepared each and every Red Sox fan for moments like those few seconds before Crawford homered. Still, they hope against hope. Their fear and loathing are joined in one excruciating moment of tremendous dread. "Ha-ha!" I say to Red Sox fans. That's not me anymore! Not after my epiphany! I can simply sit back, completely relaxed for the first time in my life, and wait. Like the person who finally accepts death and reaches a level of serenity, comfort, and acceptance, I have inner peace. I have peace of mind. I am one with the world, because I am now a Yankees fan, and the world will never again let me down.

I believe my epiphany not only changed my future, but also my past. All pre-epiphany events have been altered in my memory. Friends tell me I experienced immeasurable suffering when the Red Sox lost a one-game playoff to the Yankees in 1978, but now I remember it as a blessed event. The births of my three boys are numbers one, two, and three on the list of big days in my life. It used to be that Pedro Martinez's humiliation of Roger Clemens, 13-1, in the postseason was number four—an extremely close number four, no offense to my kids. Someday they would have understood, but now, thanks to my epiphany, they'll be raised as Yankees fans. They'll grow up to be happier, more well adjusted, and less paranoid men with lower blood pressure. They'll have all their hair, and they'll poke fun at their grandparents who have stubbornly stayed the course. I'm sure my kids will thank me for this one day.

I love the Yankees team so much I want to marry it—for better or even better, for richer and even richer, in tight hammy and in health, until death do us part and they carve a Yankees logo onto my gravestone.

It actually felt good to imagine for a while that Tampa Bay's walk-off victory didn't cause excruciating pain. Pretending to be a Yankees fan for a few moments delayed the pain. Only a few hours later, though, genuine Yankees fans were feeling some pain of their own.

Sure, the Yankees won their opener at Toronto's Skydome behind six shutout innings from Roger Clemens, but superstar shortstop Derek Jeter separated his shoulder in a violent collision with Blue Jays catcher Ken Huckaby. Huckaby was running to cover a vacated third base. He and Jeter arrived at about the same time, so Huckaby jumped to his knees to try to block the bag. Instead, as Jeter dove headfirst for the bag, Huckaby drove his knee right into Jeter's shoulder. Jeter stayed down for 15 minutes before being lifted onto a cart and taken for X rays. He's definitely headed for the disabled list, but for how long? It could be a season-ending injury, the kind that would devastate a lot of teams not named the "Yankees." First, they're too talented to miss one player, even one as good as Jeter. Second, if he's out for an extended period of time, they'll just get another above-average shortstop. We're supposed to find out more on Tuesday about how long he'll be out. It could be that the

Yankees' opening day victory was more devastating than the Red Sox ninth-inning collapse against the Devil Rays.

Meanwhile, there was no deal announced regarding Pedro Martinez's contract. The deadline came and went, which only inspired Pedro to establish a new deadline.

"I'm just going to wait and see what happens," Pedro said in his postgame news conference. "If we reach an agreement within the next two days, that will be the only way I will talk to you guys."

Pedro added that he hadn't heard anything from his agent or the Red Sox today, because he hadn't allowed anyone to talk to him before he pitched. He said he would probably get a report of some kind when he returned to his room.

One final note of interest: Todd Walker was the 10th second baseman in ten years to open the season for the Red Sox. He'll need to start in that position every year until 2015 to tie Bobby Doerr's record of 13 opening day appearances by a Red Sox second baseman (1937–41, 1943–44, 1946–51).

APRIL 1

Who knew the Devil Rays were going to be this good? Once again they battled the Red Sox to the very last out. Once again, the Red Sox bullpen failed to protect a lead late in the game. But this time, the bullpen rallied back, stabilized, and gave the Red Sox enough time to come back and post their first win for 2003. It took 16 innings and more than five hours, but they got it. The Red Sox needed to use 20 players, and the teams combined to throw 566 pitches, but it was worth it in the end. And I'll say this: it's a good thing it was the Devil Rays, because not a lot of other teams would have stranded 21 base runners, 12 of them in scoring position. The Red Sox are not looking especially good at the start of the season.

But the Red Sox were saved by a couple of strong relief performances from Steve Woodard and Brandon Lyon, two guys who went through spring training almost unnoticed, but who pitched their way onto the team to throw three shutout innings apiece. Lyon, released by the Toronto Blue Jays, got the win.

Along the way, Bobby Howry gave up a two-run homer to light-hitting shortstop Rey Ordonez in the eighth inning. That tied the game 8-8. Each team had one close play at the plate. In the 12th inning, Sox utility man Damian Jackson threw Travis Lee out at the plate. Lee crashed hard into catcher Doug Mirabelli, who held his ground but sprained his ankle in the process. In the 15th inning, Devil Rays rookie Rocco Baldelli, out of Rhode Island, fired a strike to nail the slow-footed Trot Nixon at the plate.

Kevin Millar was left to provide the game-winning homer in the 16th. The Red Sox won, 9-8. Millar had pinch hit for Jackson only two innings earlier.

No doubt, the focus will be on Howry's having blown a late lead, much the same way Embree and Fox had done in the opener. But after the Ordonez homer, the Sox bullpen threw 8 2/3 scoreless innings. I'm going to believe the collective failures of Embree, Fox, and Howry are just early season flukes, rather than indications of serious problems. The home-run hitters for Tampa Bay were Terry Shumpert, who, discounting his four seasons with the Colorado Rockies, had hit 18 homers in his ten other big-league seasons; Carl Crawford, whose home run was his career third; and Ordonez, who has averaged 1.1 homers per year during his eight-year career. You might wonder what Jason Giambi or Alex Rodriguez could do against the Sox relievers if that Devil Ray trio can take them out of the yard, but I think Embree, Fox, and Howry are good pitchers who will have many more successes than miscues.

I still firmly believe this Red Sox bullpen is better than the one that went 15-22 with a 4.25 ERA last year—with or without Ugueth Urbina, who, by the way, gave up a game-winning homer on Opening Day against the Blue Jays last year. But should this bullpen falter out of the gates, there will undoubtedly be revisionist historians who will pine for the days of the Great Oogie. And I have to admit, I'd feel better if someone who had "done it" was doing it now, but let's not forget that in 2002, Urbina only saved two games in which he needed more than three outs. Fourteen of his 40 saves came when the Sox had a three-run lead, and he only saved one game in which he came in with the tying run on base. He was good. He was relatively dependable. But his stats are like the Watergate tapes—a big part of the story is missing.

APRIL 2

It's still not as easy as it's supposed to be. Red Sox win, 7-5, but these Rays are bothersome. Aubrey Huff took Derek Lowe deep to make it a 7-5 game in the fifth inning. Another home run from a guy who doesn't hit many, against a Red Sox pitcher who doesn't give up many. Lowe gave up only 12 home runs in 219.2 innings last year, and Huff has hit only 35 homers in 987 career at bats. The Red Sox bullpen needed to come through in a pressure situation again. Mike Timlin retired all six batters he faced, and then Chad Fox, who gave up that homer to Carl Crawford in the opener, got Crawford to end the game. Fox saves Sox. I like it.

What I don't like is that the Devil Rays have scored 19 runs in three games against the Red Sox, and that they're 8-for-8 in stolen bases. As harbingers go, this is not a good one.

APRIL 3

As it should have been from the beginning: Sox win 14-5. They take three out of four from the Devil Rays. All is right with the world. Casey Fossum went five innings, striking out eight, and allowing three runs. He gets the win, and if he's going to consistently pitch against weaker teams' fourth and fifth starters, he could end up with a lot of wins. A big moment was when Tampa's Rocco Baldelli hit a one-out triple, and Fossum struck out the next two batters to get out of his first inning of the new year unscathed (nobody likes to be scathed).

Special thanks to the Chunichi Dragons who gave up their rights to Kevin Millar. He went 3-for-5 with four RBI in the finale—giving him monstrous numbers through four games—six hits (two homers and two doubles), five runs, and six RBI.

Bobby Howry was able to preserve a nine-run lead in the ninth. Whew! It's on to Baltimore next. How good can the Orioles be? They just lost two out of three against the Cleveland Indians.

APRIL 4

We have officially traversed from the subliminal to the ridiculous. The message may have been subtle, but it has been received. The Red Sox will torture their fans even more than usual this year. But here's how I see it. Since the torture of not winning a World Series in 85 years will soon end, perhaps we can expect the day-to-day torture to increase exponentially throughout the season. That might explain the opening day collapse, followed by a 16-inning tussle, and now tonight's bizarre and excruciating finish in Baltimore. It hasn't been easy, but the Red Sox have won four of their first five games.

Quick facts: the Red Sox take an 8-1 lead into the seventh inning, thanks in part to John Burkett's solid five innings, Jason Varitek's second home run of the year, and Shea Hillenbrand's league-leading ninth RBI. Steve Woodard gives up a pair of runs in the seventh. No big deal. Alan Embree pitches a scoreless eighth. The Red Sox lead 8-3 and hand the ball to Ramiro Mendoza. It won't be long now. Wrong!

Mendoza proceeds to give up a series of hits and a couple of quick runs. The inning's first strange play occurs on a Tony Batista base hit to left field. With two outs and the Orioles down by five, the slow-footed and ancient B. J. Surhoff wheels around third, trying to score. Manny Ramirez makes a good throw to the plate. The ball arrives in time, but Varitek inexplicably doesn't block the plate.

"I screwed up," said Varitek, which I guess means it *was* explicable.

Now it's 8-5. Then 8-6 on a base hit by Melvin Mora. Mendoza has so far given up three runs on five hits. Why is he still out there? I thought the beauty of not having one true closer is that the manager can yank a pitcher anytime he's not getting the job done. Mendoza clearly needed help, and though Chad Fox was warming up in the bullpen, he never got the call.

Now, with runners on first and third, Baltimore's Geronimo Gil sends a one-hopper to the wall in left center. A run scores as Ramirez bare-hands the carom to Nomar Garciaparra, standing on the outfield grass. Nomar wheels and fires a strike to the plate. This time Varitek doesn't "screw up." He blocks the plate and tags out Deivi Cruz. The Red Sox win, 8-7.

"I threw my best pitch—the sinker—and the ball didn't sink," Mendoza said. "Bad day."

These guys are nothing if not honest.

This, by the way, has nothing to do with the "closer by committee." If Mendoza were still with the Yankees, and Joe Torre had decided to save Mariano Rivera and not use him in an 8-3 ball game, then Mendoza certainly would have been called upon to mop up in the ninth inning. And he would have been expected to do the job. This wasn't a pressure situation where you need a guy with experience to close out a tight ball game. This was, as Mendoza said, nothing more than a "bad day." And I love a team that wins on the bad days.

Five games into the season, the Red Sox have scored 42 runs. Shea Hillenbrand leads the American League in RBI, and Jason Varitek is the leading hitter with a .571 batting average. He also leads in the ever-popular category of on-base percentage, and with six extra base hits in 17 at bats, he also leads in slugging percentage. This is also great news because the Red Sox have won four of five and really haven't gotten much production out of Nomar or Manny. Wait till that starts happening. The games won't be that close then.

Also, the Red Sox should benefit from an incredibly easy April schedule. Their first 20 games are against Tampa Bay, Baltimore, and Toronto. Even if they play as badly as they have so far, they could be 16-4 by then. Don't be surprised.

The Yankees learned today that Derek Jeter won't need surgery and should only miss about four to six weeks. Jeter will get a second opinion from Dr. James Andrews in Birmingham, Alabama, on April 7. The Yankees are undefeated (4-0), but at least Jose Contreras has an ERA of 19.29 in 2.1 innings pitched.

APRIL 5

Pedro's pitched twice this year, and the Red Sox have lost both games. How does that happen when his ERA is 0.60? Look no further than Chad Fox, who's now 0-2 with a 13.50 ERA. You see, for the fifth time this year, a Red Sox game went down to the final out, and for the fourth time, it was because of the bullpen. Fox came into a 1-1 game in the ninth inning and proceeded to give up a walk, a double, an intentional walk, and finally a bases-loaded walk to Tony Batista. The Orioles "walk off" with a 2-1 win. Pedro's eight-inning, six-strikeout, zero-walk performance was wasted.

Say what you will about the bullpen, but one overlooked fact from this game is that Pedro was outpitched by Baltimore's Jason Johnson. Pedro was facing an inferior lineup and doing a wonderful job. But in the final analysis, he gave up a run and Johnson didn't. Granted, Johnson only went 6 1/3, but he didn't allow a run against the Red Sox offensive juggernaut, while Pedro did get touched up for a run. Jerry Hairston, now batting .360 lifetime against Martinez, tripled in the sixth and scored on a ground-ball out.

Jason Varitek said it best, "Pedro pitched great. The kid on the other side was doubly as good today."

Still, it's a shame that Pedro's given up just one run in 15 innings and doesn't have a win to show for it. The Red Sox only managed three hits and needed four walks in the ninth inning to tie the game. Shea Hillenbrand struck out with the bases loaded to end the threat.

At least the Yankees lost their first game of the year. And they lost because their bullpen blew a late lead to the Tampa Bay Devil Rays. Where have we heard that before?

APRIL 6

Boston 12, Baltimore 2. Sure, now the Red Sox bats come back to life! The Sox have scored a major league-leading 55 runs in seven games, but only five of them in Pedro's starts. That tells you they're averaging 10 runs per game when somebody other than Pedro is pitching.

It was a career day for "Mister April," Shea Hillenbrand. He homered, doubled twice, and drove in a career-best six runs—giving him a major league-best 15 RBI. Hillenbrand also had a huge April last year, batting .341 with five homers and 23 RBI. He says the trade talks are definitely motivating him.

"I think it can drive you. It's driving me."

And he just keeps driving in runners, even though he's ignoring the Red Sox emphasis on on-base percentage. As a team, the Red Sox have walked 40 times already, with only two of them issued to Hillenbrand. He's also only scored three runs, which says more about the bottom of the Sox lineup.

Tim Wakefield will be key to the Red Sox season, and so far so good. After another solid outing from him today, Little said, "Wakefield has been in a groove since the first of spring training. He's just been outstanding. We've got to knock on wood, but he's been automatic every time he takes the mound."

APRIL 7

Other than "You're under arrest," "What's that rash?" and "Yes, it's malignant," the worst three-word phrase in the English language for baseball fans is "No game today." Fortunately, the never-boring Red Sox made news anyway by choosing this off day to pick up Pedro Martinez's $17.5 million option. Basically, the team blinked. But Pedro's happy, and that's all that really matters, isn't it?

I'm surprised the Red Sox bothered to do this, because it does nothing for them and nothing for the fans. It only guarantees Pedro more money than any pitcher in history. But as far as the fans are concerned, we knew

Pedro would be back next year—assuming he stayed healthy. And the Red Sox didn't have to pick up the option until November. They think they kept the door open for negotiating a long-term contract, because they believe Pedro would have slammed that door shut if his option weren't picked up. That's where I think they were mistaken. Pedro has as much to lose as the Red Sox. If he had let his wounded pride get in the way and refused to negotiate with the Red Sox during the off-season, he would have had to pitch all next year worrying about getting hurt. I don't think he would have taken that gamble.

Besides, Pedro makes me angry—like so many other ballplayers today. He says he wants to finish his career in a Red Sox uniform, but that's not true. He wants the most money available to a pitcher of his stature. Guaranteed—if the Red Sox offered him a six-year, $90 million contract right now, he'd say "No!" That's $15 million per year and a major monetary commitment by the Red Sox, but it's not market value—represented by Randy Johnson's recent two-year, $33 million deal, or by Manny Ramirez and Alex Rodriguez, who make upwards of $20 million per year. You see, if Pedro really wanted to finish his career with the Red Sox, he would, and they'd welcome him with open arms and multiple millions. But if Pedro doesn't hear the right number, he'll be just as happy finishing his career with the Yankees or Dodgers or Texas Rangers—all of whom would pay his king's ransom.

Pedro has just become another Roger Clemens to me. Clemens talked a lot about Red Sox history and how much it meant to him to be part of the organization. The Red Sox offered him a "decent," though clearly not a wonderful, contract, but Clemens left anyway to join the rich and storied history of the Toronto Blue Jays. Pedro would do the same if it meant getting the biggest contract, because to him, having the biggest contract means he deserves the most respect. I hope the Red Sox don't cave in to his demands during the off-season. I'd rather root for someone who wants to be here.

Principal owner John W. Henry said today, "We wanted Pedro to know that this organization is committed to him." But I'd like to know that Pedro is committed to the Red Sox organization.

Looking back at the first "week that was," the Red Sox bullpen threw 27 innings and gave up 17 runs. That will get better.

Shea Hillenbrand leads the major leagues with 15 RBI. Nomar Garciaparra leads the American League in runs with nine. Johnny Damon's hitting .172, and Manny Ramirez has done almost nothing—no homers, five RBI. That's fine. He'll hit, and when he does, he could carry the team for a while.

APRIL 8

Let's just say Pedro Martinez is "full of it." Upon his arrival in Toronto for the start of a three-game set, Pedro met with several members of the media to discuss the stalled negotiations for a long-term extension of his contract. His statements were full of more bad lies than a public golf course.

First, he indicated that he would have taken less money "now" on a long-term contract, but since no deal was struck, his price tag will be going *up* at the end of the season.

"They could have gotten me for less money at this point. That's going to be off the table. They know. They agreed to that."

The explicit lie here is that he would have taken less money; the implicit lie is that he wants to finish his career in Boston. If he's already threatening to get "whatever" on the open free-agent market, then he's admitting that the highest bidder will win his services, which means he couldn't care less about staying in Boston. Also, there's no way he would have taken less money. Pedro clearly wants more.

Then he says, "I don't want to be compared with anybody," and proceeds to compare himself to several players.

"I'd put [my numbers] against Randy (Johnson), against (Greg) Maddux, against anyone in the last 10 years and you'll see. Kevin Brown, drop my numbers against his. (Mike) Mussina, (Curt) Schilling, Roger (Clemens), anybody. Put up my numbers there. Look at their salaries. Look at what Randy Johnson got at 39 years old."

Pedro's been doing his research. He knows what the other pitchers are getting, and he wants more than any of them.

Let's count the number of references Pedro made to his health. He said, 1) "At 33, being a free agent, if I'm healthy I can get whatever"; 2) "I'm just going to let it go, but it's not going to be there in November, not the same offer. God willing, if I stay healthy, I'm not planning on leaving that on the table"; and 3) "If I'm healthy, what I can do, what I've done, the experience I have and what I can bring to the team. You tell me."

It's on his mind: "If I'm healthy." Nobody else talks like that. The Red Sox are hesitant because they have doubts, the same doubts Pedro has. I think it's simple. The Red Sox should come up with an offer they think is fair, and that they are willing and able to pay, and stop right there. If Pedro takes it during the off-season, fine. If he doesn't, he can pitch like a Cy Young candidate in 2004, at which time the Red Sox will be equal players bidding on Pedro. If their offer is four cents more than the next highest bidder, Pedro will stay in Boston. And if Pedro gets hurt anywhere along the line, the Red Sox can pull their offer off the table, just like he says he's done. Fair is fair.

Finally, if it's not already incredibly obvious how selfish and arrogant Pedro is, consider this: when the Red Sox picked up his option, they, in effect, handed him $15 million. The option is for $17.5 million, and there's a buyout of $2.5 million. So, Pedro knows that if he were to get seriously injured this year, he'll still get $17.5 million next year, instead of just $2.5 million. The Red Sox didn't have to pick up his option. In fact, they shouldn't have. But they did it as a gesture of good faith and goodwill. Fat lot of good it did them!

Pedro is completely unappreciative, because he's so self-centered and self-serving that he believes the Red Sox should have done it anyway. $15 million! And it bought them nothing—no appreciation, no loyalty, no future considerations, no hometown discount. Instead, 24 hours later, Pedro had returned to a "me" against "them" mentality. The guys who just handed him $15 million are still the bad guys. They're still the ones who owe him a certain amount of respect. They're still the guys who will have a gun to their collective heads with Pedro's finger on the trigger. At the very least, Pedro should have kept his disappointment and frustration private. If this truly was his last day talking about his contract until the end of the season, couldn't he have spent this day talking about how great the Red Sox organization is, or how hopeful he is that everything will be worked out because he loves the Fenway Faithful so much?

I hope he pitches well this year. I hope the Red Sox win every one of his remaining starts. I hope he stays healthy. But I hope he hears a smattering of boos at the home opener on Friday—which looks like it will be cancelled because of snow. Where's global warming when you need it?

Fenway fans are certainly willing to boo their own. Ask Derek Lowe. Coming off his 42-save season in 2000, Lowe came out in 2001 and went 1-4 with two blown saves in April. He says, "I was booed off the field." He eventually lost the closer's job to Ugueth Urbina, and by the end of the year, Lowe was back in the starting rotation. It all seemed to work out for him. He threw a no-hitter the following April 27 against Tampa Bay, and finished the year with 21 wins, making him the first pitcher to win 20 or more games in a season *after* he had saved 40 or more games. Atlanta's

John Smoltz and former Red Sox pitcher Dennis Eckersley both had their 20-win seasons *before* their 40-save season.

Lowe never appeared destined for greatness. Sure, he was an all-league player in baseball, basketball, soccer, and golf when he was at Edsel Ford High School in Dearborn, Michigan. But he wasn't selected until the eighth round of the 1991 amateur baseball draft. When the Seattle Mariners finally gave up on him, he was traded to the Red Sox on July 31, 1997, along with Jason Varitek, for closer Heathcliff Slocumb. It's now considered one of the more lopsided trades in baseball history.

But it didn't look very good when Lowe began the 1998 season with an 0-7 record as a starter. Pushed to the bullpen, he went 6-3 with a 2.63 ERA in 74 appearances in 1999. The decision was made to make him the closer, and he promptly saved 42 games in 2000.

Now, he's a starter again, and again he's struggling. After just two starts, he's 1-1 with a 7.94 ERA, having walked six in 11 1/3 innings. He took the loss in Toronto last night, 8-4. It's hard to pinpoint the source of his problems. Clearly, he's leaving his cutter up in the strike zone—when he's able to find the strike zone. But Lowe had surgery for skin cancer in January, and after getting 60 stitches on his nose, he had to shut down his off-season conditioning, which could have set him back during spring training. Or, this is just another bad April, which he's had before. Or he's missing pitching coach Tony Cloninger, who hasn't been with the team for a few weeks now while he's being treated for bladder cancer.

Whatever it is, Lowe needs to right the ship in a hurry. The Sox are 5-3.

APRIL 10

"There's the Yankees and the A's, and then there's everybody else," says baseball guru Peter Gammons of ESPN, explaining why the Red Sox shouldn't bother to compare themselves to the Yankees. It's the wild-card theory. Nobody believes the Red Sox can win the Eastern Division, so they should concentrate instead on beating out the White Sox, or Twins, or the A's, Angels, or Mariners for the wild card.

Let's not forget the Blue Jays. They went 44-32 after the All-Star break last year, and they enter tonight with a five-game winning streak (the first three at Minnesota, and the other two against the Red Sox). Their ace Roy Halladay will be on the hill. The Jays could be this year's surprise team. Let's hope not.

APRIL 11: THE HOME OPENER

Former Red Sox player and long-time employee, 90-year-old Charlie Wagner stepped up to the microphone and said, "Let's play ball!" But nobody did. Just 42 minutes after the scheduled start of the game, it was postponed due to rain. Based on the weather reports, nobody believed they were going to get this game in, but the Red Sox evidently wanted to hold the opening day ceremonies with Lou Rawls singing the national anthem and Ray Charles performing an inspirational and emotional rendition of "America the Beautiful."

During the pregame introductions, the fans cheered Pedro Martinez and booed the bullpen. Perhaps they would have been happier had they known that Alan Embree and his 12.27 ERA were going on the 15-day disabled list. At least they won't have to worry about him for a while. Embree's got a sore shoulder, which may explain his loss of velocity. Hopefully, he'll be a lot better when he comes back.

There seems to be a lot of negativity surrounding a team that's on pace to win 96 games and is playing .600 ball—all on the road. Granted the bullpen has struggled, but the Sox are 6-and-4.

APRIL 12

After the day part of a day-night doubleheader was rained out, the Red Sox finally played their home opener Saturday night. And this time, Pedro heard the boos. He also had a staredown with a fan in the first row behind the Red Sox dugout.

"The first thing I heard (from fans) once I got to the dugout was a reminder of how much I got (my contract) extended to. That's not anything new. I heard that in '98 when I was here for the first time. When I had my first terrible game at that time, I heard about every cent I signed for—for about a week."

Even though Pedro admitted he deserved the boos, he couldn't keep himself from pausing at the top of the dugout steps to glare at an offending fan.

"I just wanted to take a close look at the person who said that. I hope I see him again the day he claps and I'll look at him again, just keep him in mind as a person."

How bad was it? Well, Pedro's ERA went from 0.60 to 5.12. That's pretty bad. And that's what happens when you give up 10 runs in 4 1/3 innings. The last time we saw something like that from Pedro was on July 18, 1999, when he gave up nine runs in 3 2/3 innings against the Marlins. It happens. But coming on the heels of his failed contract negotiations, his threats to leave, and his sour attitude, it was pretty dreadful timing. Plus, the Red Sox lost, 13-6, to Baltimore, so the team is now 0-3 in games Pedro's started this year.

Also today, Red Sox third base coach Mike Cubbage collapsed and had convulsions in the third base coach's box before the start of the sixth inning. He's a diabetic and had mistakenly given himself too much insulin. He was given an IV with sugar and quickly rebounded, but it was an eerily frightening scene before they carted him off on a stretcher.

APRIL 13

After Derek Lowe threw seven shutout innings in tonight's series finale with the Orioles, Grady Little had Tim Wakefield pitch the final two innings. The number two and three starters in the Sox rotation combined to throw a 2-0 shutout. It was among the most palpable indictments of the bullpen so far. Little demonstrated a complete lack of faith in his relief corps and further denounced the bullpen by announcing that Wakefield, who missed a start on Saturday, would also be available on Tuesday.

APRIL 15

The new Mendoza Line: 4 IP, 13 runs, 17 hits. That's what Ramiro Mendoza has done after opening the season with two scoreless innings, and he nearly blew another one tonight. This time the bullpen bandits pilfered the victory from Casey Fossum. Fossum was nearly spectacular and left after seven innings with a 5-1 lead. A lead like that should be safer than Fort Knox, but this team is all about hard knocks.

Mendoza and Mike Timlin combined to give up four runs in the eighth inning, leaving it to Shea Hillenbrand (4-for-5) to bounce one up the middle with the bases loaded in the ninth inning. The Red Sox won, 6-5, but the "Pen of Iniquity" reared its ugly head once again.

Grady Little said, "I find myself anxious waking up in the morning, thinking about the late innings. I might start coming up to the clubhouse to watch those late innings on TV."

Hey, it's no picnic on TV either.

So far committee members Embree, Timlin, Fox, Howry, and Mendoza have pitched a total of 28 innings, and they've allowed 62 base runners! Meanwhile, Ugueth Urbina picked up his fifth save of the season today, and his ERA is 1.35. He's excelling with the Texas Rangers, while the Red Sox have a total of two saves—and one is from a starter, Tim Wakefield.

The most perplexing culprit has got to be Mendoza, because there were no indications that he would perform this poorly. Sure, some folks claim the Yankees must have known something like this was possible since they just let him walk, but the evidence suggests Mendoza still has plenty of ability. He pitched in 62 games last year, going 8-4 with an ERA of 3.44. True, he gave up 102 hits in 91 innings, but that's not the first time in his career he's allowed more hits than innings pitched. He only gave up eight home runs—the fewest in his big-league career. He walked only 16 batters—also the fewest in his career—and that 3.44 ERA was the lowest he'd posted since 1998. He was solid again this spring. So it seems there were no signs he was capable of this kind of treachery. Or were there?

Further research reveals that last April Mendoza gave up seven runs in his first four appearances—a combined three innings. His ERA after his first six appearances was 10.13. And as late as May 17, his ERA was still at the "high-yield IRA" rate of 6.06. Apparently, he's very capable of prolonged slumps, particularly at the beginning of the season. This is why I maintain that the Red Sox bullpen—while it may never rival the 1990 Cincinnati Reds' "Nasty Boys"—will reach a level of acceptability as soon as the "unusual suspects" return to their respective levels of mediocrity.

Of course, the five-man committee has already lost two of its charter members. Embree hit the disabled list, and Howry was demoted to the Red Sox Triple-A ball club in Pawtucket. Opposing batters have roughed Howry up to the tune of a .478 batting average. He was terse upon his departure, but even he'd have to admit he's got some things to work out.

APRIL 16

There's a new name for the Red Sox bullpen: The Lyon's Den. Twenty-three-year-old Brandon Lyon pitched a 1-2-3 ninth inning for his first big-league save, and the Red Sox won in their final at bat for the third time this season. It was a reversal of fortune as the Red Sox bullpen held off Tampa Bay long enough to rally back. Trailing 4-2 in the eighth inning, David Ortiz came up with a two-run single to tie the game, and Jeremy Giambi followed with a two-out double off the center field wall. The Red Sox won their third game in a row and may have found a closer—at least temporarily—and a cheap one at that! Lyon makes only $325,000 a year.

After a rookie season in which he went 1-4 with a 6.53 ERA, Lyon was waived by the Blue Jays back in October. Blue Jays GM J. P. Ricciardi said that Lyon never developed the way they thought he would, and that he'd lost some of his confidence. Of course, Toronto had been hoping he could be a starter. The Red Sox were hoping he could eat up some innings in middle and long relief. Now, who knows?

And let me say this: Red Sox Nation ought to be ashamed of itself. Booing the bullpen, mocking management for a closer-by-committee theory, and having an overdone Chicken Little mentality that the "sky is falling." All this while the Red Sox are winning.

The question these negative blowhards like to ask is, "Yeah, but who are they playing?" You know who they're playing? They're playing the schedule. They're playing teams within their division. They're playing teams with a combined record of 16-26. And one of the reasons those teams have a losing record is because they're 5-9 against the Red Sox. You know what the combined record of Anaheim, Oakland, Minnesota, and Chicago is? 32-27. And you know how many times the Sox play those teams? Thirty-one. That's all. Throw in the Yankees, and it's up to 50 games against the projected best in the American League. And how many games do they play against Tampa Bay, Baltimore, and Toronto? Fifty-seven. Throw in Detroit, and it's up to 66 games. As easy as the schedule is at the beginning of the season, it's probably easier at the end when they'll play their final 14 games against Tampa Bay, Baltimore, and Cleveland—all teams that figure to be way out of the race and giving some big-league time to their minor-league players. There's almost no way this team can fall out of contention. The schedule's too easy, and they're that good.

They're 9-and-5 and Pedro goes tomorrow. So, I think you could make the case that the sky, in fact, is *not* falling.

By the way, are people aware that Chicken Little, Henny Penny, Ducky Lucky, Loosey Goosey, and Turkey Lurkey all get eaten by Foxy Loxy at the end of yet another horrific children's tale? Be careful reading to your children. I got caught in the middle of *Ladybug, Ladybug* before I realized its climax is, "Your house is on fire, your children are gone."

So you see, little Tommy, the house burned down, and all the children perished. Nighty night.

APRIL 17

There were two big developments today. First, Pedro Martinez got his first win of the year, beating the Tampa Bay Devil Rays 6-0. Then he chose to zip the lip, and zip it good. Ex-zip-it A: Pedro threw seven shutout innings at the Rays, throwing 92 pitches, 59 for strikes, and allowing just two hits. Ex-zip-it B: he left without saying a word to the media.

Another athlete who thinks silence is punitive. Apparently, media criticism concerning his last start is evidence to Pedro that the media has been disloyal to him. And they must be punished. Let's see, when spring training started, Pedro said he wasn't going to talk about his contract or extension. That lasted about a day. I wonder how long this silent treatment will last? I give it about a week.

Meanwhile, his performance against the D-Rays speaks loudly and clearly about what kind of pitcher Pedro Martinez has become. He's a seven-inning specialist. He's like a guy who's on the clock at work from nine to five, but leaves at three, saying, "I did my job. Now it's up to the night crew."

When it comes time to talk about his contract, Pedro will compare himself to other dominant pitchers in the big leagues like Randy Johnson, Curt Schilling, and Barry Zito. Pedro's ERA, wins, and strikeout-to-walk ratio certainly put him in that stratosphere—perhaps even at the top.

But it's worth noting that on the same day Pedro got lit up by Baltimore, Schilling also had a miserable start. And while Pedro bounced back with seven innings against the light-hitting D-Rays, Schilling went the distance against the high-powered Colorado Rockies—*in* Colorado. Schilling threw a four-hit shutout. Pedro needed Mike Timlin to pitch the final two innings to get the 6-0 win.

This is not an isolated example. It's the latest illustration of a long-running trend. Pedro hasn't gone nine innings since August 29, 2000. That was also against Tampa Bay, a truly masterful one-hit, 13-strikeout shutout. Pedro's had three complete games over the past two seasons; all were eight-inning losses. From 1996 to 2000, Pedro had five straight seasons with more than 200 innings pitched, topping out at 241.1 in 1997, but he hasn't thrown 200 innings in either of the past two seasons. Now, 200 innings for a Cy Young-caliber pitcher really shouldn't be much of a challenge. A guy makes about 33 starts and throws about seven innings per start. If you do the math, it adds up pretty quickly. Schilling has thrown more than 500 innings in the past two years. Johnson has *averaged* 248 innings pitched over the past six seasons. Those guys are horses. Pedro is an incredibly talented, often overpowering, immensely competitive—little pony. But you just know the Red Sox will eventually "pony up" the dough.

APRIL 18

In less than a day Pedro began talking to the media again. "I don't care," he said. "I just got tired. I don't have anybody to blame. I don't have anything to say. I just don't want to talk. I don't feel like it."

He was asked if he'd be willing to talk sometime later, and said, "Maybe not now, not the end of the year, not ever." Or tomorrow?

Pedro also says he won't speak for Manny Ramirez anymore either. So, now you've got a team with three superstars—Pedro, Manny, and Nomar—and two aren't speaking; the other one never says anything interesting anyway. This could be a very good year after all.

The Sox won their fifth in a row, 7-3, against Toronto. It's a decent 11-5 start to the season, but we shouldn't forget that the Sox have played three teams that they went 42-15 against last season.

APRIL 20

Happy Easter. The Red Sox extended their winning streak to seven games with a dramatic, come-from-behind 6-5 win over Toronto yesterday. And in case nobody's noticed, the bullpen has thrown 15 1/3 scoreless innings in a row. That's a nice comeback after giving up 34 earned runs in 41 1/3 innings to open the season.

This was an especially nice win because the Red Sox were trailing 5-0 to Toronto's ace, Roy Halladay, who won 19 games last year. But the Red Sox rallied, tying the game on a Nomar Garciaparra two-run double in the eighth, plus Nomar's walk-off homer in the ninth.

The Red Sox are the third-best team in baseball right now, behind the Yankees and San Francisco Giants. But even if they finish the season as the second-best team in baseball, they probably won't win their own division. Yankees starters are 13-0.

At least there's turmoil in Yankeeland. Joe Torre decided to send Jose Contreras to the Yankees' Triple-A affiliate in Columbus, Ohio, but owner George Steinbrenner overruled Torre, sending Contreras to the team's minor-league complex in Tampa, Florida, instead.

"I'm angry," Torre said. "If he wanted to send a message, he could have told me on the phone the other day. He certainly doesn't have to send me a message that he's the boss. We all know that. I don't say that sarcastically, I say that literally, because that's what he is."

After years of uncharacteristically fading from view, the Boss is much more visible this year. He criticized Derek Jeter in the spring, had his issues with David Wells's book, and now he's getting in the face of the man who has led his team to four World Series championships. There's trouble in paradise, but it's still not a "paradise lost."

APRIL 21

It may have been Patriots Day in Massachusetts, but it wasn't Red Sox day at Fenway. The winning streak snapped at seven.

Meanwhile, Yankees starters improved to 14-0. And the devil's team has out-homered its opponents this year, 39-5. We're dead.

APRIL 23

It looks like the story in the Red Sox bullpen has become "The Lyon and the Fox." Grady Little said he plans to use Brandon Lyon and Chad Fox as ninth-inning closers.

"These guys know where they're going to pitch now," said Little. "They kind of showed us they're the ones who oughta be pitching then. That's what we've been looking for ever since we left spring training. It looks like those are a couple of guys we're not scared to go to and a couple of guys who aren't scared to be out there. That's what we need."

Little's statement verifies he never really bought into Red Sox management's view that the team did not need a closer. He says he's been looking for one since spring training. It was evident that Little intended to find someone he could trust in the ninth inning. He desperately wanted it to be Chad Fox, who seems to have the nastiest stuff, but Fox stumbled out of the gate. Now, he's pitching better, so Little's going back to him. He'd probably be willing to make Lyon his guy, except Lyon's too young and untested. The hard part for Little will be to remain committed. Each of these guys is bound to falter, and when they do, will Little start looking for someone else?

Meanwhile, more misery from the Yankees. Roger Clemens went eight innings for his fourth win this year, and Yankees starters improved to 16-0. According to the Elias Sports Bureau, that makes them the first rotation to start a season 16-0 since the United Association's 1884 St. Louis Maroons.

They continue to win without Derek Jeter or Mariano Rivera, and with Jason Giambi batting a paltry .200. Once Giambi starts hitting, and the other two come back, the Yankees could be really good.

How many other teams have a $33 million pitcher who can't even make the team? (That's Jose Contreras, by the way).

APRIL 26

Ike and Tina Turner had a healthier relationship than the media has with the Red Sox right now. Add Nomar Garciaparra's name to the list of Red Sox players taking a stand against the media. The Sox shortstop, currently in an 0-for-19 slump, says he won't be available for pregame interviews unless a request is made 24 hours in advance. He also won't be available on the first day of a new series. But he will condescend to do postgame interviews.

So, let's see. You've got Pedro Martinez and Manny Ramirez not talking at all, and Nomar talking only on an extremely limited basis. These are the Red Sox three highest-paid players. They are the fan favorites. When does team management step in and tell these guys they've got a responsibility to speak with the media? Players and coaches are often fined for not making themselves available to the media during the NCAA basketball tournament or the Super Bowl. I think these guys should be fined, too. Even if it was for a relatively insignificant amount, it would still send a clear message that what these players are doing is wrong and unpopular with the organization.

Of course, this is only a major story because of the star status of the three players involved. I think if Damian Jackson or Kevin Tolar had a sense of humor, they'd call a news conference and announce some ridiculous set of ground rules for their interaction with the media.

"I, Kevin Tolar, have decided I will only speak to the media for up to five minutes on the days I throw more than 50 percent first-pitch strikes. Are there any questions? Is this thing on?"

APRIL 27

I read in a magazine recently that researchers have determined that stress truly does cause acne. They were able to prove this long-presumed theory by conducting comprehensive tests on mice. So, apparently, there's a bunch of stressed-out mice with zits running around, probably worried they're going to get cancer.

I mention this because if stress truly causes acne, I can't imagine there's a Red Sox fan who isn't riddled with whiteheads right now.

Pedro Martinez left after seven innings with a 4-2 lead against the Angels. Brandon Lyon gave up a run in the eighth. In the ninth, Chad Fox gave up the tying run. It was "failure by committee" once again. But the Red Sox got back-to-back home runs on consecutive pitches in the 14th inning from David Ortiz and Jason Varitek to win the game 6-4.

"It's got to stop," Grady Little said. "I can't afford this feeling every night."

I think he's starting to break out like a very worried mouse.

APRIL 28

Chad Fox was placed on the 15-day disabled list with a strained left oblique. Nobody shed a tear. In his first month with the team, Fox blew two saves and lost two games. His ERA isn't bad (3.86), and he's only given up one run in his last seven appearances, but when he's been bad, he's been costly. Still, he leads the team with three saves.

APRIL 30

The world of strange but true baseball stories needs to be updated after today's Red Sox comeback to beat the Kansas City Royals, 5-4. This was another wild one!

The Red Sox scored three runs in the ninth inning, when the Royals committed two errors and hit three batters. That's right. They hit three batters in one inning! The only other time that's happened in the ninth inning of a game was September 17, 1928, when the Chicago Cubs hit three members of the Boston Braves. Alan Embree ended up getting the win after throwing just one pitch.

Ramiro Mendoza failed again and was charged with two runs in the ninth inning. Embree finished the frame by coming in with two outs and getting Brent Mayne to fly out to center on his first and only pitch of the game. The Red Sox trailed 4-2 heading into the bottom of the ninth.

After Todd Walker led off with a base hit, K.C. closer Mike MacDougal hit Nomar Garciaparra on the elbow, and Manny Ramirez singled to drive in Walker. Kevin Millar followed with a sac fly to score Nomar and tie the game at four. MacDougal was lifted after he hit Shea Hillenbrand on the elbow. His replacement, D. J. Carrasco, hit Johnny Damon on the foot, which loaded the bases. Jason Varitek hit a slow bouncer to first that was mishandled by Mike Sweeney, and Ramirez scored the winning run.

It was the Red Sox 18th win, tying a franchise record for the month of April. They finished the month just three games behind the Yankees. As good as that is, I can foresee a scenario in which the Red Sox play very well all season long, but finish each and every month three games behind the Yankees. So, they could end up playing .650 baseball and be 18 games out of first place. Thank God for the wild card.

3

Committee Canceled

MAY 1

It only took one month for the Red Sox to abandon the closer-by-committee approach. With "the Fox in the hole" (Chad Fox on the disabled list), 23-year-old Brandon Lyon has been told he's the closer.

Meanwhile, tonight's game should be archived under "Baseball's Code for Dunderheads." After three Red Sox were hit in the ninth inning last night, Casey Fossum's 12th pitch of the game was blasted over the fence for a two-run homer by Mike Sweeney. Then his 13th pitch went *behind* Kansas City's Raul Ibanez. Without warning, Fossum was summarily ejected. Keep in mind, the pitch didn't even hit Ibanez.

So, three Red Sox batters were hit, and *no* Royals hitters were plunked, yet the Red Sox were put in a position in which their starting pitcher was gone in the first inning. It's blatantly unfair, but it's the rule, and it's all about intention. I don't think the Royals pitchers were throwing at the Red Sox last night. But there's little doubt that Fossum *was* throwing at Ibanez. According to the rules, the umpire has the right to toss Fossum out of the game. He could have just issued a warning, especially since Fossum missed his target, but intentionally throwing at a batter is cause for ejection.

And I do like the umpire's interpretation of justice. It's always bothered me that someone found guilty of *attempted* murder gets a lighter sentence than someone *convicted* of murder. Why does one guy catch a break simply because he was incompetent? Trying to kill someone deserves equal punishment as actually killing someone, because the criminals are equally dangerous to society—assuming the attempted murderer improves. I'm OK with the idea of punishing intent. And Fossum was an idiot!

"It just got away from me," Fossum said. "I had given up a home run, I was mad at the previous pitch. I talked before about the game speeding up on me. Instead of just relaxing, I got up there and wanted to fire the ball as hard as I can and you can't do that. It hurt me today. I was out of the game."

What a crock! The pitch was a foot behind Ibanez. Could he have been any more obvious than that? A pitch up and in might have only produced a warning, and it would have served the same purpose. If he really wanted to hit someone as payback, couldn't he have waited until the sixth or seventh inning? Instead, he put his bullpen in a nearly untenable position.

But it all turned out fine in the end. Steve Woodard was called upon in the emergency situation and pitched 4 2/3 innings, allowing just three runs. Mike Timlin followed with 1 2/3 shutout innings. Jason Shiell pitched a scoreless eighth. And newly anointed closer Brandon Lyon pitched a 1-2-3 ninth inning to pick up the save.

The Red Sox scored single runs in the sixth, seventh, and eighth innings and won 6-5. Kansas City came into town 17-5, and the Red Sox swept them in three straight. The Red Sox are now 8-1 in one-run games. Last year, they were 13-23 in the close ones. Also, this was the seventh game this year that they won in their last at bat. Last year, they only had 10 wins all season that came in their final "ups." If teams like the Twins, Royals, Angels, or A's were winning that many games in their final at bats, people would be talking about "magic" or "destiny." But when one of the "big boys" does it, there's more talk about the reasons they're not winning more easily. But I'm calling it destiny!

By the way, Kansas City's Kris Wilson hit Johnny Damon with a pitch in the sixth inning and wasn't ejected.

MAY 2

More from the new millennium's version of the Mendoza Line. Today,

Ramiro Mendoza pitched to three batters, recorded no outs, and gave up three runs. Alan Embree followed by pitching to four batters. He also recorded no outs and gave up three runs. Mendoza and Embree now have ERAs of 10.47 and 14.40, respectively.

The Sox lost, 11-7. In five of their 10 losses, they've given up 10 or more runs.

MAY 3

Pedro Martinez remains silent but deadly. And to extend that thinly veiled metaphor, he had plenty of gas today. But the surprise in his performance wasn't that he completely dominated the Minnesota Twins, or that he struck out 12 in the Red Sox 9-1 victory, but that he completed the game. Even after the Red Sox scored seven runs in the sixth inning (the most runs they've scored in one inning this year), and took a 9-1 lead after seven, Pedro stayed in the game. Normally, Pedro gets pulled with a victory all but guaranteed, and even this bullpen could be trusted with an eight-run lead. But Pedro is becoming quite the workhorse. After his first nine-inning complete game in more than two years, he's now second in the American League in innings pitched.

The Red Sox have done a masterful job of bringing him along. In his first four starts, Pedro threw 91, 92, 92, and 92 pitches. Now, he's thrown more than 100 pitches in each of his last three starts. He's been able to limit his pitch counts by working effectively and throwing a high percentage of strikes. In seven games, Pedro has thrown 696 pitches—243 balls and 453 strikes. That means that 65 percent of his pitches have been strikes. He's had six outstanding games and one clunker, and all signs indicate he should be able to go out every five or six days and throw between 100 and 120 pitches—which should get the Red Sox at least seven innings every time. Right now, he's pitching like a genuine, front-of-the-rotation ace, the kind that chews up innings, picks up wins, and fills everyone in the organization with confidence.

Pedro has been everything he thinks he is, and everything the Red Sox want him to be. And that's very, very good. But it will make him that much harder to deal with come contract time.

MAY 5

After losing 9-4 to the Twins yesterday, the Red Sox avoided a tornado on their way to Kansas City. But disaster struck anyway.

The Red Sox are still playing their version of Extreme Baseball—taking most of their games right to the limit. No lead is safe, and no deficit insurmountable.

This time, the Red Sox fell behind 5-0. Derek Lowe—who now sports an 11.12 ERA on the road—gave up two-run homers to Desi Relaford and Michael Tucker. Lowe was gone after just 3 2/3 innings, having allowed seven hits and four earned runs while walking three. But Ramiro Mendoza was uncharacteristically brilliant. He threw 3 1/3 scoreless innings, which gave the Red Sox time to come back. And they did.

Nomar Garciaparra hit a two-run homer that tied the game at 5-5 in the eighth, and Jason Varitek hit a two-out solo blast in the ninth to give the Red Sox a 6-5 lead. But the Royals, who were attempting to become the first team to open a season with 11 straight home wins since the Tigers of 1911, would not be denied.

The Royals loaded the bases with one out against Brandon Lyon. Lyon struck out Ken Harvey, putting the Red Sox one out away. But the very first pitch to Relaford was a slider that ran too far inside. It hit Relaford on the left leg, forcing home the tying run. Still, there were two outs—one out away from extra innings.

"I lost the game for us, it was as simple as that," Garciaparra said after the game.

That was a bit of an overstatement. But there was enough truth to it that nobody bothered to argue. Garciaparra, whose throwing error in the first inning led to an unearned run, made his second error of the game, his eighth of the season. It was a hard ground ball right at him. The runner on second may have obscured his view of the ball momentarily, but it was certainly a ball that Garciaparra should have handled. He went down on one knee to make sure he would field it cleanly, and still somehow the ball found a hole between his legs and continued untouched into left-center field. Instead of extra innings, the game was over.

It's now officially the closest thing the Red Sox have come to a slump all year. They've lost three of their last four. It's a shame, too, because the Yankees have gone 5-5 over their last 10—which tells you they're barely a .500 team. Ha, ha.

MAY 6

The Red Sox handed the Royals their first loss of the season at "Turn your head and" Kaufman Stadium. Casey Fossum demonstrated once again his ability to pitch very well for relatively short periods of time. After putting up six goose eggs and allowing just two hits, Fossum finally faltered in the seventh inning, giving up three runs on three hits. But the Sox bullpen picked him up and held on to win, 7-3.

MAY 7

It's time to start noticing that the honor roll of role players is on a roll. In last night's victory, Doug Mirabelli had four base hits. The backup catcher is supposed to give the first-string guy a rest, and if he does more than that, it's a huge bonus. Mirabelli's played in 14 games, driving in six runs and scoring seven. I'd say he's been quite a bonus.

Today, Steve Woodard got his first win with the Red Sox, and Brandon Lyon pitched a perfect ninth for his third save. These two youngsters barely made the team out of Fort Myers. When the Red Sox fell behind 6-1 after six innings, it was David Ortiz who led off with a walk, and pinch runner Damian Jackson who stole his seventh base in eight tries. Jackson has only had 27 at bats in 20 games, but he's got those seven steals, and he's thrown out a runner from each of the three outfield positions. He's been a significant upgrade over Lou Merloni as a utility player.

Even Jeremy Giambi came up with a couple of base hits and an RBI today, lifting his average all the way up to .153. Woodard, Lyon, Jackson, Mirabelli, Ortiz, and Giambi are basically a Who's Who of "who are you?" But the Red Sox couldn't have come back to win this one 9-6 without them.

Except for Mirabelli, all of them are spending their first seasons with the Red Sox. Theo Epstein and Grady Little did a wonderful job finding them, choosing them for the 25-man roster, and using them in the right places so far this year.

And you really can't say enough about Bill Mueller. His versatility has helped him get into 26 of the first 34 games, playing five games at second, 20 at third, and one at shortstop. He's yet to commit an error, and he routinely makes superb defensive plays. And, by the way, he's hitting .346. Without question, the best team the Red Sox can put on the field on any given night has Mueller at third and Shea Hillenbrand at first.

Still, Mueller is one of those curious signings, and a poster child for the sign of the times. This is a guy who has almost always been a part-time player and has never hit more than 10 home runs or driven in more than 59 runs in a season. Yet, he'll make $4.5 million over the next two years—

which is actually a pay cut from the $3.3 million he made in 2002. That still seems like a lot of money for someone who isn't considered an everyday player, but there's no debating his value to the team—at least so far.

You'd have to figure former San Francisco Giants manager Dusty Baker isn't surprised. When Mueller played for him, Baker predicted that Mueller would one day win a batting title. That's high praise for a guy who hit .268 the only year he played in more than 150 games (2000). Of course, Baker's bold statement was made before Mueller tore up his left knee crashing into an unpadded portion of the wall at Busch Stadium in 2001. He had follow-up surgery on the knee last spring, so this is really the first time in three years that Mueller has been healthy. At the age of 32, he's now starting to live up to his potential. Plus, he's a perfect clubhouse guy.

In February 2001 Mueller told the *Chicago Tribune*, "I don't need the publicity or the endorsements. I want to make the stars around me bigger stars. I love to play and I love to win. You don't dream about being famous. You dream about being a hero to your teammates."

And this spring he told the *Providence Journal*, "You want to be known as a good person first. Sometimes, that means putting your teammates ahead of yourself. You go out and try to help the younger guys."

I think I'm in love.

Also today, the Red Sox claimed left-hander Bruce Chen off waivers from the Houston Astros. With Chen's salary set at only $700,000, the Red Sox consider the 25-year-old "low risk." I remember when the Braves thought he'd be an effective starter during the 1999 season. But they threw him in the pen the following year, then traded him to Philadelphia, with whom he started 15 games and won three. Then he was a Met, and then a Phillie again.

Since the beginning of 2000, Chen has been with the Braves, the Phillies twice, the Mets twice, the Reds twice, the Expos, the Astros, and now the Red Sox—each team waiting for him to live up to his potential. Sox GM Theo Epstein said, "We think he can help us now in the 'pen from the left side. We think there's still some upside left to him. It's been a bit of an enigma as to why he hasn't replicated his minor-league success in the big leagues. Maybe a change of leagues will help."

Maybe.

Meanwhile, the Yankees continue to stumble. Their loss last night was their third in a row, leaving the Red Sox and Cubs the only teams yet to lose three in a row. For the Yankees, it was also their fifth loss in their last eight games.

But they bounced back today with another impressive outing from Mike Mussina, who improved to 7-0.

MAY 8–10

The Red Sox lost two out of three in Minnesota. In the first game, they were shutout by the combined efforts of Johan Santana, LaTroy Hawkins, J. C. Romero, and Eddie Guardado. It was the first time the Red Sox had been shut out since last August—not surprisingly against the Yankees.

Mike Mussina had tossed a three hitter, beating Pedro Martinez, 7-0. Martinez was the victim of the Twins' shutout as well, complaining about stiffness in his groin. He's not expected to miss his next start, though.

"It's nothing to be alarmed about," Grady Little said. "He felt something down around the groin area, but he didn't feel it when he was pitching in the fourth or fifth inning. We'll evaluate it and take him out tomorrow and make sure nothing's wrong."

Mussina's shutout was the fourth time in 12 games that the Red Sox had been held scoreless, while the Twins' shutout was the first time in 65 games that the Red Sox had failed to score. It's a curious streak that doesn't mean a whole lot, especially when you consider the Kansas City Royals now have the longest streak of consecutive games without being shut out.

But their record is just 32-38 during the streak.

After beating the Twins, 6-5, in the second game of the series, Derek Lowe let off another stink bomb. He left after four innings, with the Red Sox in an 8-0 hole. Six of the runs were earned. His road ERA is now a well-publicized 11.57. At home, he's 2-0 with a 0.95 ERA.

"Why the difference, it's absolutely beyond me," Lowe said. "It's very frustrating because you know you can do so much better in every outing. You look forward to the next start because you figure it's going to be the one that gets you going."

To their credit, the Red Sox scored in each of the last five innings, including twice in the ninth, and almost pulled off an amazing comeback. They lost 9-8, but the tying run was on second base when Bill Mueller grounded to short to end the ninth-inning rally.

When you consider Lowe's abysmal start (3-3, 6.52), Manny Ramirez's pedestrian numbers (4 HR, 24 RBI), and Nomar Garciaparra's sub-.200

batting average with runners in scoring position—not to mention the bullpen's being about as steady as Crispin Glover after nine mocha lattes—it's amazing and fortunate the Red Sox remain only three games behind the Yankees.

MAY 13

God have mercy on the man who doubts what he's sure of.
—Bruce Springsteen, *Brilliant Disguise*

Doubt. I was consumed with doubt, probably for the first time this season. Sure, I've had moderate levels of uncertainty before, but nothing to compare with the misgivings I felt during the series opener against the Texas Rangers.

Manny Ramirez hit his first home run in 52 at bats (since April 27), and Trot Nixon also homered to give the Red Sox a 2-0 lead, while John Burkett shut down the potent Rangers attack for five innings. Then, it happened again. Just as Burkett was shifting into cruise control, the wheels came off. He gave up a three-run homer to Juan Gonzalez and left in the sixth inning trailing, 4-2. This has been Burkett's modus operandi in his last four starts. Last time out, he shut out Kansas City for five innings, then gave up six runs in the sixth. Before that, he shut out Minnesota for four innings, then gave up one in the fifth, and two each in the sixth and seventh innings. And before that, he threw four shutout innings against Anaheim before giving up three in the fifth. So, his ERA in the first four innings of his last four starts is *zero*. After that, he's been awful.

The Gonzalez homer was so deflating. It made me feel like the Red Sox were not only going to lose this game, but that the "team of destiny" label I had given them a few months ago was about to be ripped off.

But as Kahlil Gibran said, "Doubt is a pain too lonely to know that faith is his twin brother." Or, as Ambrose Bierce once said, "Who never doubted, never half believed. Where doubt is, there truth is—it is her shadow."

It's comforting to know that doubt is a by-product of faith. Gibran and Bierce would have you believe you can't have one without the other. And I certainly had them both during tonight's game.

The Red Sox won! And they did it with three runs in the eighth inning, making it the eighth time this season they've secured a win in their last at bat. It's the seventh time they've won a game in which they trailed going into the seventh inning. It's their 11th come-from-behind win, and they're now 10-2 in one-run games. It feels like a team of destiny again!

Trailing 4-2 in the eighth inning, Shea Hillenbrand reached on an error by third baseman Hank Blalock. The door was open. Trot Nixon struck out. The door was only slightly ajar. Jason Varitek singled Hillenbrand to third. Here we go. Johnny Damon singled to score Hillenbrand, and pinch runner Damian Jackson advanced to second. The tying run was in scoring position. Todd Walker's base hit to right scored Jackson, and Damon went to third. Tie game. Only one out. Nomar Garciaparra doubles off the wall. Damon scores the go-ahead run. That's all the Sox would get, or need.

It was a big win, but not as big as the loss two days ago in Minnesota.

"I think that was our biggest game of the season," said second baseman Todd Walker. "Everybody believes when that happens you can do it again. So now two runs down doesn't seem that much."

Brandon Lyon pitched a scoreless ninth, making him a perfect 5-for-5 in save opportunities. (The loss against K.C. on May 5, when Nomar made an error in the eighth inning, didn't count as a blown save because Lyon was already the pitcher of record entering the ninth.)

In any event, I'm now ashamed of having doubted the Red Sox are a "team of destiny." From now on, I'm going to listen to people like Mark Twain, who said, "When in doubt, tell the truth." Or Benjamin Franklin, who said, "When in doubt, don't." Or perhaps, Bill Blass, who said, "When in doubt, wear red."

And I've got one more, though I "doubt" you're interested. It's the one I agree with most, and it's the one that assures me doubt will be a constant companion no matter how good or bad things look for the Red Sox this year. It comes from Voltaire, who said, "Doubt is not a pleasant condition, but certainty is absurd."

Like, I'm so sure!

Derek Jeter returned to the Yankees lineup and went 1-4 against the Anaheim Angels, but the Yankees lost, 10-3. It was Mike Mussina's first bad game of the year. He gave up a couple of homers and three earned runs in five innings, raising his ERA to 2.02 and dropping his record to 7-1.

Has anybody noticed that the Yankees have lost six of their last nine games, and eight of their last 14?

That's a slump, people. That is most definitely a slump. And all of those games have been against the West—Texas, Anaheim, Seattle, and

Oakland. They've been shut out twice in those 14 games, and held to three runs or fewer *seven* times.

The Sox are two games back—three games closer than they were 14 games ago.

MAY 14

The Sox close to within one game of the Yankees. New York loses its seventh out of 10 while the Red Sox beat the Rangers, 7-1, behind five solid innings from Casey Fossum, two from Ramiro Mendoza—who has now thrown 8 2/3 consecutive scoreless innings—one from Mike Timlin, and one, the ninth, from Robert Person.

It was the easiest win the Red Sox have had in a while. And once again, the Red Sox much-maligned bullpen is quietly enjoying a hot streak. In the last nine games, the committee has allowed four runs in 29 innings, for a 1.24 ERA.

MAY 15

When Pedro Martinez walked off the mound after six innings, the Red Sox led 7-0. By the time the home half of the inning was over, it was 10-0. Pedro didn't come out for the seventh. The Red Sox completed the sweep of the Rangers, 12-3. They outscored Texas 24-8 during the series.

Meanwhile, the Yankees snapped their second three-game losing streak of the season and maintained their one-game lead over the Red Sox. Now, they'll change opponents. The Angels come up from New York to play three at Fenway Park, and the Rangers head to the Bronx for a weekend series against the Yankees.

MAY 16–17

Two days in a row the Red Sox and Yankees have both lost. So, in essence, the Red Sox have missed two opportunities to move into a first-place tie.

The second game of the Angels series may have helped put Red Sox rightfielder Trot Nixon into the "Bonehead Hall of Fame." It's Nixon's custom whenever he catches the third out of an inning to flip the ball to a fan along the right-field line. At least, he typically waits until there are three outs. Not this time.

With runners on first and second, and only one out, Angels shortstop David Eckstein hit a soft fly ball to right. Nixon made the easy catch and instinctively tossed the ball to a young boy in the stands.

"I just threw the ball up in the stands, it was a bonehead play," Nixon said. "I've made mistakes in my life, and I bounce back from them. It was just stupid. I'm going to be fine. This stuff makes you stronger, even though you don't want it to happen to you."

Because the ball was now out of play, both base runners were allowed to advance two bases. That meant a run scored on what was ruled a throwing error. Ya think? The play didn't directly affect the outcome of the game, because the Red Sox were already down 3-2, and they wound up losing 6-2. But Nixon certainly took a lot of heat for his forgetfulness. A gentle razzing was in order, but plenty of fans wanted Nixon either yanked out of the game or benched the following day. To his credit, Grady Little did neither. Nixon, a hard worker who throws his body around and gives an honest effort every day, simply forgot how many outs there were. It appeared more egregious because he flipped the ball into the stands, but there have been countless times when players have lost track of the outs for a moment. How many times have you seen a first baseman get the putout at first and start to run off the field prematurely, or an outfielder make a catch and fire the ball toward a base to get a potential runner only to realize that was the third out? It happens.

My advice to Nixon, if hecklers start to get on him about remembering there are only three outs in an inning, is to look at the aforementioned hecklers and say, "Excuse me, but there are *six* outs in an inning—three in each half." It wouldn't erase the bonehead nature of his mistake, but the one-upsmanship might silence the harassment momentarily.

4

The Yanks Are Coming

MAY 18

Don't tell me the baseball gods aren't watching. On the eve of the Red Sox and Yankees' first meeting of the year, the teams are tied for first place. We've got ourselves a race! After 43 games, the two rivals have identical 27-16 records, but they sure took different routes to get there. The Yankees—who got off to their best start in team history at 18-3—have lost six of their last seven, seven of their last nine, and nine of their last 13. The Red Sox have been much steadier and have yet to lose more than two games in a row.

But thanks in large part to John Burkett, the Red Sox finally caught 'em. Burkett was at his best in salvaging the final game of the series against Anaheim. He went seven innings, allowing just one run, and the Red Sox won, 5-3. The Yankees, on the other hand, were swept at home against the Rangers for the first time.

One other note: the Yankees called Jose Contreras back up from Triple-A. So, the Sox will get an up-close and personal look at the guy they desperately wanted during the off-season—only he'll be in the other dugout. So far, signing Contreras is one of the best moves Sox GM Theo Epstein "didn't" make. Still, Epstein told me recently that he expects Contreras to be a very good big-league pitcher soon. Let's hope it doesn't happen in the next three days.

MAY 19

I know "flated" is not a word. But I feel somehow I must have been "flated" before the start of the Yankees–Red Sox game tonight, because at about 7:15, I was most assuredly *de*-flated. Alfonso Soriano—single. Derek Jeter—double. Jason Giambi—two-run single. Bing, bang, boom! After only four pitches, the Yankees had a 2-0 lead. Before Casey Fossum got out of the first inning, it was 5-0. Fossum pitched exceptionally well after that. He allowed only one more hit and no more runs over the next five innings, but the Red Sox never really figured out David Wells. The portly left-hander scattered nine hits, and the Yankees took round one, 7-3.

It's a shame that first inning took all the wind out of the sails of Red Sox fans. Until then, there had been something special in the air. Thousands of fans showed up early. The number of media on hand was at least triple that of an average regular-season game. Granted, that had a lot to do with the entourage of Japanese reporters who follow Hideki Matsui around like lapdogs. But this series was getting extra-special attention, and deservedly so. The ballpark was filled with opening day anticipation, but unlike the actual opening day, there was no rain. It was a beautiful evening. The Yankees were in town. The Red Sox were in first place for the first time all year, albeit tied. And the game turned out to be a dud. The best part of the day was Roger Clemens's press conference.

I don't often find Clemens endearing, but he is always engaging. On this day, he was at his most entertaining. He joked that he wishes he could send opposing teams out to "get hammered" the night before he pitches, so that winning his 300th game would be that much easier. He joked that he's happy to have a solid nickname like Rocket, because so many Hall of Fame pitchers—like Lefty Grove and Walter "Big Train" Johnson—are known by their nicknames. But his best quip was, "I come up here and find out that Manny (Ramirez) isn't talking. Pedro (Martinez) isn't talking. Nomar (Garciaparra) isn't talking. I guess that's why they've got me doing this press conference."

As I stood there listening to Clemens, a question suddenly struck me. I hadn't thought about it before, but as it settled in my brain, it made sense. Up went my hand, and I asked, "Roger, you've pitched during a time of offensive explosion, a time when even 500 home runs isn't respected like it once was. So, if today's hitters are going to be diminished in a historical perspective, do you think today's pitchers should be elevated and given more respect?"

It wasn't a very good question, because it essentially asked Clemens to say, "Yes, I'm better than the pitchers of another era because today's hitters are stronger, the ball is livelier, the ballparks and strike zones are smaller, etc." And he wasn't about to say any of that. Instead, he replied, "First of all, 500 homers is 500 homers"—a reference to Texas Rangers' first baseman Rafael Palmeiro's recent accomplishment, which spawned debate as to whether or not 500 homers should automatically put a player in the Hall of Fame. Clemens thinks it should, and I agree.

But back to my question, because although Clemens wouldn't answer it directly, it's something that baseball fans should address. While it hurts me a little to say this, a case can be made that Roger Clemens is the greatest pitcher of all time! For the sake of argument, I'll make that case. And I'm only going to consider 300-game winners, so guys like Sandy Koufax, Bob Gibson, and Greg Maddux don't even get discussed.

Let's quickly dismiss all but one of the modern 300-game winners. Clemens is clearly better than the likes of Don Sutton (324 wins), Phil Neikro (318 wins), and Gaylord Perry (314 wins). Nolan Ryan (324 wins) is a tribute to longevity, having pitched for 27 seasons, which means he averaged only 12 wins per year. Tom Seaver measures up with Clemens, having finished with 311 wins, a .603 winning percentage, and a lifetime ERA of 2.86. But Clemens has won 66 percent of his games, and his lifetime ERA of 3.15 is just as impressive as Seaver's when you consider the premise that the game has shifted in favor of the hitter. Plus, Clemens had six Cy Young Awards, twice as many as Seaver, and six 20-win seasons— one more than Seaver. It's close, but I'd give the edge to Clemens.

The one guy from the postwar era who you can't so easily dismiss is Steve Carlton. This guy was a monster! Consider that in 1972, he *completed* 30 games! He threw 346 innings that year, and 10 years later, at the age of 37, he completed 19 games and threw for more than 295 innings. He won his fourth and final Cy Young Award that year. Carlton had 254 complete games to Clemens's 116, but even with 136 more starts, Carlton only had 55 shutouts to the Rocket's 45. Carlton, who pitched for a lot of bad teams, had a winning percentage of just .574, and his lifetime ERA is identical to Clemens's (3.15). So, again we return to the argument that there is more offense in today's game, which makes Clemens's ERA "better" than Carlton's. That's a tough call, because you have to wonder if Clemens would still have anything left at the age of 40 if he were to throw 5,217 innings like Carlton did. Instead, Clemens will finish his career (assuming this is his last season) with more than 1,000 fewer innings than Carlton.

If you're still with me, and you agree that Clemens is the best of the so-called modern-day pitchers, we still have to address the old-timers. First, Cy Young himself—511 wins, but alas, he never won a Cy Young Award. (That's a joke). Complete games: 749. That's also a joke. Instead of being incredibly impressive, a stat like that disparages the kind of baseball they were playing in the 1990s.

Walter Johnson? Pitched from 1907 to 1927. So, for the first 12 years of his career, the biggest home-run hitter in the league was Gavvy Cravath. Who? That's what I said. Cravath led the major leagues in home runs from 1913 to 1915 with 19, 19, and 24. It wasn't until 1920 that Babe Ruth shocked the baseball world with 54 homers. But the biggest knock against a guy like Johnson is the 531 complete games, and .599 winning percentage. Those two stats tell you that it wasn't at all uncommon for Johnson to be outpitched by his opposition. He was apparently completing a lot of games that he ultimately lost. So his lifetime ERA of 2.17 is less extraordinary because the average pitcher of his day was nearly as good as he was.

You can't say the same for Christy Mathewson. True, his career started in 1900, but it only took him 17 years to amass 373 wins. He had 12 straight seasons with more than 20 victories—four with more than 30—and a career high of 37. His winning percentage is even better than Clemens's, and his lifetime ERA is 2.13.

And that leaves only Warren Spahn. When I spoke to former Major League Baseball commissioner Fay Vincent, he immediately targeted Spahn as the best pitcher ever. Vincent pointed out that, because of World War II, Spahn didn't win his first game until he was 25 years old. Routinely making about 36 starts per year (only slightly more than today's pitchers), Spahn won 363 games over a 21-year career. He had 13 20-win seasons, but his lifetime ERA was 3.09. I'd say that was relatively high based on the era in which he pitched. He led the league in wins eight times, but in ERA only three. Clemens, on the other hand, has led the league in wins only four times, but in ERA six times. To me, the ERA stat is the most important, because it points more directly to how dominant a pitcher is in relation to opposing hitters as well as to his pitching peers.

When it's all said and done, it looks to me like you're left with Clemens, Carlton, Mathewson, and Spahn. I'm giving the nod to Clemens. And believe me, I'm none too happy about it.

MAY 20

I can still remember my initial reaction when I heard the news: "You have *got* to be kidding me!" It wasn't spectacularly original, but it contained equal levels of anger, frustration, and numb resignation. There wasn't an ounce of surprise, however. Pedro Martinez was hurt, and he wasn't going to pitch tonight—against the Yankees! It was upsetting, but it was about as shocking as finding out the sun would rise tomorrow.

Of course he was hurt on the day of the season's most important series to date! He is at all times either hurt, worried about getting hurt, or getting over a hurt. This time it's his right lattisimus dorsi muscle. He felt a twinge there while long-tossing on Monday, and again today. So, about four hours before he was scheduled to start, he was scratched. He left Fenway Park early to have an MRI. The results will be revealed tomorrow. Until then, and quite possibly not even then, nobody will know how long he'll be out. Such is the plight of Red Sox fans forever tied to the capricious nature of Pedro's health. "*If* he's healthy, the Red Sox have a chance." "*When* he's healthy, he's the best pitcher in baseball." "*With* him, the Red Sox are contenders. *Without* him, they're sunk."

Not to beat a dead horse, but this is exactly why Pedro Martinez is not a horse, and therefore not worth signing to a long-term extension. A team deserves to see some sort of return on its investment, and there's no convincing case that the highest-paid players in the game are bringing in money, fans, ratings, or advertising dollars. The Red Sox have sellout crowds or near-sellout crowds whether or not Pedro pitches. The Texas Rangers could finish in last place whether Alex Rodriguez is playing shortstop every day or not. With their cushy television deal, the Yankees would make money—potentially even more money—whether or not their payroll was $179 million (luxury tax included). When Roger Clemens went to the Toronto Blue Jays for three years and $31 million, he won two Cy Young Awards, but the Blue Jays went nowhere *and* had diminishing crowds. So, they traded him away. He performed remarkably for them, but as a revenue stream, he was more like a puddle.

So, should the Red Sox guarantee an ingrate upwards of $50 million over the next three years when the aforementioned ingrate is a constant source of worry and hopefully will make 28 to 30 starts per year? Pedro will make $17.5 million next year, which breaks down to about $583,000 per start, or approximately $5,830 per pitch. I'd love to see his agent bring statistics like that into negotiations. "Look, the best pitchers in the game are making well over $6,000 per pitch, and we think Pedro's value in today's market is $8,400 for strikes and $5,900 for balls. Anything hit foul, of course, is a strike, even if it was out of the strike zone, and if there were two strikes on the hitter. And to show you what good sports we are, we'll throw in warm-up pitches and side sessions for free. Whaddaya think?"

I think the end is near.

So anyhoo, above the din of despair around the ballpark, you could hear "Chen music." Bruce Chen, the left-hander who came over from Houston and had thrown a grand total of 3 1/3 innings in the American League, was chosen to replace Pedro Martinez in a game against the New York Yankees. His opponent? Jeff Weaver. That was the silver lining. Weaver had given up 18 runs in his previous 25 innings. He could be had.

The game played on. Alfonso Soriano began the evening by homering on the first pitch. No Pedro, no problem. Derek Jeter followed by singling, stealing second, and later scoring on a sacrifice fly. The Red Sox had fallen into another hole, but this time they climbed out—only to climb back in, and then back out.

The Red Sox did get to Weaver, and led 4-3 after four innings. But then former Yankee Ramiro Mendoza got lit up. Four straight singles produced just one run, but the Yanks scored two more on a sacrifice fly and a ground out, taking a 6-4 lead. Mendoza's ERA continues to look more like a 1990's mortgage rate: 7.48.

But this was a game of "my bad bullpen is better than your bad bullpen." And in some kind of poetic justice or just plain irony, Jose Contreras stank worse than Mendoza. Contreras loaded the bases in the seventh, then jerked his head back quickly to see the ball that David Ortiz roped into the left-center-field gap. The Ortiz two-run double was part of a five-run inning. Contreras's ERA is 15.63. Again I say he might be the best move the Red Sox never made.

Once the Red Sox roared back, there was still the "Lyon's share" of the work to be done. Now, Red Sox fans are slow to give unconditional love to anyone—especially a young closer they'd never heard of until this spring, and the first thing they *did* hear about him was that he'd been released by the Toronto Blue Jays. So, any affection for Brandon Lyon is bound to be conditional—specifically, until he proves himself in a real pressure situation. The kid needed a dominating performance against a contender, or, better yet, a rival.

Robin Ventura. Strike three. Alfonso Soriano. Strike three. Derek Jeter.

He struck him out! Lyon struck out the side in the ninth inning to secure a 10-7 win in the second game of the Yankees series. It was certainly impressive, but before he gets any love from the Red Sox fans, he'll have to do it again…and again.

Strange days indeed. Despite the news that Pedro Martinez would be out indefinitely, the Red Sox beat the Yankees. So, was this a good day? I think that depends on the word "indefinitely." Because as everybody knows, "*If* Pedro Martinez is healthy…"

MAY 21

Very clever, those Red Sox. By having Oscar-winning composer John Williams throw out the ceremonial first pitch, they were able to conjure up images of Larry Lucchino's "Evil Empire" comment without directly referring to it. Williams wrote the music for *Star Wars*, so that's what blared from the loudspeakers while he strode to the mound and tossed the first pitch. Nice touch.

Meanwhile, Roger Clemens went in search of his 299th career win. He was booed when he first walked on to the field, about 30 minutes before game time. He was booed again when he went to the hill in the bottom of the first inning. And he was routinely heckled and harassed throughout the six innings he was out there. From my seat along the third baseline, I personally yelled, "Hey, Roger! Congratulations on 298. That's a good weight for you!"

But Roger had the last laugh, and he did it in what has become typical Roger fashion. He left the game after six innings and with the score tied at two. Then the Yankees scored in the top of the seventh, giving Roger the victory, 4-2. The Yanks won the series. And they're back in first place by a game.

Red Sox starter Tim Wakefield finally retired Soriano and Jeter in the first inning, but Jason Giambi followed with a solo home run. So, for the third straight night, the Red Sox came to bat already trailing. That didn't last long, however, because Nomar Garciaparra answered right back with a two-run shot that put Boston ahead.

Wakefield matched Clemens for six innings, but with two outs in the seventh, Jorge Posada singled. Robin Ventura walked, and Raul Mondesi soft-served a base hit up the middle. Posada scored what proved to be the winning run.

"Mondesi just hit one off the end (of the bat)," Wakefield said. "There's nothing you can do about that."

The game's other big moment was when Bill Mueller lined a shot back at Clemens with two outs in the sixth inning. The ball grazed Clemens's pitching hand. He was attended to by the trainer, and threw a couple of pitches to make sure he was all right. Then he struck out Doug Mirabelli to retire the side. That was the last batter he'd face. Clemens's record at Fenway Park is now 99-55.

As for Pedro Martinez, Red Sox team physician Dr. Bill Morgan says that the MRI didn't show any rips or tears in the lat muscle, which is good. He's calling it a "strain" and says Pedro could be on the hill by the middle of next week. That would potentially make him available for the last game of the second Yankees series in New York, but Morgan wasn't offering any guarantee. He mentioned that Pedro—who still isn't talking to the media—was in good spirits and reported that he felt about 60 percent better on Wednesday than he had on Tuesday. That's a measure that means absolutely nothing. Just show up someday with a ball in your hand and pitch, would you, please?

MAY 22

A day off for the Red Sox and an extremely "off" day for the Yankees. Not only did they lose to the Blue Jays, as Andy Pettitte dropped his fourth straight start, the Yankees also learned that their All-Star center fielder Bernie Williams will probably be out for four to six weeks with torn cartilage in his left knee. Williams had just gone 0-for-13 in the Red Sox series, and had obviously been struggling. This could be why. Williams plans to get a second opinion before having surgery that would sideline him for up to six weeks, but with Nick Johnson already out, this is a significant blow to the King of the East.

Following that bit of news, the Yankees lost to the Blue Jays, 8-3. It was Pettitte's 206th career decision and his first four-game losing streak. Only Whitey Ford (306), Juan Marichal (267), Ed Reulbach (227), and Mike Mussina (208) had longer streaks without losing four in a row.

And look out for the Blue Jays! They're now 16-6 in May, and they've cut their deficit against New York from 11 1/2 games to 3 1/2 games. I thought this was going to be a two-team race.

MAY 23–25

The Red Sox took the first two from the Indians, 9-2 and 12-3, but lost the series finale, 6-4. They finished their home stand 7-5. Nomar Garciaparra extended his hitting streak to 24 games—a streak made all the more incredible because it began after an 0-for-19 slump dropped his average to .248.

The Yankees left Boston, went home, and lost four straight to the Blue Jays. The Yankees have lost seven in a row and 10 of their last 11 at home. They only managed to score 10 runs in the four games against Toronto, and on Sunday, they went 0-for-18 with runners in scoring position. They've now gone 52 straight innings at home without scoring more than one run in an inning.

"We like to think we're something special, and to be something special, we have to handle bad times," Joe Torre said. "And this is one of those times."

Bad times for the Red Sox as well, but nothing unexpected. For the fifth time in his career, Pedro Martinez was placed on the 15-day disabled list. The move is retroactive to May 16, which means Martinez can pitch on Saturday in Toronto—if he's healthy.

Grady Little assessed things this way, "Pedro looks like he is not going to be ready for this series (and) he is not going to be ready for Wednesday, but in all likelihood, he will be ready to pitch on the weekend in Toronto."

The Red Sox called up Matt White from Pawtucket. Whew! That's reassuring.

MAY 26

Memorial Day. Afternoon game. Roger Clemens going for his 300th career victory…at Yankee Stadium…against the Red Sox. Clemens flew in several of his former Red Sox teammates, such as Rich Gedman, Marty Barrett, and Spike Owen—who I'm sure were just happy to receive free tickets to something. The anticipation was high, and unavoidably delayed. First, there was a rain delay. Then there was a "Reign Delay."

The game was about to start some 90 minutes past its originally scheduled time, but even before Clemens threw his first pitch, there was controversy. Red Sox manager Grady Little went to the home plate umpire, Bill Miller, and pointed out a commemorative 300-win patch on the back of Clemens's glove. After Miller and crew chief Joe West talked to Clemens on the mound for a few moments, a bat boy came out of the dugout with a new glove for Clemens. Little had asked for the switch to be made, claiming that the patch could be distracting to Red Sox hitters. It seemed like gamesmanship to me, but Clemens was unfazed. He retired the side in order.

That was the only time he'd accomplish that.

Shea Hillenbrand knocked in a run with a base hit in the second inning. Boston scored twice in both the third and fourth innings to take a 5-0 lead. And Clemens was finally knocked out in the sixth inning. He received a standing ovation after being charged with eight runs on 10 hits (and eight of the hits against him came with two strikes). He threw a season-high 133 pitches on his way to dropping the series opener, 8-4.

Clemens lost, and the Red Sox won. It was the best combination since Reese's had the good sense to put peanut butter inside their chocolate. It was the Yankees' eighth straight loss at home, their longest skid at home since they lost 10 straight in 1986—which just happens to be the last time the Red Sox went to the World Series.

But I'm not nearly as confident as I think I should be. The Red Sox are 2 1/2 games up on the Yankees, which means they'll definitely leave New York in first place. But that's not much of a lead considering the Yankees have gone 8-16 in May. That's because the Red Sox are just 13-10 this month. Neither team is playing lights out, and most people have more confidence in the Yankees' ability to right their wayward ship. I'm not quite as convinced, however.

Nomar Garciaparra had two hits to extend his hitting streak to 26 games. He's now hitting .313, raising his average 65 points since the streak began. And he's just four games shy of joining Ty Cobb and George Sisler as the only men with two hitting streaks of at least 30 games. Nomar had a 30-game streak in his rookie season of 1997.

Not to be overlooked is the Red Sox new fan favorite, Bill Mueller. He worked his way into the everyday lineup by hitting .315 in April. He's now hitting .383 with 11 multi-hit games in his last 20 starts. He's 34-for-78 in May. That's a .436 average. Hey, maybe Dusty Baker was right. There could be a batting title in this kid's future. However, he doesn't have enough at bats right now to qualify for the title. Most likely, he will by season's end.

MAY 27

Nobody likes to be drubbed. But the Red Sox got a drubbing from the

Yankees today—11-3. Derek Jeter, switched to the leadoff spot, began the home half of the first with a home run. Robin Ventura homered in the second, and Todd Zeile homered in the fifth. Other than those three mistakes, Bruce Chen—starting in place of Pedro Martinez again—was pretty sharp. He left after five innings with the Red Sox trailing 4-2. The wheels didn't really come off until Matt White couldn't get out of the eighth inning. The new kid on the block was charged with all six runs the Yankees scored that inning. Welcome to the big leagues, and enjoy that 81.00 ERA!

Nomar Garciaparra's hitting streak ended at 26 games. Those darn Blue Jays won their sixth in a row.

Meanwhile, David Wells developed a bruised right calf after getting hit by a batted ball in his last start. So, the Yankees announced that Jose Contreras will start in place of Wells on Friday in Detroit. Wells, who makes a $135,000 bonus per start, wasn't happy to learn he wouldn't be starting.

There was plenty of speculation that the decision was made by Yankees owner George Steinbrenner, but Joe Torre said it was his decision based on the reports from his medical staff. Torre is definitely getting some heat from above. Steinbrenner told the New York papers that he got Torre the players he wanted, so it's up to him to turn things around.

One other note: Bernie Williams went ahead with arthroscopic surgery on his left knee. He'll be out until July.

MAY 28

The Yankees did it to us again. After Mike Mussina pitched brilliantly—allowing only a solo home run to Shea Hillenbrand in the eighth inning—the Red Sox managed to tie the game by scoring four runs in the ninth inning against the usually unflappable Mariano Rivera. The Red Sox had a chance to take the lead, but Hillenbrand was thrown out at the plate on a great play by Alfonso Soriano for the final out of the inning.

With Hillenbrand on second base, the score tied at 5-5, and two outs, Trot Nixon ripped a ground ball to the right side. Jason Giambi moved to his right. Soriano moved quickly to his left. The ball bounced off Giambi's glove and appeared to be heading for right field. Because of the deflection, Soriano had overrun the ball, but he reached back with his bare hand and knocked the ball down. Soriano slid on his backside but bounced up quickly enough to retrieve the ball and throw a strike to the plate. Hillenbrand was charging for the plate and made a nice move around catcher Jorge Posada, but just a fraction of a second before Hillenbrand reached for the plate with his left hand, Posada tagged him on the chest. We headed for the bottom of the ninth still tied.

It was an amazing comeback for the Red Sox, who had trailed 5-0 in the Bronx against a commanding Mike Mussina and one of the game's most reliable closers. But the game was far from over.

Brandon Lyon came in to pitch the ninth. After he retired the first batter, Hideki Matsui lifted a fly ball to deep left field. It barely missed the outstretched glove of Manny Ramirez and one-hopped the wall for what should have been a routine double. But Ramirez got to the ball and uncorked a wild throw that missed the cutoff man. The ball rolled along the stands past third base and past Lyon, who was making an effort to back up the play. By the time Lyon slid on his knees to stop the ball near home plate, Matsui had coasted into third base. The winning run was on third with one out. What would you do, with Soriano and Giambi coming up?

Well, Grady Little opted to walk them both. This is not the first time he's elected that strategy. On July 21 of last year, the Red Sox led the Yankees 8-7 in the ninth inning—also in New York. Giambi reached on an infield single. Bernie Williams singled to right, and just like Ramirez, Trot Nixon committed a costly error. The ball went under his glove, and by the time he ran back to get it, Enrique Wilson (who pinch ran for Giambi) had scored, and Williams had moved around to third. So, the game was tied with the winning run on third. Grady Little had Ugueth Urbina intentionally walk Robin Ventura and Raul Mondesi to load the bases. Urbina "unintentionally" walked Posada, forcing in the winning run. The Yankees won, 9-8.

Back to today's action. With Matsui on third, Lyon intentionally walked Soriano and Giambi. Again the bases were loaded, and Posada was the batter. The Red Sox would later complain vehemently about what they believed should have been a called strike three, but it mattered not. Just as he had done some 10 months earlier, Posada walked. Another walk-off walk! Different pitchers, different year—same uniforms, same results. The Yankees spoiled what would have been a near-miraculous comeback for the Red Sox, winning the game 6-5, and taking the series, 2-1.

The Red Sox lead is back to half a game. The Yankees improved to 29-0 when leading after eight innings. The Yankees holding on to a late lead is about as sure as death and taxes. Or about as sure as the fact that I'll never know why I seem to love everything banana flavored, but I really don't like bananas.

MAY 29

The word of the day is "proactive." It's not a word frequently used when referring to the Boston Red Sox, but this time it fits. Instead of waiting and ultimately reacting to what the Yankees might do before the trading deadline, the Red Sox made a terrific, timely, and proactive deal with the Arizona Diamondbacks. Sure, it took six months from the time the deal was first proposed, but it's proactive nonetheless.

The Red Sox finally traded Shea Hillenbrand. He's second on the team in RBI, one behind Nomar Garciaparra. He was an All-Star third baseman last year, and he's been playing a fantastic first base. But he'll barely be missed. And in return the Red Sox got Byung-Hyun Kim. Where do we begin?

Let's start with Hillenbrand. Talk about history repeating? Last May 29, Hillenbrand had 39 RBI. On the same date this year, he's got 38. He finished last year with 83 ribbies. That's 39 in two months, and 44 more in four months, which indicates a rather sharp cooldown in the second half of the season. Now, with Hillenbrand gone, Bill Mueller becomes the everyday third baseman, and David Ortiz will see regular playing time over at first. I'm willing to bet that Ortiz has better offensive stats from this point forward than Hillenbrand does. Hillenbrand will give the Diamondbacks next to nothing. He doesn't hit for power—despite his 18 home runs last year, he hit 13 of them before the All-Star break, and he's hit just three so far this year. He hasn't homered at Fenway Park since May 26 of last year, a span that covers 316 plate appearances. Those who say he'll hit for more power in Arizona point to the fact that only 10 of his 33 career home runs were hit at Fenway Park, suggesting that as a line drive hitter, Hillenbrand was hurt by the Green Monster. I'd be just as quick to point out that he only has 33 career home runs. That's not a lot, no matter where you're playing. His 23 road homers came in 170 games. The guy's about to turn 28 years old. He's not about to bust into a 40-home-run guy.

Red Sox GM Theo Epstein said, "It was difficult to trade Shea Hillenbrand, but this trade was about winning the World Series, and we think it brings us closer to doing so."

He's absolutely right.

Epstein also said, "We wouldn't be able to make this trade if it wasn't for Bill Mueller."

Right again.

Mueller's emergence made Hillenbrand that much more expendable. Of course, now the Sox have to hope Mueller stays healthy, because they don't have a reliable backup on the hot corner anymore. They've called up infield prospect Freddy Sanchez from Triple-A, but he's more of a middle infielder. He's known for his defense, but he's leading the International League in hitting at .391 and has a .484 on-base percentage. His call to the big leagues has come a bit earlier than expected, but it will be interesting to find out what the Sox have in Sanchez. He could be the heir apparent to Nomar Garciaparra.

Now—about Kim. The Red Sox announced that he'll start in place of Pedro Martinez on Tuesday against Pittsburgh. But as soon as Martinez is healthy again, Kim will go to the bullpen.

"We feel like he'll be a starter in the future," manager Grady Little said. "But for us to be the best club we can be when Pedro comes back, he'll surely be working in the back of our bullpen."

As it should be. Kim was a lights-out closer for the Diamondbacks last year. He's a 24-year-old, submarine-throwing right-hander who has held opponents to a .197 batting average during his five-year career. Say again— five-year career, 24 years old. Last season he was 8-3 with a 2.04 ERA while converting an Arizona franchise-record 36 saves in 42 opportunities. And in the rarely talked about category of "tough saves," he led both leagues with six.

Heading down the stretch last year, he helped lead Arizona to the Western Division title by allowing just three earned runs in his last 22 appearances. That's a 1.05 ERA during crunch time. That's what the Red Sox need right now.

Kim always wanted to be a starter, however, and the Diamondbacks gave him a shot during spring training. He earned a spot in the rotation, and while his 1-5 record is less than impressive, his 3.56 ERA is bound to help. And there's no doubt that Kim, because of his peculiar sidewinding delivery, is much more effective as a closer than a starter. If a hitter only gets one chance to face him, that hitter is at a distinct disadvantage. By the third at bat, the hitter's disadvantage dissipates somewhat. I think that's what happened to Kim in his most famous performances.

Many baseball fans remember the 2001 World Series, when the Diamondbacks played the Yankees. In Game Four, Kim gave up a two-run homer to Tino Martinez in the bottom of the ninth that tied the game. Then he surrendered the game-winning home run to Derek Jeter in the 10th.

The next night, Kim gave up a two-run homer to Scott Brosius in the ninth inning. Television cameras caught Kim dropping to his knees in abject disappointment, the pain of his failure tactile. The Diamondbacks eventually lost that game in 12 innings, but they won the Series. Still, there were coast-to-coast rumblings that the youngster from Korea might never recover from his collapse on the big stage.

"At the time, it felt like I was in hell," Kim said. "But now, as I look back, it was a learning experience. Now, I feel like I'm in heaven."

Wouldn't you know, the guy the Red Sox get to improve a pitching staff that ranks 23rd in the major leagues with a 4.92 ERA has a bad history with the Yankees. He'll fit in nicely, because he was already one of us.

Reports out of Arizona tell us that Kim is a bit of a quirky loner. He'd have to be somewhat of a loner—the man speaks Korean. As for quirky, that relates to his work and sleep habits. He apparently works unceasingly on his windup, and often throws immediately *after* a game. His coaches have become frustrated because he throws too much.

Meanwhile, his teammates in Arizona called him "The Lion"—as in the 1961 song by The Tokens, "The Lion Sleeps Tonight." Apparently, his ability to sleep is legendary, and there was a time when it was problematic. In 1999, Kim was known to leave the bullpen and fall asleep in a nearby room. He'd have to be *woken* up in order to warm up.

MAY 30

John Burkett is no longer allowed to pitch against the Blue Jays! Back in April, he gave up seven runs in 2 2/3 innings. Tonight, he gave up eight runs in two innings. Sox lose, 13-2. It was a reversal of fortune for the Sox and Yankees. Last weekend, while the Yankees were being swept by the Blue Jays, the Red Sox moved into first place. Tonight, while the Blue Jays were beating up on the Red Sox, the Yankees moved back into first place.

That's because the Yankees shut out the Tigers in Comerica Stadium. Jose Contreras got his first big-league start and threw seven shutout innings at the Detroit Tigers. Contreras K'd six and only gave up two hits. Granted, it was the Tigers, who have only scored 154 runs, the fewest in the major leagues. So, the Yankees definitely put Contreras in a position to succeed. But he went out and did it. If he keeps doing it, and pitches like the Yankees (and the Red Sox) think he can, that won't be good for Boston.

MAY 31

The Blue Jays and their modern-day version of "Murderer's Row"—Carlos Delgado, Vernon Wells, and Josh Phelps—toppled the Red Sox again, 10-7. Delgado and Wells rank first and second, respectively, in RBI in the major leagues.

This game turned once Casey Fossum took the mound in the sixth inning. Despite having retired the side in the fifth, it was clear that Fossum was struggling. But Grady Little sent him back out there, and the game was quickly lost. Toronto scored five times in the inning, and Fossum was charged with nine runs in 5.1 innings.

In his six starts between April 15 and May 14, Fossum gave up 12 runs in 31.1 innings, which equates to an ERA of 3.47. Quite acceptable. But since then, he's made three starts, giving up 19 runs in 17.1 innings. That's an ERA of 10.00. Utterly *un*-acceptable. In all, Fossum is 4-4 with a 5.86 ERA.

By the way, the Blue Jays scored those 10 runs today even though Delgado and Wells went a combined 0-for-7 without scoring a run or driving one in. It was the bottom five guys in the Jays order who went 9-for-18, with eight RBI and nine runs scored. The Jays set a new one-month club record by winning 21 games in May, and they scored 10 or more runs in six of those wins.

Note to self: the Blue Jays are for real.

5

The Blue Jays Are Coming

JUNE 1

Add Tim Wakefield to the list of wholly ineffective starters. He only lasted four innings, giving up six runs on 10 hits. Then Matt White put on another putrid performance. Thanks in part to a team record five doubles in the fourth inning, the Red Sox scored four times. They eventually scored seven runs against Toronto's ace, Roy Halladay, though Halladay got the win anyway. When White entered the game in the sixth, it was tied 6-6. He promptly gave up three runs and never made it out of the inning. The Red Sox ultimately lost this one, 11-8, which means they gave up 34 runs in the final three games of the series. Yet for some reason, the pitchers aren't being called upon to answer nearly as many questions as the manager.

Show of hands—how many people think they could be an offensive co-coordinator for an NFL team? Put your hands down, you delusional freaks!

How many think they could draw up the appropriate play during an NBA time-out? All right, maybe a few former college players with disproportionately healthy egos.

But how many people think they're qualified to manage the Boston Red Sox? Absolutely everyone, plus everyone else, and everyone else's brother. No experience required.

That's why so many people feel they have the authority—both intellectually and morally—to openly criticize Grady Little. They talk behind his back right under his nose. And that's no easy trick.

The rumblings and ramblings have heated up again recently. Little's being lambasted for having brought Casey Fossum out for the sixth inning. But what's being omitted from the criticisms is the fact that it was Fossum who stank like a hockey team's locker room.

Little's biggest mistake during the team's losing streak was sending Burkett (2 IP, 8 runs), Fossum (5.1 IP, 9 runs), and Wakefield (5 IP, 7 runs) to the mound. Granted, it was Little's decision to walk the bases loaded in New York, but the *only* reason the Red Sox dropped five in a row is because their starters gave up 31 runs in 22.1 innings, and not one of them got past the sixth inning. When someone has a heart attack, you'll notice they grab their left arm. But Grady Little is prescient. When he walks toward the mound and grabs his left arm, it's because a heart attack is *about* to happen.

If it looks like the Red Sox have a Little problem, consider what's been happening in New York. Joe Torre should start worrying about the possible side effects from all the "stupid pills" he's been taking. Apparently, in addition to hair loss and mild intestinal discomfort, those pills can also cause a man to take a team that has won four World Series titles and lead it to an 11-17 record in May. Even with the injuries to Bernie Williams and Nick Johnson, the Yankees have the best lineup in baseball, and a pitching staff that's as intimidating as the "Four Horseman of the Apocalypse"—plus Jeff Weaver. So how could they be so bad for so long? Must be the manager.

The Red Sox have slumped for the same reason the Yankees have slumped—pitching. Or more specifically, bad pitching. And to rephrase with added editorial comment—pitching that stunk so bad it could make your eyes water, your nose run, and, in extreme cases, induce vomiting. That's right, the Red Sox pitching hasn't been anemic—it's been bulimic.

I don't agree with everything Little does. For instance, I wouldn't have started David Ortiz against Cleveland southpaw Brian Anderson on May 24. But Ortiz had three hits that day, including a double and a three-run homer off Anderson. Manny Ramirez also had three hits that day, and was given the following day off. Personally, I'd play Ramirez into the ground. I also don't think I'd hand the ball to Matt White ever again. He's one of those Rule 5 guys, and apparently Rule 5 states explicitly: "Said pitcher, henceforth to be referred to as Gas-on-the-Fire, is prohibited from retiring the side until a minimum requirement of three runs has been scored." White has complied dutifully.

Those who want to stomp on the manager suggest the Red Sox should bunt more, run more, and play more fundamentally sound baseball. That's just vague enough to be simultaneously accurate and unfounded. The biggest Little complaint is that he calls on the wrong pitchers at the wrong times. But I ask you, is there a right time to call on any of those guys? The best thing the bullpen coach can do these days is take the phone off the hook, or at least set up an answering machine that says, "Sorry, we can't get anyone out right now. Please leave a message, and we'll get back to you when one of us finds an ounce of talent." BEEEEEP.

I'm confident that when Pedro Martinez comes back or Byung-Hyun Kim becomes the closer, the Red Sox manager will suddenly become a Little smarter.

Meanwhile, Derek Lowe rejoined the team after stopping in Boston to have a new growth removed from his nose. Doctors will do a biopsy to determine if the skin is once again cancerous. Lowe greeted reporters by saying, "Yeah, I'm ugly. I know." He seems optimistic based on what doctors told him following the procedure.

Let's hope he's OK and that his pitching improves.

JUNE 2

"Yeah, trade me now, faggot!" That's how I'll remember Shea Hillenbrand. I didn't hear him say it, but I've since read about his ill-advised, politically incorrect dare to Red Sox GM Theo Epstein. Hillenbrand uttered the classless phrase on WAAF radio a couple of days before the trade was actually made. He was probably trying to be funny while talking to some rock jocks, but it's about the dumbest thing I've ever heard an athlete say publicly about his boss. I'm sure it came from frustration over being the subject of trade rumors for so long, but even the dumbest, coarsest, most despicable athletes don't often resort to offensive name-calling. But Hillenbrand didn't stop there.

"There's no distraction that can contend with playing in Boston," Hillenbrand told reporters in Arizona, adding, "It's nice to meet reporters who are decent people."

Since Hillenbrand was always treated with respect and given due praise from the Boston media, I'd have to assume he's referring to the media's treatment of other players—like his good friend from last year's team, Carl Everett. This is the same Carl Everett who head-butted an umpire and threatened his former manager Jimy Williams—who had had the audacity to ask Everett why he once abandoned the team for two days. Hillenbrand played hard and well while he was in Boston, but he left without an ounce of class.

Once the trade was complete, Epstein boarded a plane for Toronto so he could meet with Hillenbrand and tell him about the deal in person. It was a respectful and unnecessary gesture on Epstein's part, but Hillenbrand was unimpressed.

"I could care less what Theo did. I would have been more appreciative if he had given me a phone call when he found out because I could have flown out that night. The last flight was at 7 o'clock. I could have been here with this team."

Of course, even though expedience was so very important to Hillenbrand, he didn't join the Diamondbacks for *two* days after he received the face-to-face news. So it's doubtful he would have made that 7:00 p.m. flight.

And then there was this absolute load. Former Red Sox and current Diamondback infielder Carlos Baerga said, "Shea told me Manny (Ramirez) cried when he heard. Manny said, 'They trade everybody. They got rid of Urbina. They traded Hillenbrand.'"

Puh-leeze! First of all, Manny cried? Big tears rolling down his face? Like trading Shea Hillenbrand was akin to a death in the family? C'mon. Let me just say unequivocally—Shea, I don't believe you. Manny did not cry. And not just because "there's no crying in baseball." But because you're just not worth it.

Secondly, Ramirez's bemoaning a lack of loyalty is ridiculous. What kind of loyalty did he show the Indians when he bolted for more money? And whom will he blame when Pedro Martinez bolts from Boston for the same reason? C'mon, big boy, you can't seriously be whining about evolving rosters in Major League Baseball as if the Red Sox are the only team to make transactions.

JUNE 3

While the Red Sox were rained out in Pittsburgh, the Yankees were naming Derek Jeter the 11th team captain in Yankees history. George Steinbrenner is clearly looking to light a fire under his team, and he couldn't wait to do it. Instead of introducing Jeter as the team captain when the Yankees returned home, he simply told Jeter during a telephone conversation before the start of the Yankees series in Cincinnati. Steinbrenner is clearly frustrated and beginning to show signs of panic.

First, he complained about the interleague schedule, and now he makes a midseason move that suggests the Yankees are in need of leadership.

Steinbrenner even said that Jeter will be "the most important Yankees captain ever," adding, "I felt we needed the leadership."

They also need to start playing better. In the series opener against Cincinnati, the Reds got a two-out single from Juan Castro that drove home the game-winning run. The Yankees lost, 4-3. And the only reason the Reds were still in the game at all was because they got one run when Alfonso Soriano couldn't turn a double play. They got another run on Andy Pettitte's throwing error—which followed two wild pitches that allowed another run. The Yankees have committed eight errors in their last four games. It's truly amazing how badly they've played for such an extended period of time.

But the Red Sox haven't been able to take advantage of the Yankees' slide, and that's due in large part to the absence of Pedro Martinez and its domino effect on the rest of the starters. Pedro hasn't pitched since May 15, and the Red Sox have gone 5-10 since then. And since Derek Lowe's complete-game victory against Cleveland on May 23, no Red Sox starter has gone more than six innings. That's a pathetic stretch that covers eight games, during which the starters are 2-4 with a 9.88 ERA. This will only get better when Pedro comes back, and that won't happen for at least another week.

"It's worse than I thought," Martinez said today. "I didn't know the lat was so influential, but it's getting better. Hopefully, it will continue to react well."

This is especially aggravating because of the natural proclivity to believe that an injured player—especially one who doesn't have a broken bone—could come back sooner. And it's worse in this case, because the doctor sat there in the Red Sox dugout soon after examining Pedro and said there was no tear, no significant damage, and basically no problem. Yet by the time, Pedro pitches again, it will have been about a month since he suffered what was diagnosed as a "strain."

JUNE 4

The Red Sox swept a double header from the Pirates while the Yankees lost. Boston is back in first place. It took two great starts from Byung-Hyun Kim and Derek Lowe to make Grady Little look like a genius. Kim and Lowe each went seven innings, allowing just one earned run apiece. The Sox won, 11-4 and 8-3.

These were two easy ones. Manny Ramirez went 4-for-4 in the opener with a homer, two doubles, and four runs batted in. Trot Nixon had a home run in each game and knocked in four runs. Todd Walker extended his hitting streak to 19 games. Nomar Garciaparra tripled in each game, becoming the first player in the majors to triple in four straight games since Sammy Sosa did it in 1994.

Speaking of Sosa, that brings us to the corked bat incident. On June 3, Sosa used an illegal bat against the Tampa Bay Devil Rays. It was discovered when the bat broke as he hit a weak grounder to second base. The event immediately became the biggest story in sports. Sosa's image was tarnished, and his 505 career home runs were called into question. Some people believe Sosa's explanation that he uses the corked bat to put on home-run-hitting displays for the fans during batting practice, and that he accidentally brought it with him to the plate. I and others consider it implausible that in the nearly 8,000 times he's gone to the plate, the one time he carried a corked bat with him he was caught. I believe the number of times he's used a corked bat is somewhere between one time and every time. I also believe we'll never know the truth.

But the story of "Sammy and His Corked Bat" has gotten everyone talking—even Manny Ramirez. For the first time this season, Manny had something to say.

"People are making a big deal about a corked bat or this and that. But you still got to hit the ball," he said. "I think what Sammy did, he didn't know that was his bat, so he took it to the plate. Sammy's so big, he don't need that to hit home runs. So now everything he's accomplished, now people are going to think he used cork all the time. I don't think so. I think he's innocent and people need to support him because of all the things he's done for baseball. Maybe he's telling the truth."

And maybe not.

But Pedro Martinez has taken the issue to an odd and irresponsible extreme, claiming that a racially biased media is blowing the issue out of proportion simply because Sosa is Dominican.

"If it was Mark McGwire, it would still be a big deal," Martinez said. "But not like this." And because 76 other bats belonging to Sosa were checked and determined to be cork free, Martinez believes that exonerates Sosa, and said that all those in the media who vilified Sosa should run the stories of Sosa's innocence with equal passion.

"I'm not defending Sammy for cheating," Martinez said. "I'm just saying, 'Treat everybody the same way, that's all.' I want to see the same campaign go on now to pull him up, to justify whether it was a mistake or whatever."

The only problem with Pedro's rationale is that the 76 other bats don't prove Sosa's innocence. Only the one bat, the one with the cork in it, proves anything—and that's guilt. He's guilty of one incident of wrongdoing. Nobody can dispute that. Everyone's free to believe it was an innocent mistake, but everyone is equally free to believe it wasn't. I'll add this point, however. I submit that every player on the Cubs knows for sure whether Sosa frequently uses a corked bat, and while I've heard opposing players like Pedro and Manny run to Sosa's defense, I haven't heard any of his teammates say that Sosa would never do something like this on purpose. They've supported him as their teammate, but they've come up a little short in the area of denial.

But Martinez's accusations of racism in the media are completely unfounded, and they reveal a lot about Pedro's ego and pettiness. He implied it was racism that cost him the MVP award in 1999 when two voters left him off their ballots entirely. Those voters said they didn't think a pitcher should be eligible for the MVP award, but Pedro called them racist. By the way, Ivan Rodriguez—who's from Puerto Rico—was the MVP that year.

Martinez also intimated there was more racism last year when A's lefty (and white guy) Barry Zito edged him out for the Cy Young Award.

"We might be Latin and minorities, but we're not dumb," Martinez said. "We see everything that happens."

Zito went 23-5 last year while pitching on a playoff team. Pedro was 20-4 and led the league in ERA and strikeouts. A case could be made for either pitcher, but I don't think any voters broke the tie by going with the Caucasian. It makes me angry that Pedro does.

But Pedro saved his most ludicrous comment for last. Referring to a reporter for Fox television who has been especially disbelieving and critical of Sosa, Martinez said, "Even that guy at Fox, this guy said, 'Hey, let's go, smile,' as if that's something that's supposed to be fun. (Expletive), I'm going to go and hunt the guy down."

Happy hunting!

JUNE 5

It was just one of those days. The Pirates got a stolen base from a guy who hadn't stolen a base in three years plus a game-winning pinch-hit single from a guy who was an 0-for-14 pinch hitter, and the Red Sox lost, 5-4.

The Yankees tied a club record with 10 doubles and avoided being swept by the Reds. The Yankees are back in first place by half a game, but they're still having problems.

David Wells has a contract that guarantees him a $135,000 bonus for each start from his sixth through his 17th, but he gets nothing for relief appearances. After pitching in 5.2 innings in relief earlier in the week, Wells wants a little something for the effort.

"I took one for the team," Wells said. "I could have said no, but I'll do what it takes to help the team. I think they should pick up my incentive for that. I think that would be a nice thing to do."

The Yankees have given no indication that they'll do that, nor have they picked up Wells's $6 million option for next season. Wells doesn't expect to be back.

"Just because of the way things are going, especially when the Boss doesn't talk to you," Wells said. "It hurts every day coming in here, knowing the Boss is still mad at you inside, knowing that I've done everything I possibly could do to win our friendship back. It's just something I have to deal with every day, and it stinks, because I like joking with him and having fun."

I remember when the Yankees just played baseball, played it very well, and won championships. There's something drastically different about this Yankees team. It's hard to identify exactly what it is, but I think I like it—a lot!

JUNE 6

Sammy Sosa received an eight-game suspension for using a corked bat. His appeal will take a few days, which means he'll be playing in the Cubs-Yankees series at Wrigley Field this weekend. He went 1-for-4 tonight as David Wells beat the Cubs, 5-3, and he'll be in the lineup when Roger Clemens tries for a third time to win his 300th game.

Meanwhile, the Red Sox lost to the Brewers, 9-3, and dropped a game and a half back in the standings. Tim Wakefield was hit by a pitch in the ankle in the second inning and was forced to leave the game. The injury doesn't appear too serious.

Also, the Yankees traded minor-league outfielder Marcus Thames to the Texas Rangers for the switch-hitting Ruben Sierra. Sierra called Joe Torre "a liar" in 1996 when he was with the Yankees and not getting the playing time he thought he deserved or that Torre had promised him. It's a relatively insignificant move by the Yankees, who are looking for some left-handed hitting help while Bernie Williams and Nick Johnson are laid up.

JUNE 7

Good news and bad news. First, this game against the Milwaukee

Brewers was simply the best comeback of the year for the Red Sox. Of all the games they've won in their last at bat (now up to nine), this was the most dramatic. However, Casey Fossum left the game after just one inning because of soreness in his left shoulder. This smells like the disabled list to me, but we'll find out on Monday when he's checked out by the team doctor in Boston.

As for the game—with Fossum out, the Brewers jumped on Robert Person and Byung-Hyun Kim for eight runs in four innings. The Red Sox were in a 10-4 hole after five innings, but it wasn't 10-4 over and out. This was just beginning.

Bill Mueller pinch hit for Kim in the sixth inning and blasted a solo home run. Then Kevin Millar pinch hit for Allen Embree in the seventh inning and blasted a grand slam. Suddenly, the Sox were only down 10-9.

Milwaukee brought closer Mike DeJean in for the ninth inning, and after David Ortiz (who had homered earlier) struck out, Trot Nixon drove a pitch that was low and away out toward left center. It could be. It might be. It was! Gone! The game was tied at 10.

The next batter was Jason Varitek. Gone! Varitek was the sixth different Red Sox hitter to homer in this one, and the Red Sox came from six runs down to take the lead, 11-10.

Brandon Lyon had already thrown two innings, so it was up to Mike Timlin to close it out in the home half of the ninth. And he did. It was the first time this year the Red Sox won a game in which they were trailing after eight innings. They've won 10 times when trailing after six innings, but had been 0-24 when behind after eight.

But the absolute best news of the day came out of Wrigley Field, where Roger Clemens failed for a third time to win his 300th career game. And this wasn't some ordinary, run-of-the-mill loss. This was jump-up-and-down glorious. It was dramatic. And it was controversial.

Clemens pitched magnificently for six innings and was nearly matched pitch for pitch by Cubs fireballer Kerry Wood. This was a wonderful matchup between the only two men to ever strike out 20 batters in a game.

Clemens has done it twice—truly amazing! Wood did it in the fifth start of his career—also incredible.

Through six innings, Clemens had given up two hits and was working on a shutout. Wood had surrendered just one hit, but it was a home run to Hideki Matsui. So, it's a 1-0 Yankees lead through six. In the seventh, Clemens began with a strikeout of Corey Patterson, but Sammy Sosa followed with a base hit. And then Moises Alou walked, putting runners on first and second with one out.

Suddenly, Joe Torre bounds out of the dugout and touches his right arm. Clemens is done!

It was shocking. Clemens was throwing a two-hit shutout while on a quest for his 300th win, and Torre was pulling him after just 84 pitches. Even more astonishing, Clemens was being replaced by Juan Acevedo, whose ERA was a shade under *seven*. What was Torre thinking?

We later learned that Torre was thinking about Clemens's health. The Rocket was fighting an upper respiratory infection that was making him a little weak, and the next base hit would bring home the tying run. Since Clemens wouldn't be coming back out for the eighth inning, that would remove any chance he'd have of getting his big victory that day. So Torre gambled—and lost.

The first pitch Acevedo threw was dropped into the left-field stands by Eric Karros, a three-run homer that put Clemens on the losing end of a 3-1 score. The Yankees eventually lost, 5-2. I can't even imagine what the fans and media in Boston would have put Grady Little through if he had made the same decision and it had blown up in his face like that.

Clemens, who issued a postgame statement saying that his upper respiratory infection didn't affect his pitching, but expressed no anger or frustration about having been pulled from the game, dropped to 6-4. He'll try again in five days against the Cardinals at Yankee Stadium.

JUNE 8

The Red Sox 12-game trek through New York, Toronto, Pittsburgh, and Milwaukee ended with an easy 9-1 win over the Brewers. Kevin Millar homered twice, and the Sox finished the road trip 5-7.

The most important development of the days away was the resurgence of Derek Lowe. Today, he threw six innings, allowing just one earned run. Unfortunately, the reason he left was because he had a blister on his right thumb.

Still, over his last five starts, Lowe is 3-0 with a 2.55 ERA.

JUNE 9

Casey Fossum landed on the disabled list today after an MRI showed he has a minor case of shoulder tendinitis. Rest is recommended, and his full recovery is expected in a couple of weeks. The Red Sox will be looking for someone to replace him in the rotation, either from the bullpen or the minor leagues.

Also, Red Sox pitching coach Tony Cloninger has taken a leave of absence from the team so he can battle his bladder cancer full time. So, the Red Sox hired Dave Wallace, who was a vice president for the Los Angeles Dodgers. Wallace will be asked to solve the problems of the Red Sox bullpen, which is currently sporting an unsightly 5.83 ERA.

"Anybody who thinks I'm coming in as a miracle worker is crazy," Wallace said.

Call me crazy, but that's what I'm hoping for.

JUNE 10

The St. Louis Cardinals came to Fenway Park for the first time since the 1967 World Series, and there was more heartbreak for Red Sox fans this time around. The Red Sox rallied from five runs down, only to lose, 9-7, when Brandon Lyon surrendered a couple of runs in the ninth inning. The Red Sox dropped back into second place, a half game behind the Yankees.

Red Sox hitters weren't able to do much against Cardinals starter Woody Williams, but that changed in the seventh inning. Down 7-2, Todd Walker doubled, Nomar Garciaparra tripled (his league-leading ninth triple), and Manny Ramirez homered (his fourth in five games). That knocked Williams out of the game and cut the deficit to 7-5.

The Red Sox were able to tie it when Jason Varitek blasted a two-run homer in the eighth, but for the seventh time in their last 13 games, Red Sox pitchers allowed nine or more runs. Their staff has fallen to 27th in the major leagues.

The Yankees also have pitching woes to be concerned about. Jose Contreras was placed on the 15-day disabled list with a right shoulder strain. That's a significant loss for them, because Contreras had found his groove as a starter, winning both his starts and posting a 1.29 ERA.

So, the Yankees will be without him, and they'll be without Juan Acevedo. Three days after blowing Roger Clemens's potential 300th win, Acevedo was released. At the time of his dismissal, Acevedo was 0-3 with a 7.71 ERA. It stinks a little bit that the Yankees can just cut a guy loose who's making $900,000.

JUNE 11

On the night Pedro Martinez returns to the hill for Boston, the Yankees were no-hit for the first time since 1958. The games at Fenway Park and Yankee Stadium ended at nearly the exact same time. Don't try to tell me there aren't any baseball gods up there jerking us around. They love this stuff. And so do I.

Taking on a strong Cardinals lineup, Martinez was nothing short of awesome. Apparently, he pitches very well on four weeks' rest. He threw 47 pitches (33 of them for strikes), struck out three, and allowed just two hits in three scoreless innings.

"I was actually locked in (despite) the time away from the mound," Martinez said. "I'm pretty much back on track. Tomorrow is going to be a big day, definitely. But I'm right away jumping ahead and saying I'm going to feel better according to what I feel right now."

The Red Sox hitters seemed inspired by Martinez's return. They scored seven runs in the second inning on their way to a season-high 19 hits. And John Burkett, throwing in predetermined relief, pitched in with six solid innings. The Red Sox won, 13-1.

Could this signal a turnaround for the Red Sox? We'll find out. But Martinez's value to the team, despite his pitching only every five or six days, may best be reflected by the team's 9-13 record while he was out. The staff ERA was a pathetic 6.29. *If* he gets back to full strength, *if* Lowe truly is back on track, *if* Kim stays in the rotation, and *if* Burkett can put together a few more performances like tonight's, then the Red Sox starting rotation just might be able to hide the bullpen's continued deficiencies. Did that seem like a lot of *if*s?

As for the Yankees, Joe Torre said it best: "It was a total inexcusable performance. Whatever kind of history it was, it was terrible. It was one of the worst games I've ever been involved with."

Six Houston pitchers combined to no-hit the Yankees for the first time since Hoyt Wilhelm beat them 1-0 in 1958.

"I've never been a part of a no-hitter where my team was no-hit," said Derek Jeter. "It's embarrassing. It should be. If you're not embarrassed by it, something is wrong with you."

The embarrassment and distress were written all over the Yankees' faces during the final innings. It was clear that the Yankees couldn't believe this was happening to them. This is what they do to everyone else. It had to be a most humbling experience for a team that thrives on its own justifiable arrogance.

"We're getting a taste of our own medicine," Jeter said. "These are the things we've been doing to teams throughout the years and even in the first month of this season. It's not a good feeling. You have to remember it, because you don't want to feel like this again. We're just getting kicked when we're down."

It sure didn't look like a no-hitter in the making when Astros starter Roy Oswalt left the game after his second pitch of the second inning. He had aggravated a groin strain. Advantage Yankees. But then five relievers combined to toss a no-no-no-no-no-no-hitter. And quite uncharacteristically, the Yankees appeared to quit. Eight Yankees in a row struck out before Hideki Matsui grounded out to end the game.

Torre held another closed-door meeting with his floundering club, one that's gone 16-24 after an incredible 20-4 start.

"Right now, it's not pretty," Torre said. "I don't feel good about myself, either. I'm the leader of this squad. I'm not putting it all on them, because I'm responsible for it."

Still, the Yankees remain the most fearsome team in the American League, and they're only half a game behind the Red Sox. Who would be surprised if they suddenly won 20 out of 24 games again and started to run away with this thing? There are absolutely no indications that they're about to do that, because they look utterly lost, but a team that good can't play that badly forever. Or can they?

JUNE 12

Game of the year! No doubt about it. A fantastic game filled with intrigue, drama, comebacks, and of course second-guessing. But as great as it was, it was just another in an exasperating series of character-building losses for the Red Sox. Once again, they showed a "never say die" mentality—and then died, so to speak. After two unlikely comebacks in the ninth and 10th innings, the Red Sox lost the "game of the year" in 13 innings, when a third comeback fell one run short.

With the Red Sox trailing 2-0 in the eighth, Cardinals outfielder Jim Edmunds hit a solo home run off Alan Embree. Who knew what a costly run that would be? In the ninth, Jeremy Giambi led off with a walk (which is the only thing he seems to do well), and Jason Varitek followed with a two-run homer. Now, with nobody out, the Red Sox were only down a run.

Johnny Damon grounded to first, but Todd Walker reached on a base hit to center. Pinch runner Damian Jackson stole second. Gutsy call by Grady

Little. If Jackson had been thrown out, Nomar Garciaparra would have been standing at the plate with two outs and nobody on. Instead, the tying run was at second base, with only one out and the heart of the Red Sox lineup facing Cardinals reliever Cal Eldred.

Garciaparra put on an incredible at bat. Unable to get a pitch he could handle, Nomar just kept fouling them away until he got one he liked. He fouled off five pitches, and on the 11th pitch of the at bat, he drilled a long fly ball to center field. It banged off the wall about four feet from being a home run. Jackson scored easily, and Garciaparra went into third base standing up with his 11th triple of the year. The game was tied at 3. The Red Sox still had only one out, and their winning run was 90 feet away.

Cardinal Manager Tony LaRussa opted to walk Manny Ramirez intentionally. No surprise there. Then he walked Kevin Millar intentionally. Still not much of a surprise, since he had pulled the same move two nights earlier. In the eighth inning of a tied game, LaRussa walked the same two hitters in order to put the game in David Ortiz's hands. Ortiz popped up to end the inning, and the Red Sox eventually lost the game.

"It's not a question of walking someone," LaRussa said. "It's a matter of who you pick to beat you."

So, LaRussa does the same thing here. This time, he brings in a tough lefty, Steve Kline, to face left-handed hitter Trot Nixon. Keep in mind, there's one out. All the Red Sox really need is a fly ball to the outfield. Garciaparra has good speed at third. The right-handed swinging Freddy Sanchez is on the bench. Should Little pinch hit for Nixon? Probably. But he let Nixon hit. Nixon fouled out to first. Two down.

Now, it's up to switch-hitter Bill Mueller. He flies out to right. LaRussa's strategy works again, and we head into extra innings.

In the 10th, LaRussa sends J. D. Drew up as a pinch hitter to face Brandon Lyon. The first pitch he saw was like a dog without a leash—it left the park. It was a two-run homer, giving the Cardinals a 5-3 lead. Lyon got out of the inning without any further trouble.

In the home half of the 10th, the Red Sox made two quick outs against left-hander Jeff Fassero. It was up to Johnny Damon to keep hope alive. And he did, with a beautifully placed bunt down the first base line. He was safe on an extremely close play.

Time for another strange move by Grady Little. With another lefty on the hill, he pinch hit for Jackson (a righty) with David Ortiz (a lefty). Granted, Ortiz has been swinging a hot bat and is hitting .323 against lefties, so it wasn't a crazy move, but it wasn't exactly going by the book.

Ortiz responded with a wall-scraping double to left. Jackson scored to make it 5-4, St. Louis. Now it was up to Nomar again. He swung at the first pitch, then it appeared Fassero was trying to unintentionally "intentionally" walk him. He threw three straight balls that were well off the plate, and a fourth one had Nomar heading for first base. But the home plate umpire called it a strike. All right, Nomar got another chance to swing the bat. Base hit to right-center field. Pinch runner Freddy Sanchez scored easily, and the game was tied at 5.

Again LaRussa intentionally walked Ramirez. But he surprisingly pitched to Kevin Millar with the winning run at second base—at least he started to. Once the count got to 2-1, LaRussa ordered Fassero to intentionally walk Millar, leaving the bases loaded once again for Trot Nixon. Now there's no one left to pinch hit, and for the third time in this amazing game, Nixon left the bases loaded. He grounded into a force play to end the inning. Nixon left 12 men on base.

The game stayed tied 5-5 until the 13th inning. In Ramiro Mendoza's second inning, he gave up a leadoff single to Kerry Robertson. He was sacrificed over to second, and a grounder to the right side put him on third with two outs. Little, perhaps taking a page out of LaRussa's handbook, decided to intentionally walk the always dangerous Albert Pujols. But instead of also walking Jim Edmunds, who had homered earlier in the game, and who swings from the left, Little had Mendoza throw to him. With right-handed-hitting Scott Rolen watching from the on-deck circle, Edmunds blasted a three-run homer over the wall in left—8-5 Cardinals. Rolen grounded out to third to end the inning.

More miracles in the bottom of the 13th? Not quite. Ramirez walked, Millar singled, and Nixon singled—8-6. Bill Mueller grounded into a double play, and Millar scored—8-7. But those were two big outs, and now the bases were empty.

Jeremy Giambi walked. He's good at that. He went to second base on a wild pitch. And here we go again. LaRussa has Varitek intentionally walked so that his right-handed pitcher, Estaban Yan, can pitch to left-hander Johnny Damon. This was the exact same strategy that had failed to work for Little. Damon flied to right. Game over.

"It was one of the most bizarre games I've been in," Little said.

Garciaparra added, "It was just an incredible game on both ends. The Cardinals battled. They pulled it off. They didn't give up. We didn't give up. If you're any kind of fan, there's nothing you can say bad about that game on both ends."

JUNE 13

Once I finally accepted the inevitability of it, watching Roger Clemens win his 300th game was an exhilarating sports experience. It was a heavyweight championship fight, the Super Bowl, and a last-second three-point shot all rolled into one. And it had the added dimension of being a history-making moment—and a history-making "series" of moments. That's the way baseball plays itself out. Moment by moment. Momentum by momentum. No clock. Waiting to exhale. It's never over, Yogi tells us, until Jason Giambi scoops up a ground ball and steps on the bag. That was the moment Clemens was finally able to turn awkwardly and hug pitching coach Mel Stottlemyre and manager Joe Torre.

It was a moment that Clemens almost missed. Like every starting pitcher who gets pulled, Clemens retreated to the locker room, where he showered and shaved. In the ninth inning, he decided to put his uniform back on and return to the dugout.

"Just being able to thank each guy on the field that I hugged on the field, it was amazing," Clemens said. "I'm glad it's done."

He was overpowering from the start, striking out the side in the first inning and picking up career strikeout number 4,000 in the second (Cardinal shortstop Edgar Renteria was the victim). Clemens threw 120 pitches over 6 2/3 innings, finishing with 10 Ks and leaving with a 3-2 lead. Once again it was up to the bullpen. And it nearly faltered.

It was a little surprising to see Joe Torre come out and get Clemens after he retired the first two batters in the seventh. But the pitch count was high, and Torre wanted his lefty, Chris Hammond, to face Cardinals left-hander J. D. Drew.

"I told Roger after the game, 'I used to be popular here before you started doing this stuff,'" said Torre. "You have to do what you think is the right thing. I'm just glad it worked out. I would have booed too if I was sitting in the stands."

It was the right thing to do, but it almost turned out all wrong. Drew bunted his way on, and another base hit put runners on the corners. But Hammond escaped by getting Jim Edmonds to ground out.

A two-run homer by Raul Mondesi provided a cushion, and Mariano Rivera closed it out. The Yankees won, 5-4. And Clemens became the second pitcher to win his 300th game in a Yankees uniform. Phil Neikro was the other, but he won his 300th at Toronto in 1985. Clemens is the first Yankee to reach the milestone at home.

"To have these two milestones that I was able to attain on the same night here, it couldn't have worked out any better," Clemens said. "Four thousand and 300 put me with some great men that have ever stepped on that mound. I'm very happy to be able to catch these guys."

It took him 18 days and four tries after his 299th win, but it was inevitable. And it turned out to be well pitched, well earned, and quite special.

My biggest concern right now is that with this distraction behind them, the Yankees will shift into overdrive again. They're real good, and it's about time they started showing it. This could be the springboard.

The Red Sox, meanwhile, got a strong outing from Ryan Rupe, who was called up to take Casey Fossum's place on the roster and in the starting rotation. The Sox beat the Astros, 4-3. Also, Pedro Martinez reports he's feeling fine and will throw between 70 and 80 pitches on Monday against the White Sox. And how about this for convenience? A day after another implosion—this one a three-run homer to Jim Edmunds—Ramiro Mendoza is placed on the disabled list with tendinitis in his right knee. I wonder if he told the Red Sox about the pain in his knee, or if they told him.

JUNE 15

The Red Sox and Yankees both swept their National League opponents, but the Red Sox had to work a lot harder to do so. It took a Manny Ramirez RBI single in the bottom of the 14th for the Red Sox to outlast the Astros, 3-2. It's only the second time this year the Red Sox have won when they've scored fewer than four runs. They're 2-9 when that has happened.

Oh, what a relief the bullpen was for a change. Byung-Hyun Kim started and pitched into the seventh inning, surrendering only a two-run homer to Richard Hidalgo. Then Mike Timlin, Brandon Lyon, Alan Embree, and Jason Shiell combined to throw eight shutout innings. Timlin has been dependable all year. Ditto for Lyon. Embree is off the disabled list and hitting in the mid-90's again on his fastball. And Shiell is just a gutsy guy up from the minor leagues for the second time this year.

Strange to say, and it's probably too soon to say, but the Sox bullpen looks good right now. The Yankees seem to have turned the corner and could be getting ready to go off on another hot streak. But it feels like the Red Sox are prepared to stay right with them.

JUNE 16

Having Pedro Martinez back in the rotation is supposed to feel better than this. He's made two starts since his interminable stint on the disabled list, going three innings his first time out and five innings tonight. Gradually, his pitch count will increase. In the meantime, though, he's not doing the team a lot of good. True, he left tonight's game against the White Sox with a 2-1 lead, but it's a lot to ask of any bullpen to hold a team scoreless for nearly half the game—especially this bullpen. Ryan Rupe will wear the horns for this one, because he gave up a three-run homer to Joe Crede, and the Red Sox lost 4-2. But truth be told, the Red Sox lost this game because they couldn't score enough runs, and because Pedro couldn't last another two or three innings.

Meanwhile, there's lots of talk about impending deals. The Yankees and Red Sox are both interested in Texas closer Ugueth Urbina, the guy the Red Sox chose not to keep during the off-season. Also, the Red Sox have had several talks with the New York Mets about their heart attack closer, Armando Benitez. There's also reported interest in Houston closer Billy Wagner, Mets starter Al Leiter, and, of course, Bartolo Colon. I expect the Red Sox to make one more substantial move, but not the Yankees.

An average French history student can tell you the "do-nothing kings" reigned from about 638 to 751. They were ultimately deposed by Pepin the Short. I never took French history, so I had to look it up, and I did so merely to reference the fact that this year's New York Yankees are the modern-day "do-nothing kings." Baseball's royalty tends to be a royal pain when it comes to making in-season improvements. Have a weakness? Go out and get Raul Mondesi from the Blue Jays (July 1, 2002). Need another arm for the pennant drive? Trading Brett Jodie and Darren Blakely to the Padres for Sterling Hitchcock should help (July 30, 2001). Looking for a left-handed bat? Ricky Ledee will get you David Justice from the Cleveland Indians (June 29, 2000). And if that's not enough offense to get you where you're going, just wave that magic scepter, and Jose Canseco will become available (August 9, 2000). Sure, it may cost you $1 million for 56 days' work, but you're the Yankees; you can afford it.

The list of helpful additions heading to the Bronx is nearly as endless as it is one sided. They got David Cone from the Blue Jays in July 1995 for Marty Janzen, Jason Jarvis, and Mike Gordon. They got Chad Curtis from the Indians in June 1997 for the weathered David Weathers. Two years later, Geraldo Padua went to San Diego for Jim Leyritz. Who do you think got the better of those deals? You have to go all the way back to 1988 to find a deal in which the Yankees got snookered. That's when the Yankees sent Jay Buhner, Rick Balabon, and Troy Evers to Seattle for Ken Phelps. Phelps hit .224 after the trade, and the Yankees finished fifth in the East. Phelps was traded to Oakland a year later. As George Costanza's father said on *Seinfeld*, "*How could you trade Buhner?*"

And while I'm at it, let me attempt to clear up one rather large myth about the Yankees. They don't make these one-sided trades because they're such good talent evaluators. The teams they're trading with know they're getting long-shot talent in return. But they make the deals anyway, because they're dumping salaries. The Yankees don't make these deals because their farm system is so fantastic, either. They don't need a great farm system. All they need are warm bodies. That's also why they're able to hold on to the handful of great talents they develop every 20 years or so. Think about it. From 1981 to 1995, the Yankees were a bad team going nowhere. Finally, they were able to draft and develop guys like Derek Jeter, Bernie Williams, Jorge Posada, and Andy Pettitte. Wonderful work there.

But for all the credit the Yankees get for being a well-run operation, their greatest skill is identifying the best free agent on the market and paying that player the most money. You think it takes a genius to recognize that Jason Giambi is better than Tino Martinez? That Mike Mussina would be a nice addition? That keeping Williams away from the Red Sox is a sound idea? That trading for Roger Clemens after his second straight Cy Young Award makes sense? When comparing the Yankees to the Red Sox, you need only remember that the Yankees generally don't do anything better, except spend more money in the most obvious places.

But this year, the Yankees will "do nothing," or darn close to it. No offense to Ruben Sierra, but he's nothing. (All right, maybe that's a little offensive). But Sierra will turn 104 on his next birthday (38 actually), and he had a grand total of 275 hits over the last *five* seasons. He was picked up merely as a stopgap measure. His switch-hitting ability will come in handy until Nick Johnson returns from the disabled list. Then Sierra, who's making $600,000, will be cast away like Tom Hanks and his volleyball friend, Wilson. There will be rumors, inquiries, and intrigue. There always are. When teams are looking to pawn off some high-priced talent, they'll always look first to baseball's pawnshop. But when the trading deadline nears, the Yankees will have about as much movement as a constipated man in a straight jacket. Or, if you prefer, let's just say a pimply faced, introverted mute has more moves than the Yankees will be making this year.

The reason the Yankees will be a bigger "do-nothing king" than Larry is because they need nothing. Unless there's a significant injury to one of their starters, they're set in that department. Closer? Got one of the best. Go around the infield. Seems pretty solid. Even at third, while getting Mike Lowell from the Marlins would be an upgrade from Robin Ventura, it would not make a big difference. In the outfield, they'll be adding Bernie Williams to the lineup in a few weeks, and he'll stand between Hideki Matsui and Raul Mondesi. So, do you really think the Yankees are going to make a serious bid for Pirates outfielder Brian Giles, as has been reported? The New York papers are also throwing around the name of Carlos Beltran of the Kansas City Royals. Another great talent, but where would he play? Whose place would he take? If Bernie Williams is more seriously injured than we've been led to believe, then the Yankees would likely jump at a big name like Giles or Beltran. Otherwise, they'll do nothing.

They won't get Ugueth Urbina, because they already have a better closer, and they'll be concerned about Urbina's willingness to accept a setup role, and his ability to do the job. Urbina has never been especially good in the eighth inning or in non-save situations.

So, while the baseball world waits for the Yankees to step up to the plate and take a big swing at a guy like Urbina or even Bartolo Colon, I expect them to go for someone more like Gabe White. And I don't say that disparagingly. The Yankees' only real weakness remains in their bullpen, and the Reds' left-hander would be a decent addition. His ERA is 3.94, and his salary is $2.35 million. Both are numbers the Yankees can handle.

But c'mon! If Gabe White is the best they can do, then perhaps you'd agree they really are the "do-nothing kings." Of course, I could be wrong. After all, these are the Yankees, and I could see them getting Urbina just to keep him away from the Red Sox. I could see them scooping up Colon, and putting Jeff Weaver *and* Jose Contreras in the bullpen. I could see them getting their payroll to the verge of $200 million. But doesn't it seem more likely that the Red Sox, who aggressively went after Kevin Millar, Bill Mueller, David Ortiz, a host of relievers, and, most recently, Byung-Hyun Kim, will make the bigger splash before the trading deadline?

That's the way I'm looking at it. I think that if you're looking for a Blockbuster in the Bronx, you'll find one at 2554 White Plains Road. They're offering five-day rentals on *Deliver Us From Eva*. Be kind. Please rewind.

JUNE 17

The Red Sox got an up-close and personal look at the guy they've coveted since the start of spring training, Bartolo Colon. What they saw, they undoubtedly liked. But they beat him, and his record dropped to 6-7. Colon leads the league with five complete games and is a definite horse who could help the Red Sox immensely, but I hope it's not at too high a price. By the All-Star break, Colon's ERA should be hovering around 4.00. He'll be a .500 pitcher, plus or minus a game or two. He'll have $4 million left on his contract. And he'll be able to walk away at the end of the year. I can't imagine the White Sox can ask for very much. I think the Red Sox could get away with offering a decent prospect out of the minor leagues—which would make Theo Epstein GM of the Year, in my opinion.

Remember, Epstein wouldn't pull the trigger on a deal of Casey Fossum and Shea Hillenbrand for Bartolo Colon. Then he traded Hillenbrand for Byung-Hyun Kim. Now, if he's able to acquire Colon for something less than Fossum, he will have effectively gotten Kim and Colon for Hillenbrand and a prospect. That would truly be amazing!

By the way, ever since Kim joined the Red Sox rotation, the team's starters are 6-0 with an ERA of 3.05 over a span of 14 games. Unfortunately, the bullpen's record during that span is 2-6. Putting Pedro into the mix has been even more beneficial. In the seven games since Pedro's return, Sox starters have had an ERA of 2.72, and the team is 5-2.

JUNE 18

A day after Roger Clemens appeared on the *Late Show with David Letterman* and delivered the Top Ten List, he flirted with a no-hitter. Clemens is one of seven 300-game winners who's never thrown a no-hitter, and he didn't quite get there tonight. Instead, for the second time in his career, he watched the no-no go away after 7 1/3 innings. The first time it happened, he was with the Red Sox. Cleveland's Phil Clark hit a one-out single in the eighth. Clemens also fired a one-hitter during the American League Championship Series in 2000 against the Mariners. This time he was facing the Tampa Bay Devil Rays, the team he had insulted the night before on national television.

You see, the Top Ten List was about things that Clemens has learned during his time in the big leagues, and number four on the list was this: "The best practical joke? Tell a teammate they're traded to the Devil Rays."

He was equally insulting to the Red Sox, though nobody made too big a deal out of it. "Number three: It doesn't matter if you win or lose. Well, it didn't when I was on the Red Sox." And while we're here, number two was: "Good nickname: Rocket. Bad nickname: Lard-ass." The number one thing Roger has learned? "Adjusting your cup doesn't do anything…just makes you feel good."

Good stuff. And that's what he brought to the mound against the Devil Rays. His no-hitter was snatched from him when Marlon Anderson went the other way and hit a clean single to left. Clemens left after eight, but the Yankees needed a bases-loaded single by Alfonso Soriano in the 12th to beat the Rays.

The Yankees have won six of their last seven, during which time they've picked up two games on the Red Sox and now lead by 1 1/2 games.

Meanwhile, after the Red Sox lost, 3-1, to Chicago's Estaban Loiaza, their lead over the Blue Jays is down to half a game. After a disappointing May, the Sox are just 7-7 in June.

Before the game in Chicago, the Red Sox announced that Bobby Howry is done for the year. Howry only made four appearances this year, posting an ERA of 12.46 before being sent down to Pawtucket with elbow problems. Now he needs surgery to repair damage to his ulnar nerve. His days with the Red Sox could be over. The team has an option worth $2.5 million for next year, or they could opt out for just $200,000.

Yankeeland still isn't a happy place, despite the team's recent resurgence. Joe Torre told the Fox News channel that George Steinbrenner has been more of a distraction this year than he'd like, and that he'd like the occasional pat on the back from The Boss.

"At times I'd like (him to) just give me a little more credit that I know what I'm doing. Conversations happen all the time. Over the 7 1/2 years I've been here, they continue to happen, but it's never been as public as it has been this year. It started last year when we lost to Anaheim. He was very upset, and I was, too. And then he got on Jeter…he got on my coaches. The change is he went public with a lot of it and it's gotten in the newspaper."

Keep yapping, George. And maybe someday you'll accidentally happen upon the answer to this question, and then you can tell us all: if the Michelin Man is made out of tires, why is he all white?

JUNE 19

The offense is going cold. Last night was the first time all year the Red

Sox were held without an extra base hit. Tonight, it happened again. This time the vaunted attack that has averaged six runs a game was held to three singles—one hit through the first nine innings. But the Red Sox still managed to win. Strange game, this baseball.

Three walks and an error resulted in a run and loaded the bases for Trot Nixon in the first inning. He responded with a two-run single, and it looked like the Red Sox were off and running. But they didn't get another hit until the 10th.

Derek Lowe pitched in and out of trouble throughout his six innings, and the bullpen held the weak-hitting White Sox at bay until the Red Sox could get the game winner in the 10th. Johnny Damon extended his hitting streak to nine games with a game-winning single that scored Bill Mueller. Damon has raised his average by 20 points (to .259) during the streak.

Brandon Lyon threw the final two innings to pick up his third win of the year.

The Blue Jays won for the eighth time in nine games and remain just half a game behind the Red Sox. The Yankees were rained out in Tampa Bay. Their lead over the Red Sox is back down to a game.

JUNE 20

No game today. Too much rain in Philadelphia. They'll make this one up on Labor Day. Meanwhile, the Blue Jays and Yankees both won. So, the Sox are now 1 1/2 games back—*tied* with Toronto. The Blue Jays aren't slowing down at all. After their 21-8 May, they're 11-5 in June. But who made up their schedule? After getting swept by the Cardinals, the Blue Jays have dominated the likes of Pittsburgh, Cincinnati, the Cubs, Baltimore, and now Montreal. Of that group, only the Expos and Cubs have a winning record, and the Jays lost two out of three against Chicago. Looking ahead, the Blue Jays play 13 of their next 19 games against *really* bad teams—Baltimore and Detroit. Of course, after Philadelphia, the Red Sox play 10 straight against Detroit, Florida, and Tampa Bay—who have winning percentages of .257, .480, and .338. So forget I mentioned it.

JUNE 21

This one hurt so much it's going to leave a mark. The Red Sox blew a 2-1 lead in the eighth inning, and a 3-2 lead in the 12th inning when Philadelphia's Jim Thome hit two game-tying solo home runs. In the 13th inning, the Red

Sox scored twice with the help of Nomar Garciaparra's sixth hit of the game. That's right! The man went 6-for-6! But the bullpen blew the lead again. This time it was Rudy Seanez surrendering a two-run pinch-hit homer to Todd Pratt, a 36-year-old journeyman backup catcher who's never played in more than 80 games in a season. It was his first home run this season and his second hit this month—which equals the number of hits he had all of last month. Todd Pratt beating you with a home run is just not supposed to happen.

This game had several story lines. It began with Pedro Martinez making his third start since coming off the disabled list. This time he'd be allowed to throw upwards of 90 pitches, which was expected to get him into the seventh inning. It turned out he threw 91 pitches, 65 for strikes, and gave up just one run on a solo shot off Bobby Abreu's bat. Pedro struck out seven and left after seven innings with a 2-1 lead.

Todd Walker provided the Red Sox offense with solo homers of his own in the third and sixth innings. Walker's last multi-homer game wasn't quite as long ago as I would have thought. He had two home runs for the Rockies on May 22 against Florida. He also had two home runs on June 25, 2001, against the San Diego Padres.

Pedro was relieved by Mike Timlin. One of the steadiest influences in the Red Sox bullpen, Timlin had only given up two runs in his last seven appearances (9.2 IP), and he hadn't given up more than one run since April 25. He seemed like somebody you could count on.

But Thome, the big left-handed slugger who always looks like he's wearing a throwback uniform and who signed a six-year, $85 million contract with the Phillies during the off-season, drove the ball into the right-center-field bleachers, tying the game with two outs. Thome hadn't homered in seven games and 23 at bats, so I guess he was due.

In the Red Sox ninth, Manny Ramirez batted with runners on first and second with one out, and grounded into a double play. It was not his day. Ramirez went 0-for-7, stranding 10 runners. For all the heat the bullpen will take for this loss, Ramirez is equally responsible.

The Phillies had the best early threat in extra innings, loading the bases in the tenth. But Brandon Lyon struck out Abreu. The game remained scoreless into the 12th when the Red Sox got a gift run. With Garciaparra on first, Kevin Millar blooped a fly ball into left field. Jason Michaels had a long run, but he got there in time, only to see the ball slip under his glove and roll to the wall. Garciaparra scored from first, and Millar was credited with a triple. Jeremy Giambi pinch hit for Lyon and struck out. He's now three for his last

34, and his days in Boston could be numbered. There's been talk that the Red Sox are interested in outfielder/first baseman Gabe Kapler, who was recently let go by the Rockies. Kapler would provide a right-handed bat off the bench, and even though he was cut loose, he'd have to be better than Giambi's been.

With the Red Sox ahead 3-2, Jason Shiell was brought in to close it out. He didn't. He quickly got two outs, and got two strikes on Thome. Three balls later, Thome hit one so deep, it was Freudian. Again, the game was tied. Shiell finished the inning by striking out Marlon Byrd. Too late.

But the Red Sox have more comebacks in them than a boxer. Todd Walker ripped a double to the left-center-field gap in the 13th inning, bringing home Johnny Damon. Garciaparra followed with a run-scoring single that would have been a double, had he not tripped rounding first base. Not to worry, the insurance run scored, and the Sox were up 5-3.

However, with two outs in the bottom of the 13th, Shiell gave up an RBI double to David Bell. Now, with the score 5-4, Grady Little called to the bullpen and brought in Rudy Seanez. In seven appearances with the Red Sox, Seanez had given up six runs. So, let's just say he doesn't instill a heck of a lot of confidence.

Second pitch, *gone*! Pratt hits the game winner to straightaway center field. It was an absolute killer. This one could take a while to get over. Despite the offense's recent cooldown, and the fact that they could only score two runs in the first nine innings, the Sox hitters did provide three different leads, only to see the bullpen blow each one. At some point, that has to affect a team's morale.

The Red Sox are 6-6 in Pedro's 12 starts this year. You'd certainly expect better. Of course, Pedro did leave four games this year with the lead only to watch the bullpen give them away, though I'd argue that Pedro didn't deserve to win those games, and those no-decisions were as much a reflection on the offense as they were on the bullpen. He left those four games with leads of 4-1, 3-1, and 2-1 twice. And while Pedro's ERA in those games was a minuscule 1.00, he only pitched a total of 27 innings. That tells you he averaged 6.2 innings in those games that the bullpen supposedly blew. Seems to me, he left the games when they were still very much on the line. Every once in a while Pedro needs to listen to the voice in *Field of Dreams*—and "go the distance."

JUNE 22

Let's hope it really is a three-team race in the American League East, because right now the Red Sox are the third team. The Red Sox finished up their six-game road trip 2-and-4, after dropping the finale to the Phillies, 5-0. Meanwhile, the Blue Jays' Roy Halladay won his 11th straight start, moving Toronto (now two games behind New York) ahead of the Red Sox (now three games behind New York).

Right now, the Blue Jays are exactly what the Red Sox hoped to be. They have an equally strong offense led by the absolutely sick Carlos Delgado and a not-too-shabby Vernon Wells. Wells is only 24 years old and playing in his second full season. Last year, he showed he's a player: 23 homers and 100 RBI while batting .275. He's solid. But I doubt even Toronto's front office expected that by June 22 this year, Wells would already have 19 homers with 71 RBI, and his average would be up from .246 in April to a rock-solid .308. He's gone from good to awesome in one year! And he just homered in his fourth straight game. The numbers Wells is putting up are right there with Delgado's, but no one seems to notice. Delgado's at .305, 22 HR, and 76 RBI. They're like a modern-day Mickey Mantle and Roger Maris. Amazing!

JUNE 23

C'mon, it's Jeremy Bonderman! Yes, the Red Sox won, but where's that killer offense? You'd think that coming home to face the Tigers and their 10-game loser, Jeremy Bonderman, would put a little pop in the Sox bats. Instead, they only managed two runs in six innings against Bonderman, and needed an eighth-inning home run from Kevin Millar to get a little breathing room, beating Detroit 3-1. Millar, rather quietly, has had 26 RBI in his last 23 games. He's also had four days off this month. Since he DH's a lot, shouldn't he be able to play every day?

Also, what is it about the Red Sox frequent inability to annihilate mediocre to poor pitching? They "pulled a Bonderman" when they let Minnesota's Johan Santana, pitching in a spot start, shut them out for five innings on May 9. Baltimore's Jason Johnson outpitched Pedro Martinez on April 5, then came back and beat Boston seven days later with six more effective innings. On April 23, they were beaten by Texas's John Thompson (currently 4-9, 5.71, but he threw seven innings against the Red Sox, allowing just one run). They lost to Jason Davis of Cleveland and Doug Davis of Toronto, but they jumped on Bartolo Colon for five runs in the first three innings. Go figure!

Tim Wakefield threw six scoreless innings, but left in the seventh inning with a bad back. It would be a tough loss if he had to miss any time.

Also, while the Yankees were losing to Tampa Bay, the Jays were beating

Baltimore. So, Toronto is now just a game behind the Yankees. Hard to believe that after 75 games, the Yankees have only shown themselves to be a game better than the Blue Jays.

JUNE 24

Three days after going 6-for-6, Nomar Garciaparra went 5-for-5 as the Red Sox pounced on the Tigers, 10-1. In his last nine games, Nomar has now had four-, five-, and six-hit games. He's 40-for-93 in June. Derek Lowe got the win, his fifth straight. At 8-3, Lowe is on pace to be a 20-game winner again. Surprised me, too.

Meanwhile, the Yankees "Todd Pratted" the Devil Rays. Down 9-6 entering the ninth inning, the Yankees got a three-run homer from Juan Rivera to tie the game with nobody out. Then Todd Zeile doubled home Derek Jeter later in the inning. Yankees win, 10-9. It was Rivera's first home run of the year. It was just as disappointing to see the Yankees "Pratt" the Rays as it was when Pratt's bat beat the Red Sox. You just never get used to it.

In other developments today, the Red Sox signed outfielder Gabe Kapler to a minor-league deal. Expect something to happen with Jeremy Giambi soon. The Sox can't afford to carry what unfortunately has become dead weight. They found an injury on Ramiro Mendoza when he was weighing them down. Maybe Giambi can run into some knee trouble that's a bit vague in its diagnosis. Wink, wink.

Also, the White Sox are closing in on the Twins, just 4 1/2 games back now, which puts them smack dab in the middle of the Central Division race. And that might seal the "no deal" on the Red Sox getting Bartolo Colon. If the White Sox think they can make a run in the second half of the season, they won't part with Colon, or Estaban Loiaza. But even with today's win over Minnesota, the White Sox are 36-40. If they're not at least at .500 by late July, can they seriously consider themselves a possible contender?

JUNE 25

This one will never make a list of bizarre baseball games, but it's on mine. It was a tight 2-1 game with the Sox leading in the eighth. Boston pushed one run across on a Manny Ramirez single that scored Nomar Garciaparra to make it 3-1. Then, with two outs, David Ortiz stepped in to face some 98-mile-an-hour flamethrower by the name of Fernando Rodney. Ortiz clearly couldn't handle the heat, but the kid tried to mess him up with a change-up.

Ortiz dribbled the ball to third; Tiger third baseman Eric Munson double-clutched and was late with his throw to first base. Ortiz, not known for his speed, got his first infield hit since Duran Duran was just starting to get "Hungry Like the Wolf." Bill Mueller followed with a swinging bunt. He swung with all his might, but the ball barely rolled 20 feet up the third base line. The Tigers couldn't make a play. And the bases were loaded. Damian Jackson singled. Jason Varitek hit a ground-rule double. Johnny Damon walked, Todd Walker singled, and Nomar Garciaparra hit a three-run homer, his first home run since May 24 (who knew it had been so long?). Nine runs. Seven hits. It was the stunned Tigers' turn to bat, now down 11-1. Sox win, 11-2.

The nine runs were the most the Red Sox have scored in an inning since last July 23. But the bizarre aspect of it was the two infield hits, both coming with two outs, and then eight runs scored. It's what makes the Red Sox so interesting and lovable this year. You just never know when they're going to explode offensively. It could happen when they have a small lead, or when they're in a big hole. Any time is the right time.

JUNE 26

For the first time since May 15, Pedro Martinez is the winning pitcher, though it wasn't exactly a masterpiece. Pedro got through six innings with a 6-1 lead, but was touched for a pair of runs in the seventh. Then with two outs and two on, Alan Embree came in and gave up a run-scoring single. The run was charged to Pedro, and it was a 6-4 game. Once again, Pedro would sit and watch as the bullpen pitched the final two innings of a tight ball game. Grady Little went with the surest thing he has and let Brandon Lyon get the final six outs. Sox beat the Tigers, 6-4.

Lyon ran his scoreless streak to 9 1/3 innings over his last six appearances. He may not be what's considered a "lights-out" closer, but he's 9-for-9 in save situations, and his ERA when he has a save opportunity is 0.90. Red Sox GM Theo Epstein said last week that one of the Phillies told him Lyon had the best stuff he'd seen all year. I've complained that Lyon doesn't appear to have an "out" pitch that you'd like to see from a closer, but watching him recently, I think his "out" pitch might be that slider that runs away from right-handers and eats up lefties inside. The kid looks good. But he might look even better as a two-inning setup guy in front of a more established closer. I'd feel pretty good with the starters taking care of at least six innings, and then handing the ball over to the likes of Embree, Timlin, Lyon, and a closer to be named later.

The Yankees have won 11 of 13 games since being no-hit by the Astros. They lead the Red Sox by two games. The Yankees are 47-30. The Red Sox are 45-32. And the Blue Jays, still hanging in there, are 45-34.

JUNE 27

Much like Tiger Woods winning the U.S. Open by 15 strokes, the Red Sox took all the fun out of this one. Fourteen runs in the first inning, 10 before the first out—that's a record. Johnny Damon fell a home run shy of hitting for the cycle—*in the first inning*. Two Marlin pitchers, Carl Pavano and Michael Tejera, failed to record an out before *they* were out. The Marlins threw 91 pitches—*in the first inning*. It was an incredible offensive performance, arguably the second best in Red Sox team history. On June 8, 1950, they beat the St. Louis Browns 29-4. On June 27, 2003, they beat the Marlins, 25-8. In both games there were a franchise-best 28 hits.

This late in the season the Red Sox were still able to raise their batting average three full points, from .294 to .297—*in the first inning*. It's the Red Sox fifth straight win, their eighth straight at home, and it puts them 14 games over .500 for the first time this season (46-32). Those are the good things.

Now for the bad. The game stopped for several minutes in the seventh inning when Todd Walker's line drive up the middle hit Marlins pitcher Kevin Olsen in the head. Olsen was taken off the field on a stretcher. Later reports from the hospital said he was in good condition with minor injuries.

Also, the benches cleared in the ninth inning when Red Sox reliever Hector Almonte threw a pitch behind Andy Fox. Almonte was apparently responding to Florida's Blaine Neal's having hit David Ortiz in the knee with a hard pitch in the previous inning. Personally, I couldn't believe it took until the eighth inning for one of the Red Sox hitters to get plunked. I thought it should have happened in the first inning. When hitters are that comfortable at the plate, going 13-for-14 in the first inning, something has to be done to make them uncomfortable. Throwing inside—*very* inside—wouldn't have been a bad idea. Instead, the Marlins didn't do anything until they became angry when it appeared the Red Sox were out to embarrass them. You see, in the seventh inning, Todd Walker tried to tag up and score on a shallow fly to center field. He was thrown out, but that didn't matter to Florida manager Jack McKeon, who believes that when the score is 21-5, some mercy and good judgment should be shown.

"I didn't realize your pitching was that bad here at Boston that you would try to add on a 16-run lead in the seventh inning," McKeon said.

Guess what, Jack. Your sarcasm missed its mark; the Sox pitching really *is* that bad. But even more to the point, I can't believe he expects a team to stop trying, whatever the score. Certainly, you wouldn't steal a base, lay down a bunt, or intentionally walk a batter with a 16-run lead, but if a runner thinks he can score, he should try to score. If he thinks he can stretch a single into a double, he should hustle to second base. If an outfielder thinks he can make a diving catch, he should lay his body out. And the opposing manager should keep his mouth shut!

No ground was gained on the Yankees. David Wells won his 10th game of the year against two losses. Stat of the day: Wells has only walked four batters in 123 innings. Stat of the day, part two: The Red Sox are 1-0 when scoring 25 runs or more.

JUNE 28

Nobody's perfect. Brandon Lyon blew his first save of the year, and the Red Sox suffered another devastating loss. It makes me wonder, why is it always the home run? In this one, it was Florida's Mike Lowell hitting a game-winning, walk-off, three-run homer in the ninth inning. Last week, it was Philadelphia's Jim Thome hitting two game-tying home runs and Todd Pratt hitting a game winner in extra innings. These guys couldn't hit doubles into the gap? I can't believe how snakebitten the Red Sox are by the home run ball. Remember Carl Crawford of the Tampa Bay Devil Rays, who ruined the Red Sox opening day with a game-winning homer off Chad Fox in the ninth? Well, that's his only home run of the year so far. Uncanny! It's just too late in the season for the Red Sox to still be losing games like this. On back-to-back Saturdays, they've suffered crushing defeats when victory was right in their grasp. This was a 2-2 game into the sixth inning when the Red Sox exploded yet again—this time for seven runs. A 9-2 lead should be safe, shouldn't it?

The Marlins scored four in the eighth inning and four more in the ninth to steal this one, 10-9. Tim Wakefield, who pitched marvelously for seven innings, gave up a three-run homer to Juan Encarnacion in the eighth, and said, "I'll take the blame. I gave up four runs so we were only leading by three instead of seven."

Nice attempt to take the bullet there, Tim, but a three-run lead is a pretty good cushion. This was not your fault. This one falls at the feet of the Lyon. He threw an 0-2 pitch to Mike Lowell in a spot where he could extend those gravedigger forearms and get the meat part of the bat on the ball. Lowell, who leads the National League in home runs with 25 (already a career high), drove Lyon's mistake over the fence in right center.

Nine times this year the Red Sox have lost a game in the opposing team's final at bat. If they end up missing the playoffs by three or so games—or fewer—we'll need only look back at these heartbreaking defeats. The Red Sox have also won 11 games in their final at bat, which suggests things could be worse, but right now, it's hard to see how they could be.

Before the Red Sox bullpen embarrassed itself yet again, Grady Little approached Jack McKeon to apologize for having embarrassed the Marlins the previous night, saying he disapproved of the piling on. "You see some stuff on the field sometimes that you can't believe," Little told McKeon. "That certainly was the case last night."

But I think Red Sox owner John Henry got it right. "Grady apologized?" he asked. "I disagree with that. That's old school. What about the fan who pays $50 and gives up his Friday night to come out here? Don't we owe it to our fans to play hard all the time? If we're supposed to stop trying to score, we should just put up a disclaimer on the scoreboard: 'You should go home now, we're not trying anymore.' The idea is to score runs. If not, then why are we out there? We've got a sold-out crowd, and if we're not trying to score runs, no matter what the score is, we're not playing baseball."

Gabe Kapler's debut was another point of interest. He was called up and promptly went 4-for-5 with two doubles, a triple, and a single—a greater contribution than Jeremy Giambi has made all year. Giambi, by the way, was placed on the 15-day disabled list with bursitis in his left shoulder.

"I haven't been 100 percent one time this year," Giambi said. "I've played through a lot of bumps and bruises, but that's what my job is, and that's what I get paid to do. I'm not going to use it as an excuse."

Maybe he *should* use it as an excuse. If the injury is legit, it might explain why he's hitting .173 with 13 RBI in 110 at bats this year.

Also, the Yankees swept a home and away double header against the Mets. And the bat Johnny Damon used to tie a Major League record with three hits in the first inning last night was sent to the Baseball Hall of Fame in Cooperstown, New York. Nice little hat trick for Damon.

JUNE 29

Gabe Kapler could quickly be attaining cult-hero status. After coming up a home run short of hitting for the cycle in his debut, Kapler smacked two home runs today. His two-day totals are: 7-for-9, two homers, two doubles, a triple, and seven runs batted in. His slugging percentage is 1.889. Jeremy, we hardly knew ye!

Todd Walker also homered twice as the Red Sox pounded out six home runs. The Red Sox won the final game of their homestand, 11-7, giving them a total of 45 runs in the three games with Florida, yet they only took two out of three. The Red Sox went 6-1 on the homestand, but still lost ground to the Yankees, who've won seven in a row. And the Red Sox improved to 10-7 against National League teams, a far cry from their 5-13 interleague record a year ago. The Red Sox still have a make-up game with the Philadelphia Phillies but are guaranteed to finish with a winning record against the Senior Circuit.

But the big news of the day comes from the mouth of Grady Little, who suggested the bullpen makeup will be getting a shake-up. Byung-Hyun Kim is still scheduled to start against the Devil Rays on Thursday, but Little said that's only true "as of today," adding, "Maybe tomorrow, I don't know, it might be changed by then."

What he's saying is that Kim is headed for the bullpen, where he will assume the closer's role. What he's not saying is who will replace Kim in the starting rotation. All signs point to Ramiro Mendoza, who has been working as a starter during his rehab stint in Single-A Sarasota. Today, he pitched five shutout innings, and the Red Sox apparently feel that changing his role will help. If he can be effective as a starter, it could mean a huge improvement in the bullpen. The Sox would have a legitimate and proven closer who saved 36 games last year (Kim), a reliable setup guy (Brandon Lyon), a steady influence (Mike Timlin), two effective lefties (Alan Embree and Casey Fossum, when he returns), and a healthy Chad Fox, who could be activated from the disabled list in a couple of days.

Granted, the starting rotation is immediately weakened with Kim's replacement by Mendoza, but moving Kim would allow the Red Sox to stabilize their greatest weakness (the bullpen) and continue their efforts to acquire a starting pitcher before the end of July. It all makes sense. I guess.

JULY 1

Two words: Jason Standridge. One more word: who?

He's just the latest in a string of no-names to shut down the Red Sox, who couldn't muster a run against the rookie—making his fourth big-league start—until the sixth inning. But John Burkett, who gave up three runs in the first inning and then blanked the Devil Rays for the next five, kept the Red Sox in the game.

Finally, the Red Sox came back with two runs in the ninth inning to tie the game at 3. Bill Mueller got the rally started by getting hit by a pitch. Jason Varitek followed with a double. One out later, Todd Walker drove a two-run single into right field. Byung-Hyun Kim, in his new role as closer, shut down the Rays in the ninth and 10th innings. Brandon Lyon, in his new role as "not the closer," helped the Red Sox invent a new way to lose in the 11th.

With two outs, Rocco Baldelli stole second base. A walk to Jason Tyner followed. Then Baldelli made a critical mistake. He took off for third base before Lyon went into his stretch. Not only was there very little reason to steal third in that situation, since he was already in scoring position and possesses incredible speed, but now he was a dead duck. All Lyon had to do was step off the rubber and make an accurate throw to second, and the Red Sox would have easily gotten Baldelli at third. But Lyon's throw was behind Nomar Garciaparra. The ball tipped off Nomar's glove and rolled into the outfield. Baldelli scored the winning run. So this time it was a wild pickoff throw that did the Red Sox in, not a home run.

It's not what the Red Sox need as they begin a 13-game road trip that starts with three games in Tampa Bay, ends with three games in Detroit, and has seven games against New York and Toronto sandwiched in the middle. The Red Sox, who have a paltry 19-22 road record, could find themselves drifting out of the race if they don't do well on this trip. Certainly, they need to take care of business against the Rays and Tigers, and hope to do well against the primary rivals in the East. This was an awful start. At least the Yankees' eight-game winning streak was snapped by Baltimore, so the Sox still trail by four games.

Also, before the Yankees' loss, they had won 17 of their last 20 games. Combine that with their 18-3 start, and the Yankees are 35-6 in those two amazing stretches—17-25 otherwise. It's hard to explain that below mediocre 42-game stretch, but they lost Nick Johnson and Bernie Williams for part of it. Plus, Jason Giambi and Hideki Matsui weren't hitting the ball as well as they are now. But that fearsome foursome of Mike Mussina, Roger Clemens, David Wells, and Andy Pettitte is a combined 37-18 so far. They will be tough to catch, but who knows? Maybe the Red Sox will catch lightning in a bottle and sweep the four-game series coming up in the Bronx on the Fourth of July weekend. Stranger things have happened. I just watched the Red Sox lose a game on an errant pickoff throw.

And not for nothing, but Marlins manager Jack McKeon is officially full of it. After getting pounded by the Red Sox 25-8 he said, "I'll tell you what...if I get an 18-run lead tomorrow, you can bet your sweet ass we will not steal bases, and we will hold the runners up one base at a time. OK? Mark it. Put it in your book. Put it in your pipe and smoke it for the future. We will not show the other team up."

Today, the Marlins beat the Braves, 20-1. With the Marlins up 12-1 in the sixth, McKeon pinch hit for his pitcher. Up 14-1, Ivan Rodriguez moved to second on a wild pitch. Up 17-1, Todd Hollandsworth hustled to beat out an infield single. Up 18-1 in the eighth inning, Miguel Cabrera homered for the second time when he probably could have been given the last few innings off. And up 20-1, Armando Almanza struck out the side in the ninth inning, apparently still trying to do his best to keep the Braves from scoring.

JULY 2

Finally, a game that went according to script. Pedro Martinez, who made a rather pedestrian start and was charged with four runs, put in seven innings. Alan Embree pitched an effective inning. And Byung-Hyun Kim needed just seven pitches to retire the Devil Rays in order in the ninth inning, picking up his first save with the Red Sox. Boston wins, 5-4. It's truly amazing how easy it can be when you have an effective starter followed by an effective bullpen. It's just a shame it took 82 games to end all the experimenting and put guys in their rightful places.

I say this even while the Red Sox picked up right-handed relief pitcher Todd Jones, who was released by the Colorado Rockies. He was immediately placed on the 25-man roster, and Hector Almonte was sent down to the minors. Jones is a 35-year-old veteran with 184 career saves, but he comes from the Rockies with an ERA of 8.24! Granted, ERA's tend to run a bit higher in the Rockies, but who really knows what Jones has left? Now, it's likely the first time we'll see him is in the middle of a close ball game in New York over the weekend. It'll be another in-season experiment, and most of the other ones have blown up in the Red Sox face.

Meanwhile, it's come to this. We're now ranking the Red Sox most devastating losses so far this year. Talk about an exercise in masochism. Wondering whether Carl Crawford's home run on opening day was more or less painful than Todd Pratt's home run 82 days later is a lot like debating if it hurts more when you hold your hand over a burning flame, or when you stick a pen in your ear. It's ridiculous and futile. But that's never stopped masochistic Massachusetts before. So, here goes. The Top 10 list of the Red Sox most crushing defeats in 2003, from bad to worst:

10) Paper cut: Rocco Baldelli scores on an errant, pickoff throw. Too many people made this game out to be worse than it really was. It was an extra-inning loss, plain and simple. Only the oddity of the final play even gets this game on the list. If the Red Sox hadn't rallied in the ninth inning to tie the game at 3-3, this one would have been just a blip on the radar screen. It's far less painful than most Red Sox losses, because it had little to do with the pitching staff and everything to do with the offense. After John Burkett gave up three runs in the first inning, he and the relief corps threw up nine straight goose eggs. If the Sox hitters, who had just scored 45 runs against the Marlins, had been up to their usual standards, the Sox would have won easily, but instead they managed just one run against Jason Standridge. We can forgive the offense an infrequent stinker. Having said this, don't underestimate the pain of a paper cut. They can be killers!

9) Stubbed toe: The Orioles' claim a walk-off win on April 5. If this game were to take place today, it would skyrocket up the list. But it was too early in the season to know how much pain was on the way. Pedro Martinez went eight strong innings, but the Red Sox lost 2-1 when Chad Fox walked Tony Batista with the bases loaded in the ninth. In Pedro's first two starts, he gave up one run in 15 innings but didn't have a win to show for it. I hate when that happens.

8) Finger in the eye: The game of the year went to the Cardinals on June 12. This one hurt enough to make you weepy, but it was such an incredible game, at least some of the sting was taken out of it. Remember the Red Sox scored three runs in the ninth to tie and two more in the 10th to tie it again. Nomar Garciaparra had that 11-pitch at bat in the ninth leading to his 11th triple of the year, which brought home the tying run. Then Tony LaRussa walked Manny Ramirez and Kevin Millar to load the bases with one out, and the strategy worked when Trot Nixon fouled out and Bill Mueller flied to right. J. D. Drew homered for the Cardinals in the 10th, but the Sox staged a two-out rally with Nomar getting another game-tying hit. LaRussa loaded the bases again, and Trot Nixon stranded three more runners, giving him 12 for the game. Jim Edmunds's three-run homer in the 13th gave the Cardinals enough of a cushion, but the Sox still came back with two in the home half of the inning. Sox lose 8-7. Incredible game. Tough loss. But there have been much tougher ones.

7) Pulled hammy: The Red Sox suffer a Royal pain on May 5. Nomar Garciaparra hit a two-run homer in the eighth to tie the game, and Jason Varitek hit a solo shot in the ninth to give the Red Sox a 6-5 lead. But Brandon Lyon hit Desi Relaford with the bases loaded to tie the game in the bottom of the ninth. And then Brent Mayne's ground ball to short went through Nomar's legs. Another comeback spoiled. Sox lose, 7-6.

6) Severe abdominal cramping: June 5 against the Pirates. Games like this can leave you sick to your stomach, because the players involved did things they don't normally do. When Jim Edmunds or Mike Lowell beats you—hey, it happens! But when 39-year-old Jeff Reboulet steals his first base in three years and Vladimir Nunez, who is 0-for-14 as a pinch hitter, gets a pinch-hit leading to the go-ahead run in the eighth inning—hey, that's *not* supposed to happen! Sox lost this one, 5-4. Pass the Pepto-Bismol.

5) High ankle sprain: The Redbirds leave something on the windshield on June 10. This is the game in which Jason Varitek hit a two-run homer in the eighth to tie the game at seven. The Sox had trailed 7-2, but came back only to lose it when Brandon Lyon gave up a couple of runs in the ninth inning. The pain of this one doesn't quite reach the threshold of some others, because it looked like a sure loss for seven innings.

4) Broken fifth metacarpal: Opening day. Unbeknownst to anyone at the time, this one was merely setting the tone for the rest of the season. This was the one where Fox was a goat. But we can't let Alan Embree or Nomar Garciaparra off the hook. With a 4-1 lead in the ninth inning, Embree gave up a hit, a homer, and another hit, before Grady Little called on Chad Fox. Fox struck out Toby Hall, and then Brent Abernathy hit a ball up the middle that looked like a game-ending double play. But Nomar, who fielded the ball and stepped on second, double-clutched on his throw to first. Play on! That gave Carl Crawford his chance to be a hero. But again, the crushing aspect of this loss was the fact that it was the result of a home run. Those blasts are far more deflating than a base hit or a sacrifice fly. That it was a home run from a guy who doesn't often hit home runs only makes it worse. That homer remains the only one Crawford has hit all year. Ouch!

3) Torn ACL: The Marlin that got away, June 29. Leading 9-2 after seven innings, we shouldn't have had to worry. But with four runs in the eighth, and four more in the ninth—punctuated by Mike Lowell's two-strike, three-run blast off Brandon Lyon—the Marlins, baited the night before, took the hook out of their mouths and celebrated rather swimmingly.

2) Blow to the head: Posada's bases-loaded walk on May 28. This loss was particularly painful because it was to the Yankees. Also, because the Sox came back to score four runs against Mariano Rivera to tie the game 5-5, only to lose it in the bottom of the ninth. Remember, this was the game in which Manny Ramirez threw the ball down the third base line, allowing Hideki Matsui to coast into third. This is the game in which Grady Little tried to pull a Tony LaRussa and walked both Alfonso Soriano and Jason Giambi to load the bases. This is the game in which a possible called strike was called a ball, and the next pitch was ball four. Game over.

And the number one most devastating loss for the Red Sox this year:

1) Knife to the heart: June 21 against the Phillies. Jim Thome hit a solo home run to tie the game in the eighth. He hit another one to tie the game in the 12th. And Todd Pratt hit a two-run homer in the 13th. All three of those homers came with two outs. It was Pratt's first home run of the year, his second hit of the month. A killer.

Also receiving a vote: the Ryan Rupe game on June 16. Folks, add this one to the list of games in which the bullpen blew a lead for Pedro Martinez. But he only went five innings and left with a 2-1 lead. This is another one in which the offense was a far greater letdown than the bullpen. In the sixth inning, Rupe gave up a three-run homer to the Sultan of Sweat, Joe Crede. But the Red Sox had nine more outs to try to even it up. When you only score two runs, it's not the bullpen's fault. Yeah, it hurt, but a diehard fan can walk it off. Basically, this one failed to make the list because the game-winning hit came in the sixth inning. Ha! You think that can hurt us? Red Sox fans are numb until the ninth inning. Then, if you prick us, we will bleed. We are the few, the proud, the masochists from Massachusetts!

JULY 3

Add this one to the list above. The Red Sox were leading Tampa Bay 5-3 in the eighth inning. Brandon Lyon retired the first two Rays in the eighth, but then he walked Travis Lee. Up steps Al Martin, who hasn't homered in nearly two years—a span of 160 at bats. Gone!

How does that keep happening? Guys who have no business going deep continue to frustrate the Red Sox. Martin's blast simply tied the game, but the Devil Rays won it in the 10th when Mike Timlin loaded up the bases with one out. He struck out Damian Rolls. But then Marlon Anderson ripped what would have been a double into the left-center-field gap. It only went as a single, because the winning run crossed the plate. Sox lose, 6-5. Now, they head for New York having lost two out of three against the lowly Devil Rays.

The series in the Bronx will be huge. The Red Sox are four games back and could leave Yankee Stadium either tied for first place, *eight* games back, or somewhere in between.

This will be the first time in years that the Red Sox and Yankees have played each other on the Fourth of July. The last time, the Yankees' Dave Righetti no-hit the Red Sox.

6

Fireworks in the Bronx

JULY 4

"I thought that fireworks started after it got dark," said Yankees manager Joe Torre. "They obviously started earlier today."

And they were provided by the Red Sox, who became the first team to ever hit seven home runs in a game against the Yankees. That's 103 years of pinstripe history, and they'd never been overpowered like they were today. David Ortiz, Bill Mueller, and Jason Varitek each hit two home runs, and Manny Ramirez added a supersized one that landed in the upper deck, prompting Yankees manager Joe Torre to say, "That son of a gun should have counted for two." The Red Sox took the series opener, 10-3. It was beautiful!

"Let's hope we got them all out of the way," Torre said.

David Wells hasn't been this bad all season. He served up a career-high five home runs, matching a level of futility that only four other Yankees pitchers have ever reached. Jeff Weaver was the last Yankees pitcher to give up five home runs in a game, and the only other one to do it at Yankee Stadium, and that was also against the Red Sox last year.

"The ball carried well today," Varitek said. "Real well."

Yankee second baseman extraordinaire Alphonso Soriano proved that when he took a Derek Lowe pitch that was low and away in the first inning and somehow stroked it for a home run to left field. I couldn't believe it when that ball made it over the wall. And I couldn't believe it when the Red Sox proceeded to go deep seven times. It was like a prison break. They were all going over the wall.

"It was quite impressive out there," said Boston manager Grady Little. "We were doing it against a pretty good pitcher out there, too, and it's something we're proud of."

Derek Jeter put it this way, "It's not fun to watch, but you tip your hat to them. They did a good job, especially the bottom of the order. They killed us."

He's right, too. The bottom of the order—Ortiz, Gabe Kapler, Mueller, and Varitek—combined to go 8-for-17 with eight RBI, eight runs scored, and six of the home runs. Meanwhile, the top of the order—Johnny Damon, Todd Walker, and Nomar Garciaparra—went 3-16 with no RBI and one run scored. That just proves you never know where it's going to come from. The Sox lineup runs nine deep.

It was the third time in 29 days that the Red Sox hit at least six home runs in a game. They also did it against Florida on June 29, and against Milwaukee on June 7. And that Florida game was also a Derek Lowe start, so they've homered 13 times in his last two starts. No wonder he's improved to 10-3 and has won a career-high seventh straight decision.

The baseballs weren't the only objects flying into the stands. When David Wells was pulled in the sixth inning, already having given up eight runs, he tossed his hat and glove into the stands.

"Bad glove, bad hat. Don't want that in my locker," Wells said. "It was one of those days, can't explain it."

It's certainly not going to help him mend his relationship with Yankees owner George Steinbrenner. Imagine pitching like that on George's 73rd birthday! Oh, yeah, happy birthday, George.

And while this sure feels good, the Red Sox are still three games back with the prospect of Ramiro Mendoza putting his 6-plus ERA on the line against a humiliated Yankees squad. And it's only the Yankees' fourth loss in their last 20 games. So, it's not exactly time to celebrate.

JULY 5

The new and improved Mendoza Line: five innings, six hits, one strikeout—*zero runs!* Who could have expected this? Five shutout innings from Ramiro Mendoza. The Red Sox hit three more home runs and touched up Roger Clemens for eight runs on their way to winning another easy one, 10-2. Is it possible we're about to witness a Bronx Massacre?

In 1978, the Yankees went to Fenway Park for a four-game series. They were trailing the Red Sox by four games. In what became known as the Boston Massacre, the Yankees swept the series in merciless fashion, outscoring the Red Sox, 42-9.

This time, the four-game series is at Yankee Stadium instead of Fenway, and it's the Red Sox who entered trailing by four games. But after two games, the Red Sox have outscored the Yankees 20-5, and the lead is down to two. Of course, in 1978, the series took place in September, and this is only July, but the scenarios are close enough to make you wonder, or dream.

After the Red Sox hit seven home runs yesterday, you had to expect that Clemens would throw high and tight to someone. Once Clemens recognized that the Sox hitters were a little too comfortable at the plate, he would undoubtedly try to see to it that they were made a little less comfortable. So, with two outs and nobody on in the second inning, Clemens saw his opportunity. Bam!

Down goes Kevin Millar. He was down for a few moments holding on to his right hand. Fortunately, he was able to shake it off and walk down to first base. Next pitch. Bam!

Yes! On the very next pitch, Trot Nixon took Clemens deep again. With one sweet swing of the bat, Nixon stated loudly and clearly, "Roger, we will not be intimidated!" Nixon is now 12-for-32 lifetime against Clemens, with three home runs. The ninth-inning game winner three years ago was the biggest, but this was no small achievement. This one set the tone for another blowout.

While the Red Sox roughed up Clemens to the tune of eight runs in 5 1/3 innings, including three home runs, Mendoza was pitching in and out of trouble like a wily veteran. After Hideki Matsui and Jorge Posada led off the bottom of the second with singles, Robin Ventura bounced into a 4-6-3 double play. Mendoza got out of that jam, and another one in the fifth. With two outs, Alfonso Soriano was hit by a pitch. Derek Jeter followed with an infield single. And Jason Giambi walked to load the bases. The count went to 3-2 on Ruben Sierra, and Mendoza got him to bounce back to the mound. Inning over.

The Sox led 5-0 heading into the sixth, and Clemens opened the inning by loading the bases with one out. Clemens was done, but the book on him didn't close until after Sterling Hitchcock had allowed all three runners to score.

David Ortiz, who homered twice yesterday, homered twice today. He has four multi-homer games in his career now, which means he doubled his career total in about 24 hours. Ortiz has been the biggest beneficiary of the Shea Hillenbrand trade, becoming just about an everyday player since the trade. And it's because of him that the Red Sox really haven't noticed any drop-off in their offensive production. In fact, Ortiz has done a lot more for the Red Sox than Hillenbrand has for Arizona.

Since the trade, Ortiz is hitting .340 with six homers and 24 RBI. Those numbers have come in 94 at bats. In nearly the same number of at bats before the trade (103), but spread out over the first two months of the season, Ortiz was hitting just .270 with two homers and 19 RBI. Playing regularly has helped him immensely.

Hillenbrand, however, went on the disabled list 10 days after the trade with a left oblique strain. So, he's only played in 13 games for Arizona, hitting two home runs and driving in 13. It still feels like a pretty good trade.

JULY 6

When Bill Mueller hit Andy Pettitte's eighth pitch of the game over the wall in left, the inclination was to think, "here we go again." It was the 11th home run hit by the Red Sox in 18 1/3 innings in the series, and in Pettitte's last two starts he had given up eight runs and 10 hits in 13 innings. He'd been struggling, and the Red Sox looked primed to make him suffer. But it didn't happen.

Instead, Pettitte retired 16 batters in a row from the second to the seventh innings. He went eight innings, giving up just four hits and one run. And he struck out 10 batters for the first time since May 10, 2001. He proved the old adage: good pitching beats good hitting. Pettitte, who beat the Red Sox for the second time this year, improves to 10-6, giving the Yankees three 10-game winners before the All-Star break. David Wells and Mike Mussina are the others. In his two starts against Boston, Pettitte has given up just three runs in 15 2/3 innings. He's 13-4 in his career against Boston, including a win in the 1999 ALCS.

"He's pitched some big games for us," manager Joe Torre said. "I don't know if he's pitched any bigger regular-season games than this one because of the way we were beat up the last two days."

John Burkett kept the Red Sox in the game, though he continued to struggle in the first inning. The Yankees scored twice in the first, so Burkett's now given up 15 runs in the first inning of his last seven starts. New York got single runs in the fifth and sixth innings. By then Burkett was gone, and the Sox were down 4-1. The Yankees added three more and bounced back with a rather convincing 7-1 victory. It could have been worse. New York was 1-for-12 with runners in scoring position in the game and 2-for-28 in the series before they broke through with three runs in seventh.

Nomar Garciaparra was hitless in four trips and is now 1-for-13 in the series.

Also today, Jason Varitek was the victim of an All-Star snub. The results were released, and Oakland's Ramon Hernandez was selected as the backup catcher. An awful selection considering Varitek has a better batting average, more home runs and RBI, and his slugging percentage ranks fourth in the American League. Not fourth among catchers—that's fourth among all hitters in the American League. Jorge Posada was elected by the fans to start, and there's nothing wrong with that choice. But Varitek is clearly on a par with Posada and better than every other catcher in the American League. It's easy to see that by simply looking at the statistics, but it's even more obvious to those of us who watch him every day.

We remember how important so many of his home runs have been, like when he went back to back with David Ortiz in the 14th inning to beat Anaheim on April 27. He also went back to back with Trot Nixon to help beat Milwaukee 11-10 on June 7. Varitek's homer was the game winner. And what about his ninth-inning blast against Kansas City, which gave the Sox a 6-5 lead. A clutch knock to be sure, even though Kansas City scored two in the bottom of the ninth to win, 7-6. The same thing happened to him two more times during the St. Louis series. He hit a two-run homer in the eighth inning to tie one game, and a two-run homer in the ninth inning of another to help the Red Sox tie it up—only to watch the Sox lose both games in heartbreaking fashion. And of course, he had just hit a three-run shot on the Fourth of July to give the Red Sox a 3-2 lead and open the floodgates. The stature of this catcher can be witnessed every day, and Varitek deserves to be an All-Star.

He still has a chance, because he's one of the five players on the Internet ballot for the so-called "32nd man." I hope the fans across America recognize the injustice and put Varitek on the team.

Also not making the team were Pedro Martinez, Derek Lowe, Bill

Mueller, Todd Walker, and Kevin Millar. All of them were worthy of strong consideration, but only Varitek is a true and egregious omission. Manny Ramirez was voted onto the team by the fans, and Nomar Garciaparra was named as a reserve.

But lest we believe only the Red Sox were snubbed, none of the Yankees pitchers were selected. Not one of their three 10-game winners, and not Mariano Rivera, who, although he missed the first month of the season, has 15 saves and a minuscule ERA of 1.72. Derek Jeter? Also not going. Instead, Hideki Matsui, Jorge Posada, and Alphonso Soriano—all voted to start by the fans—are the only Yankees headed for Comiskey Park for the July 15 Midsummer Classic.

The Cubs' Sammy Sosa, who plays on the other side of Chicago, will also be a no-show for the big show. He wasn't even selected as a reserve by his own manager, Dusty Baker.

JULY 7

Make it a dirty dozen. Now, it's 12 games this year the Red Sox have lost in the opponents' last at bat. Pedro Martinez and Mike Mussina locked into another outstanding pitcher's duel—every pitch proving why baseball is still the greatest game.

Another huge crowd was on hand for this one. The series drew 220,026 fans, which is the most ever for a four-game series in the 28-year history of remodeled Yankee Stadium. And today's crowd was treated to the best game of the series.

Mussina gave up a single run in the first inning when Curtis Pride misplayed a fly ball off the bat of Manny Ramirez. It turned into a double that scored Johnny Damon. After that, the Red Sox couldn't touch Mussina. He didn't give up another hit after the first inning, and retired 21 batters in a row during one very long stretch. Bill Mueller finally reached on a walk in the eighth inning.

Pedro was also throwing beautifully, finishing with 11 strikeouts, but he began the game on the wild side. It was hard to tell if Pedro was sending a message, throwing a payback pitch, or simply trying to get a tough hitter out. But on his third pitch of the game, he hit Alphonso Soriano on the hand. The home plate umpire, Ed Montague, ruled that Soriano swung at the pitch and called it strike. Still, after Roger Clemens hit Kevin Millar on Saturday, throwing at a man in pinstripes wouldn't exactly be unexpected. Pedro has the same macho attitude about protecting his teammates that Roger Clemens has. Soriano eventually struck out.

The next man up was Derek Jeter, and with his 11th pitch of the game, Pedro hit him on the hand, too. Jeter also appeared to be attempting a swing, so it's not as if Pedro was doing any headhunting. But two batters into the game, and two Yankees had been hit. It's not the kind of thing that goes unnoticed.

"I don't know what was going through his (Pedro's) mind, but if it's what it looked like, it's not good," said Yankees owner George Steinbrenner. "It's not good for his team, not good for baseball. Fortunately, both of our men are OK."

But both of his men left the game by the third inning and went to the hospital for X-rays. They both suffered bone bruises and are listed as day to day.

Pedro denied that he was attempting to hit anybody.

"Are you crazy? The guy's right on top of the plate," Martinez said. "The only way you're going to get Soriano out is inside. He hits curveballs, he hits change-ups, he leans over the plate. He's that good. You've got to give him a lot of credit. When you throw inside, you're going to hit guys sometimes. I don't try to hit anybody, it was just an accident."

We'll take him on his word, in part, because the evidence suggests there was an absence of malice in his throws. But you have to wonder if Pedro wasn't thinking about the war of words that had opened up between Clemens and the Red Sox.

In an effort to exonerate himself from having hit Millar, Clemens said, "If you've been watching the game the past five years, some guys don't know how to get out of the way anymore."

To which Millar responded, "When's the last time he hit?" Then he added, "Try to beat us for once, instead of going five innings and giving up eight runs. It's not our fault. Make some pitches."

Sweet!

David Ortiz chimed in with this beauty: "I think that guy's getting stupid. How in the world does he want Millar to get out of the way when he's throwing? There's no way."

These are the kind of comments that prove the rivalry doesn't just sit with the fans. The players are deeply invested in this. How could they not be when they've got 55,000 people hanging on every pitch?

Pedro had six strikeouts through the first three innings, but he also had already thrown 60 pitches. Once Soriano and Jeter left the game, the Yankees lineup was severely lacking. So it seemed very likely that Pedro could continue shutting the Yankees down. The big question was how long could he go? The Red Sox baby Pedro so much, they seem to chart his games with a radar gun and a baby monitor. At this rate, there was no way he could go past the seventh inning. And it certainly didn't look like the Red Sox were going to pad their lead.

And they didn't. It remained a 1-0 game through five innings. In the sixth, Jeter's replacement, Enrique Wilson, led off with a double. It was his second double of the game. How does a backup middle infielder hitting .189 manage to hit two doubles off Pedro Martinez? I absolutely love and hate this game.

Jason Giambi singled Wilson home to tie the game. It was only the sixth inning, but right there it felt like a Red Sox loss. Mussina was outpitching Pedro, and he would most likely outlast him. Then it would be up to the bullpens. I was thinking the whole time, "Be a horse, Pedro. Be a horse." But he's not. He's a marvelous thoroughbred who blazes around short tracks, but can no longer go the distance.

"If there's a blueprint for beating Pedro, that's the blueprint. Keep it close and hope for a break," Yankees manager Joe Torre said. "He doesn't give you much."

Sure enough, Pedro left after seven innings. You could call it a masterful performance. He did, after all, strike out 11, walk no one, and give up just five hits and one run. Or you could call it another solid seven innings. It's the seven innings that will always stick with me. Granted, he threw 115 pitches. But this was a game he needed to win. It was a big, big game—for both teams.

"This game was important, because we really had to win," Steinbrenner said. "We had to send them back to Boston wondering what happened. They're a very good team, an excellent team."

Nobody's really wondering what happened. Byung-Hyun Kim, pitching his second inning in relief of Pedro, gave up seeing-eye singles to Hideki Matsui and Karim Garcia to open up the ninth. Then Jorge Posada was called upon to pinch hit. Instead, *he* was hit. Kim got him on the leg. And the bases were loaded with nobody out.

Kim struck out Robin Ventura, his fourth K of the game. Now, with one out, the Sox had the option of at least moving their second baseman and shortstop back to double-play depth. Instead, they kept the infield in and the outfield shallow. Curtis Pride hit a hard ground ball to the right side. Todd Walker had to take a step to his right. He was unable to field it cleanly, and by the time he picked up the ball, his throw home was wild and late. The Yankees won, 2-1.

"It was a short hop," said Walker, who was charged with an error. "Infield in cuts down your reaction time. It was a play that should have been made. It just slipped out of my glove. It was a tough way to lose."

It sure was. Before the series started, most Red Sox fans would have been happy with a split. After the first two games, this feels like the rug has been pulled out once again. The Red Sox came in with a bang and left with a whimper, and when it was all over, they were right back where they started—four games out of first place. It's on to Toronto for three more important games against the Blue Jays. Toronto has started to play itself out of the race—losing nine of their last 13. They're three games behind the Red Sox but could catch them by series end. Certainly, stranger things have happened.

Let me just take a moment to marvel at the strange way history repeats itself. In that Pedro-Rocket masterpiece of three years ago, Pedro loaded the bases in the ninth inning. The first two batters got on, and Pedro hit a batter to load the bases. Who was that batter? Jorge Posada—same as today. I realize the situations are different, and that Pedro wasn't even in the game anymore, but in two classic pitching performances between the Yankees and Red Sox, the bases were loaded in the ninth inning by the extremely unlikely event of hitting the same guy. In that game, Tino Martinez bounced out to end the game. That was a good day. This was a bad one.

The Red Sox are 3-4 on their road trip, so far. And three of the four losses have come in the opponents' final at bat. That redundancy could be what does the Red Sox in this year.

JULY 8

Just what you'd expect: the two highest-scoring teams in the American League locked in a 1-1 tie into the 12th inning. After scoring 20 runs in the first two games of the Yankees series, the Red Sox only managed to score three runs in the next 29 innings. Granted, they faced three of the best pitchers in the American League. First, they were mastered by Andy Pettitte and Mike Mussina; tonight it was the Blue Jays' Roy Halladay, the same guy who had won his last 12 decisions dating back to April 15—and the same guy whose only two losses this year were against the Yankees.

But he's also the same guy the Red Sox pounded for seven runs back on June 1. The combined record of the three aces the Red Sox had faced on three successive nights was 31-13. So, on one hand, the Red Sox offensive struggles could be expected and explained. But on the other hand, it's worrying because that's the kind of pitching they're going to face in the postseason. So, they have to be able to win games when their offense takes a nap against some of the league's best. Tonight, they did that. But it only improved their record to 2-12 in games in which they score three runs or fewer.

Halladay went nine full innings, allowing just one run on four hits. But Tim Wakefield, who was pitching with a migraine headache, was his equal for seven innings, allowing just one run on six hits. From there, the new and improved Red Sox bullpen took over. Mike Timlin was the first out of the pen in the eighth, and left a man stranded at second base. Alan Embree gave up a leadoff single in the ninth, but he also kept the Blue Jays from scoring.

In extra innings, the Red Sox left the bases loaded in both the 10th and 11th, then finally broke through with a single run in the 12th. Johnny Damon led off with his third hit of the game and his second double of the extra innings, and Jason Varitek drove him home with what proved to be the winning run.

That's because the vaunted Blue Jay attack wasn't able to get a man on base in extra innings. Todd Jones retired all six men he faced, and then Byung-Hyun Kim pitched a 1-2-3 12th to pick up his second save of the year. It was a much needed and exceptional performance from the bullpen, and the kind of game that confirms the character of this Red Sox ball club. They're now 9-3 in games following what have been deemed "devastating losses." Those are the 12 games the Red Sox have lost in the opposing team's final at bat. This was also the 12th game the Red Sox have won in their final at bat.

Meanwhile, the Yankees were one-hit by Cleveland southpaw Billy Traber—a rookie making his eighth big-league start. So, the Yankees' lead over Boston is down to three games. Plus, there remains a hangover of anger from the Yankees series. Rogers Clemens and Kevin Millar got right into the middle of it with words that are bound to escalate the animosity between the two rivals.

"This has turned into a big old stupid thing. And it started with his stupid comment that I should have gotten out of the way of his 95-mile-an-hour fastball," Millar said. "The classy thing would have been to call the clubhouse and see if I was OK."

So, if you're counting—both David Ortiz and Kevin Millar have called Roger Clemens "stupid."

Millar added, with an obvious reference to Pedro, "If they want to get into any headhunting thing, we've got the ultimate headhunter on our side."

For his part, Pedro repeated his denial that he intentionally tried to hit Alphonso Soriano or Derek Jeter, but added that if he wanted to, he could hit them with one pitch, that he's not afraid to do it, and that he's done it before.

Baseball players have memories like Big Blue the supercomputer. Look for beanballs in Beantown when these teams meet again in late July.

JULY 9

Speaking of late July, Red Sox manager Grady Little is setting up his pitching rotation for after the All-Star break. And even though Pedro Martinez will pitch on the Saturday before the break, he's not scheduled to pitch again until the following Saturday. That means he'd miss the entire Yankees series coming up later this month. And why is Pedro's start being pushed back? Because Pedro's using the time off to fly home to the Dominican Republic, and Little says he doesn't want to pitch Pedro on the day after he returns from a long flight. I think I just had an aneurysm!

Plain and simple—Pedro should pitch on the first day back from the All-Star break. He'd have had four days of rest, and would be ready to go. If jet lag is a genuine concern, he shouldn't be going to the Dominican Republic, or he should return a day early. Is he the ace of this staff or not? Does he want to be the highest-paid pitcher in the game or not? At some point this season this guy has got to stand up and make a much greater, and far more consistent, contribution to the cause. The fact that Pedro didn't make the All-Star team meant that he wouldn't have to pitch in the game. He wouldn't have to risk injury throwing on short rest. And he wouldn't have to miss a start coming back. This is such a load of crap, the grass is starting to grow.

Meanwhile, Yankees manager Joe Torre says he intends to manipulate his rotation to ensure that Mike Mussina and Andy Pettitte will face the Red Sox again. That's as it should be. Grady Little should do the same. He should tell Pedro he's pitching the first day back, and Pedro should do what he has to do to be ready. Case closed.

The Drama Boys did it again tonight. The Red Sox scored four runs in the eighth and one in the ninth to turn a 7-3 deficit into an 8-7 lead. And then Byung-Hyun Kim, pitching for the fourth straight day, brought tension to its highest levels.

His first pitch of the game was rapped into right field for a double by Frank Catalanotto. That brought up Vernon Wells and his 81 RBI. Wells struck out on three pitches. Up stepped Carlos Delgado and his 94 RBI. Grady Little came out of the dugout to discuss the game's most feared hitter, and Kim said he wanted to pitch to him. Little conceded and walked back to the dugout wondering if he'd done the right thing.

"If I was going to let anyone pitch against Carlos, it was going to be B.K.," Little said after the game. "Because of the awkwardness of his delivery, and that Carlos had hardly seen the guy at all. We definitely weren't going to give Carlos any fastballs in the zone to hit. If he was going to beat us, he was going to have to expand the zone."

Asked if there was anyone else in his bullpen he would have allowed to pitch to Delgado, Little said, "No."

Delgado fell behind 0-2. The next pitch was a ball. Two foul balls. Another ball. With each pitch, Red Sox fans dreaded the potential outcome. We could see the ball flying over the fence and another devastating loss lying at the feet of the bullpen.

Ball three. The count ran full. Walking Delgado wouldn't be the worst thing in the world. In fact, it might even have been the preferred strategy. What were the Red Sox doing here? Don't they remember pitching to Jim Thome—*twice*? Jim Edmunds? What about Todd Pratt? Why in the world would they pitch to Delgado? He's hitting .433 with seven home runs and 63 RBI with men in scoring position. Only three guys in the history of baseball have had more RBI before the All-Star break than Delgado has. With each pitch, the anxiety and anger grew. This was ludicrous. I can't believe they're pitching to this monster.

The 3-2 pitch was swung on—and fouled off. You fools! That pitch was way too good. It was nothing but luck that the game wasn't over, or at least tied. Please, just walk the guy and take your chances with the next one.

Finally, on the ninth pitch of the at bat, the Mighty Carlos had struck out. It was a belt-high fastball, and he just swung through it. Whew! Good move. Now there were two down, and the Blue Jays sent up some guy named Howie Clark. Kim hit him with the third pitch, and the go-ahead run trotted down to first base. It's never easy!

Up next was last season's Rookie of the Year, Eric Hinske. The count ran full on him, too. And the payoff pitch—paid off. Strike three—looking. It was a low strike, maybe even a gift, but the Red Sox would take it. Kim stranded a leadoff double by striking out the side. And the three hitters who struck out had a combined 207 RBI.

Manny Ramirez got the comeback started in the eighth inning with his 21st home run of the year. Jason Varitek, who found out before the game that he was voted onto the All-Star team as the 32nd man, hit a ground rule double, driving in two more. And Nomar Garciaparra, who didn't start the game, came in to pinch hit and tied the game with a sacrifice fly.

"There were some big hits out there, and they came at opportune times," Little said. "It's nothing that we haven't been seeing a lot this year. We keep coming back, and if the door just cracks open, we've been able to crash through on a lot of occasions, and that's good."

Ramirez also led off the ninth inning, and this time he hit a triple when Hinske misplayed his long fly ball. David Ortiz brought him home with a double, and the Red Sox went on to win, 8-7. It was their 17th one-run victory this season, and the 13th time they've scored the winning run in their final at bat. It is, after all, a team of destiny.

Three things shouldn't go unnoticed. The Red Sox bullpen has thrown eight shutout innings over the first two games of the series. Derek Jeter and Alfonso Soriano returned to the Yankees lineup, and the Yankees beat the Indians. And Bartolo Colon, unable to beat the lowly Tigers, dropped to 6-8.

The Tigers are 42 games under .500.

JULY 10

Nevermind. There's been a change of mind, and a change of heart. But still the same old attitude. The Red Sox reshuffled the deck, and their ace turned up in a different place. Pedro Martinez will face the Yankees after all. Now the stated intention is to have Pedro start the *fourth* game after the All-Star break on *seven* days' rest. Then he'll be on schedule to pitch the first game of the Yankees series on July 25. It's not an awful plan, because Pedro will face the Blue Jays and the Yankees in his first two starts after the break. Plus, he'll have had plenty of rest and should be very strong for the second half. But it's still being done because of Pedro's travel plans. Pitching him the first day after the break would get him an extra start. He'd end up facing Toronto and Detroit and then the Yankees in the third game of that series. But that was never an option, because the $17.5 million man can't pitch when he's tired, and nobody has the stones to either ask him or tell him to change his travel plans.

"Pedro will be pitching against the two teams we need to beat in our division—Toronto and New York. That makes a lot of sense, too," said Grady Little. He added, "We feel like at this point in the season that another period of time off for Pedro will make him stronger for the duration of the season. He feels the same way, and looking at the long run, we feel like that's the best thing for him."

As for the action on the field, the Red Sox completed a sweep of the Blue Jays, raising their record to a season-high 16 games over .500. At 53-37, the Sox record is identical to last season's after 70 games. The biggest difference is that the Red Sox *fell* to 53-37 last year when they lost four straight games, including three in a row *at* Toronto. This is a whole new year!

The Red Sox won tonight, 7-1, and once again it was "Ramiro the Hero" putting together a magnificent start. Mendoza went another five innings, allowing just one run. That's the only run he's given up in his two starts since joining the rotation. The bullpen also deserves recognition and praise for throwing 12 shutout innings during the series at Skydome.

David Ortiz and Kevin Millar hit back-to-back homers—the seventh time this year the Sox have hit back-to-back jacks. And that's a fact!

Also a fact, the Cleveland Indians started seven rookies tonight against the Yankees—and won! Coco Crisp scored the winning run in the tenth inning.

"We had opportunities, and we hit into some double plays," Yankees manager Joe Torre said. "It's frustrating because we pitched well. It's a bad loss."

JULY 11

The Red Sox win their fourth in a row, 5-3, over the Tigers—who are just a bad, bad team. These are the declawed Tigers who have been coughing up so many hair balls since opening day you'd think they were licking Ed Asner's back. Alan Embree threw seven pitches in the eighth inning, and Byung-Hyun Kim only needed eight pitches in the ninth. The last 15 Tigers in a row were retired. Detroit drops 42 games under .500, and they've now got two guys, Mike Maroth and Jeremy Bonderman, who have 13 losses.

The Yankees also won, so their lead over the Sox remains at two games, with two to play before the All-Star break.

Also today, the Texas Rangers traded Ugueth Urbina to the Florida Marlins for three minor-leaguers. Urbina leads the American League in saves with 26, but his ERA has gone up sharply—from 2.82 to 4.19—over the past few weeks. He also has four losses and four blown saves. We'll never know how much better the Red Sox might have been if they had had Urbina—or any legitimate closer—from the beginning of the season.

JULY 12

As long as Pedro Martinez continues to be coddled and babied, the Red Sox are going to have nights like this. For the sixth time this year, Pedro pitched at least seven innings, giving up either one or two runs, and wound up with a no-decision.

"He was pretty well cooked after the seventh inning," Sox manager Grady Little said. "'Our bullpen has been doing a great job, and they did another great job tonight."

Some will blame Grady Little for taking him out after the seventh inning, but Pedro had thrown 105 pitches and was coming off a 115-pitch effort against the Yankees. The Red Sox took a 2-1 lead in the top of the eighth inning when Trot Nixon hit his 14th home run of the year. Now, with the lead and the bullpen having thrown 14 consecutive scoreless innings, I'm sure Grady Little was thinking better safe than sorry where "Pedro the Fragile" is concerned. The Red Sox were sorry when Alan Embree came in and gave up the tying run in the home half of the eighth.

"(Martinez has) pitched well all year," Embree said. "The guy is 6-and-2. He could be 12-and-2 right now. It seems like there's one guy a year (who gets snakebit), and unfortunately it's the best pitcher in the league this year. Petey is looking better every time out there."

After retiring the first two batters, Embree failed to cover first quickly enough on a slow roller to the right side. The Tigers' Warren Morris was safe at first, stole second, and went to third when Jason Varitek's throw went into center field. Still, with two outs and a man on third, Embree had a chance to work his way out of the jam. But the Sox lefty gave up a run-scoring double to Northeastern University alum Carlos

Pena—also a lefty. Another no-decision for Pedro.

Again some will say it's because Little decided to pull him after the seventh, but in truth, there was no decision to be made. Pulling Pedro at that time was automatic. And if Pedro weren't so obsessively concerned with his health, he'd be fighting to stay in these tight ball games. But he gets the luxury of taking a public stance that it's the manager's decision, and that he's just following orders. But privately, I'm sure he's grateful that Little's not putting him in a position to get hurt—*again*.

Besides, Pedro certainly should have been able to shut down the Tigers, who have scored a major-league worst 291 runs. And Pedro did for a while. After giving up a leadoff triple to Alex Sanchez to start the game, Pedro stranded Sanchez and retired 15 straight. But Matt Walbeck led off the sixth with a double and eventually scored on a sacrifice fly. It should be noted that Sanchez was hitting .262 and Walbeck .155.

Pedro only gave up one run in seven innings while striking out eight, but it wasn't just Embree who pulled this win out from under him. Where was the offense? The Red Sox—who lead the major leagues in runs scored—turn into the No-Support Hose when Pedro pitches. His ERA is down to 2.32, but his record is only 6-2 in 16 starts. And there are exactly three reasons for that: 1) The bullpen has blown five leads for him; 2) the offense has been surprisingly silent when he pitches; and 3) Pedro is a seven-inning pitcher. If he went the distance, he wouldn't have to rely on the bullpen, and any leads he lost would be his responsibility.

Tonight, other than the run against Embree, who hadn't been scored upon in 15 of his previous 17 appearances, the bullpen was solid. Mike Timlin and Todd Jones each threw a scoreless inning, giving the Red Sox time to take the lead—which they did.

Jones was especially clutch when Trot Nixon lost a ball in the lights and it turned into a triple for Andres Torres in the 10th. Two intentional walks and two strikeouts later, Jones was walking off the hill having preserved the tie game.

"We're in a pennant race, and I got to throw in a tight situation," Jones said. "I'm a former closer, so I've been in tough situations. I just concentrated on throwing my pitches."

In the 11th inning, Johnny Damon brought home the go-ahead run, and Jason Varitek added a sac fly. Byung-Hyun Kim pitched for the fifth time this week, picking up his third save of the week, and his fifth since joining the Red Sox.

It was the Red Sox 10th extra inning game this year. They're 6-4 in those games. And it was the 26th "last at bat" game this year. The Red Sox are 14-12 in those games. It was Boston's fifth straight win, improving their record to 8-5 on the road trip, so far.

It's important to remember, *it's only a game*. And I don't mean it in that way people say, "Don't worry about it. It's only a game." I mean the Yankees' lead over the Red Sox *is only a game*. The Yankees got stomped on by the Blue Jays today, so with one game to go before the All-Star break, the Red Sox trail by *only a game*.

Also today, Manny Ramirez pulled himself out of the All-Star game because of a sore left hamstring.

"It's disappointing not to go to the All-Star game, but this is for the best," Ramirez said in a statement. "My priority is to try to help the Red Sox, and I need to take care of this injury so it does not become something that will bother me for the rest of the season."

Thank you, Manny.

Chicago White Sox right fielder Magglio Ordonez was named as Ramirez's replacement.

JULY 13

It was one disappointment after another today. To begin with, Red Sox manager Grady Little got a call at 5:45 a.m. from Manny Ramirez. Manny said his mother was very ill. So, Grady told him to tend to his family. Little had already planned to give Manny the day off so he could get four full days of rest for his ailing left hamstring. So, Manny was excused from the game. And so was Pedro Martinez. He was also given permission to leave early, which is not extremely uncommon. Pedro started the game on Saturday, so there would essentially be no circumstance in which he would be used today. However, this means that, arguably the two best players on the team cut out a day early. With a chance to pull even with the Yankees on the final day of the first half, neither of those guys was interested enough to sit with and support his teammates. Plus, there were reports that Pedro didn't even wait till the end of yesterday's game to pack up and leave. So, if he's going to start his break a day and a half early, why couldn't he come back a day early to pitch the first game of the second half? Oh yeah, I forgot. That was never an option, because Pedro has to be babied more than an actual baby.

As for Manny, it's a little hard to believe. He's hustled all year, he's known as the hardest worker on the team, and he's played in all but two games. But c'mon! "My mom's sick" is akin to "the dog ate my homework." I'd hate to find out his mom is near death, but at the time of this writing, I don't believe his story.

I'm willing to grant that his mom might be sick, but unless he was afraid he wouldn't make it home before her death, he still could, and should, have waited until later today to fly home and see her. We're talking about a difference of about 12 hours. And we're talking about the difference between being there for your teammates and being available to pinch hit—or not!

Little didn't provide any details, apparently because Manny didn't either. If he had said his mom had had a heart attack, or has been battling cancer for some time and the doctors say her time is drawing near, then fine. It's understood that family matters. But she could have the flu or a migraine or simply be in a need of a sniffling, sneezing, coughing, achy-head, so-you-can-rest medicine. As far as I know, Manny's not a doctor. He makes $20 million a year, so I'll bet his mom has decent health care. Unless the situation was truly dire, arriving 12 hours earlier wasn't going to help one bit.

Someday, the whole story will come out, and I may want to kick myself for being so unsympathetic. But right now, I'm extremely disappointed to learn that winning and doing everything possible to help during a pennant race isn't that important to at least two members of the Red Sox. What it shows is that the final game of the first half meant more to the fans than it did to Manny or Pedro. The fans were at least interested enough to watch the game and root for their team. I doubt the other two even bothered to find out if the Red Sox had won or lost. What do you think the chances are that when Pedro touched down in the Dominican Republic he immediately found a television with ESPN International and started looking for the baseball scores? Those guys as much as said, "if I'm not playing, I'm not going to be there." That's not a championship attitude. It's unfortunate, and unfortunately, it doesn't surprise me about either of them.

It turned out that even the Red Sox players who showed up for the series finale against Detroit didn't really show up.

Add the name Wilfredo Ledezma to the list of no-names who have befuddled the Red Sox this year. Ledezma is a 22-year-old the Tigers acquired from the Red Sox last December. He'd never pitched above Class-A ball before this season, and this was only his second start. But he's the Tigers' version of Ramiro Mendoza, only better. In Mendoza's two starts, he's given up one run in 10 innings. Ledezma has thrown 12 shutout innings in his two starts, and now has a 14-inning scoreless streak. Today, he went seven against the Red Sox, who were shutout for the third time this year. The final was 3-0.

After scoring four runs in the first two innings of the Tigers series, the Red Sox only managed to score five more runs in the next 27 innings. And this was against the Tigers! I say that disparagingly, because the Tigers are on pace to lose 118 games this year. But that's because they can't score runs. Their pitching is right in the middle of the pack, and they've only given up a total of 12 runs in their last six games. That includes two shutout victories—like the one they got today.

The Yankees got a surprisingly strong start from Jeff Weaver (5-7) and beat the Blue Jays, 6-2. It looks like the Blue Jays were just pretenders who had a strong month or so but don't have the pitching to remain contenders. So the Yankees, who sustained injuries to star players like Derek Jeter, Mariano Rivera, and Bernie Williams, still finished the first half two games up on the Red Sox.

"Even if everybody was healthy, I'd be satisfied with 20 games over .500," Torre said a few hours before his team improved to 21 games over .500 at 57-36.

Then he added, "We've been whacked around pretty good, and our egos took a beating. Our pitchers took a beating. My coaches took a beating. So I think the fact that we're still where we are means that you didn't let it distract you from what you needed to do. I think that's the most important thing, because on a day-to-day basis sometimes so much is made of what goes wrong that you forget to look at the big picture. We play 162 games, and we can't magnify those games as much as we do."

But if we didn't magnify the games, we might not have noticed how magnificent the first half of the season was.

And it was a great first half, despite the fact that the Red Sox offense headed into the All-Star break a little early—especially Nomar Garciaparra.

Despite his three hits today, Nomar has just seven hits in his last 38 at bats, a .184 clip that brought his average down from .343 on July 2 to .319 now. In July, Nomar is hitting .200 with one homer and four RBI in 55 at bats. This after he hit .398 in June. I'd say there's a man in desperate need of a break.

Todd Walker's hitting .148 in July. And Johnny Damon's hitting .250

this month. That's not a whole lot from the top three guys in the lineup. That might explain why Manny Ramirez, who has four homers and is batting .341 in July, only has seven RBI this month. The Red Sox won seven of the last 10 games on their road trip. And in those three losses, they scored a total of two runs.

But the Red Sox offense is a giant, and it won't sleep forever. After the break, the Red Sox play their first 11 games at home. In fact, the Red Sox play 42 of their final 69 games at Fenway Park—where they're 28-12 so far. So, while the August schedule includes 17 games against the top teams in the Western division—Seattle, Oakland, and Anaheim—I still feel good about the Red Sox chances to play as well, or better, in the second half.

7

Breaking Point

JULY 14

The first half of the season was like a Magical Mystery Tour. There was magic in those 14 final at bat victories for the Red Sox, and it's a mystery how they were able to stay on the heels of the Yankees even though they lost 12 games in the opposing teams' final at bats. And of all the "feel good" stories the Red Sox experienced from Bill Mueller, David Ortiz, and the surprising return of Ramiro Mendoza, the lingering question from the first half remains: when is Pedro Martinez going to join the party?

You see, there is a boil on the butt of the Boston Red Sox that is in desperate need of a good lancing. And his name is Pedro Martinez. He's almost single-handedly ruining one of the most enjoyable and exciting Red Sox seasons in recent memory. I realize that every team and every individual has ups and downs during a long season, but in basketball terminology—Pedro's got no "ups." At least he hasn't to this point. His entire season has been one big downer.

It began on the first day of spring training when he arrived with an agenda—to get his contract extension picked up. He threatened to walk at the earliest opportunity if the team didn't show him the proper amount of respect. Then, once the Red Sox caved in to his demand, he announced that he still wasn't happy.

In Pedro's second start of the season, the Orioles jumped on him for 10 runs. After a staredown with one particularly brazen fan, Pedro announced he wouldn't be speaking to the media anymore.

On the day he was supposed to pitch against the Yankees, we found out he was injured. The first reports indicated that he would probably miss his next start, but that the MRI didn't show any muscle tears, so he might be able to pitch in the middle of the following week. Nearly four weeks later, Pedro finally returned—to pitch three innings.

During the Sammy Sosa corked-bat controversy, Pedro decided it would be an appropriate time to cry "racism" regarding his own perceived "snub" in the Cy Young Award voting last year, and the MVP voting from three years earlier.

In his most important start of the year, he lost to the Yankees when Enrique Wilson—hitting .214 at the time—doubled for the second time in the game and scored on a Jason Giambi base hit. And in his final start of the first half, Pedro left after seven innings. There has even been some speculation that he actually left the ballpark after seven innings in order to get his All-Star break started as early as possible.

We already know he wasn't available to start the first game after the break, because Red Sox manager Grady Little didn't want him to pitch the day after he flew back. But we're left wondering, if he was able to start his break a day early, why couldn't he come back a day early and get the second half started with some blaze and glory?

Did I miss something? Seriously, other than Pedro's ERA, which stands as evidence of his ability to still dominate, was there anything positive from him during the first half? It's just been one frustration after another with him.

And while it may be true that the Red Sox can't win the World Series this year without Pedro Martinez, it is equally true that the team has come a long way without him. The Red Sox won 55 games during the first half of the season, and Pedro won exactly six. Sure the bullpen and the offense abandoned him as if they were looking to catch an early flight to the Dominican Republic, but the fact remains: Pedro has made 16 starts, and the Red Sox are 9-7 in those games. The Red Sox went from May 15 to June 26 without a win from Pedro.

His contribution thus far has been negligible. If he were a hockey player, his plus/minus rating would be off-the-charts awful. But the beauty of having as much talent as Pedro has is that it can turn around in an instant—you know, *if he's healthy*. There's a phrase that has become like nails on a chalkboard. I'd rather here a scratchy record of Yoko Ono singing REO Speedwagon's "Can't Fight This Feeling" than to hear someone say, "if he's healthy." It'll end up on his tombstone some day: "If he's healthy—we've made a terrible mistake."

Some of you may agree with me (and I thank you both), and the rest might be saying that Pedro pitched well enough to win 11 or 12 games. To that I say, *no* he didn't. He pitched exactly well enough to win six games. In order to win 11 or 12 games, he would have had to outpitch the likes of Jason Johnson, Mike Mussina, and that inestimable Matt Roney of Detroit. Don't be misled by the convenient and woefully incomplete statistic that the bullpen "blew" five of his games. Pedro left those games after seven innings four times and after five innings once (the Ryan Rupe three-run homer game). Those games' scores when he left were 2-1 (three times), 4-2, and 4-1. He also left two games with the score tied 1-1. Clearly, he was pitching exceptionally well. Just as clearly, he frequently left when the outcome of the game was still very much in doubt. In what other sport does the most important player, or the best player on a team, leave at the most crucial time? Answer: only in baseball, when a guy like Pedro is lifted in favor of Ryan Rupe or Chad Fox. Pedro could have won those games, if he had been allowed, or had fought for the opportunity, to finish what he had started. It's what Randy Johnson, Curt Schilling, and Mark Mulder do. It's what the best in the game have always done.

I understand the injury risks. I don't criticize the Red Sox for feeling they have to baby their fragile superstar. What bothers me is that Pedro allows it. What scares me is that Pedro has become so obsessed with his own health that he won't put himself at risk—*ever*. Here's the nightmare: Game Seven of the World Series. Pedro's pitching a beauty. But with all his strikeouts and a couple of early inning jams, he's thrown 121 pitches through seven innings. There's still no score in the game. Pedro doesn't come out for the eighth inning.

I'd be surprised if there's anyone who doesn't think that's a distinct possibility. But don't you want a performance like that of Jack Morris, when he threw 10 shutout innings to win Game Seven for the Twins in 1991? After the ninth inning, Twins manager Tom Kelly had a short conversation with Morris that went like this:

"That's enough, Jack," Kelly said.

"I'm fine."

"Are you sure?"

"I said I'm fine. If I wasn't fine I'd tell you."

It was Morris's third start in nine days, and there was no way Kelly was going to get him out of that game.

Do you think Pedro would keep going? It's the last day of the season. Five months to rest. Biggest game. Biggest stage. What would he do? Would he glare at Grady Little, double daring him to even suggest that he was done for the night? Or would he allow the manager to make a decision that protects his future? And I know what you're thinking. You're thinking about Game Five of the 1999 American League Division Series against Cleveland. Pedro's back was hurting him, but he came out of the bullpen to pitch six hitless innings and lead the Red Sox to victory. Truly remarkable! I'd like to think something like that could happen again. But that was a long time ago, and I fear that *that* Pedro Martinez no longer exists. I might be wrong, but recent evidence and excessive coddling, at the very least, justify my concern. And that's a little sad.

With Pedro Martinez, we've learned we have to take the good with the bad. And it's been a pretty good trade-off. Because when he's good, he can be awesome. And when he's bad, he's usually just a little frustrating. But not this year. So far, following Pedro Martinez has felt like an egg-sized hemorrhoid. But a strong, productive, quiet second half just might "help shrink swelling."

JULY 15

Look for Game Seven of the World Series to be played at Fenway Park. The American League All-Stars pulled off a Red Sox-ian comeback, beating the National League stars, 7-6.

And this time it counts. For the first time, the league that wins the All-Star game gets home-field advantage in the World Series. That decision was made in order to generate more fan *and* player interest in a game that was becoming almost insignificant. After last year's game ended in a tie after both managers had used all their players, the leagues tried to come up with something to make certain that wouldn't happen again. So, they added two pitchers to each roster, and made the game matter, thus ensuring that managers would be more responsible in the way they handled their rosters. Instead of trying to make sure everybody plays, they would be trying to win the game. Imagine that! Trying to win the game. What a concept.

Hank Blalock became the 12th player to homer in his first All-Star at bat. It was a pinch-hit, two-run homer in the eighth inning off Eric Gagne, lifting the American League to a 7-6 victory.

JULY 16

The "do-nothing kings" just did something. They made a deal with their crosstown rivals, the New York Mets, and acquired right-handed reliever Armando Benitez. It's another deal in which they give up next to nothing (three low-level prospects), but agree to be the dumping ground for another team's salary woes. The Yankees will pay the remainder of Benitez's $6.75 million salary this year, which comes to $2,729,508, plus $456,434 in additional luxury tax. The deal puts their payroll up over $180 million this year, and they really don't know what they have.

Yankees GM Brian Cashman admitted to Mets GM Jim Duquette, "This is the riskiest trade I've ever made."

The risk is inherent in Benitez's regular-season inconsistencies and his postseason calamities. This year, he's blown seven of his 28 save opportunities. His six blown saves in the playoffs are the most in baseball history. And his problems at Yankee Stadium are well known.

Fans remember when Yankees shortstop Derek Jeter hit a home run in the first game of the 1996 ALCS against the Baltimore Orioles. It was an eighth-inning blast that a 12-year-old boy named Jeffrey Maier reached over the wall to get. Armando Benitez was the man who threw the pitch, and the Orioles went on to lose that game.

In the first game of the 2000 World Series between the Mets and the Yankees, Benitez failed to hold a one-run lead in the ninth inning, and the Yankees went on to win that game in 12 innings. And those aren't the only times the Yankees have witnessed firsthand a Benitez collapse. Just this year, Benitez walked four Yankees in the ninth inning, blowing a save on June 22.

Benitez's history with the Yankees goes deeper than just blowing games against them. He also triggered a ferocious brawl while pitching against them on May 19, 1998. After giving up a three-run homer to Bernie Williams, Benitez nailed Yankees first baseman Tino Martinez with a fastball right in the back. The brawl that ensued was one of the worst ever and included Darryl Strawberry's landing a haymaker to Benitez's head. Benitez was suspended for eight games and fined $2,000.

Now, he's in pinstripes and all is forgiven. The Yankees hope that he can be a reliable setup man for Mariano Rivera. The prevailing wisdom is that Benitez will pitch better with less pressure. But I believe you are what you are. And Benitez is a huge question mark that only the Yankees could afford to take a chance on.

With the Yankees' move, we're ready to begin the second half of the season. The Red Sox have been playing their best baseball over the last month. In fact, it's been some of the best baseball in the American League. Since June 4, when Byung-Hyun Kim made his first start for the Red Sox, they've gone 24-14. Only the Yankees (24-12) and Kansas City Royals (24-13) have played better. The Red Sox team ERA during that stretch is 3.55, and only the Anaheim Angels (3.34) and Seattle Mariners (3.39) have done better.

Taking into account that the Red Sox play 42 of their final 69 games at home, where they've won 70 percent of their games this year, I think the Red Sox are ready to make this a battle to the end.

JULY 17

Pedro Martinez arrived late. Typical. And I mean that. Even Pedro admits that it's typical. Completely oblivious to the kind of controversy he has stirred up during his absence, Pedro arrived and said, "It's my normal time to be here today. I normally get in sometimes a little later, but I just do my work. Those are things that I work out between the team and I. I don't {mess} with my job. I do my job. I work hard."

That level of arrogance is impossible to negotiate with. How can you talk to someone who believes being late is normal? Being late is irresponsible and disrespectful. If everyone were routinely late, there would be chaos. So, it can only be tolerated for a select few. Pedro, in his own arrogant mind, believes that he's earned the right to be "tolerated." I guess that's a good goal to have in life. Someday, I'd also like to be so talented and arrogant that people will tolerate me.

Also, Manny's mom is OK. Whew! That was close. We've since learned that his mom apparently fainted from heat exhaustion while gardening, which confirms for me that Manny's excuse was a load of crap! I'm not making light of a fainting spell. I'm just following the time line, and I'm not buying any of it.

Consider: Grady Little got a call at 5:45 a.m.. So, can we assume that Manny had just received a call as well, informing him of his mother's condition? Let's round it off and say he found out around 5:30 a.m. that his mom had fainted. I don't pretend to know the habits of older women living in the South Florida heat, but was she really gardening at 5:30 a.m.? I guess it's possible. And it's the only way Manny's story is at all plausible, because if she had fainted the previous afternoon, Manny would have already known she was OK. But if you get a call that your mom just collapsed and nobody knows at that time that it was a fainting spell, then it might be cause for great concern. Still, I feel quite positive that Manny didn't think his mom was on her deathbed. Therefore, leaving early was something he *wanted* to do, not something he *needed* to do. I would absolutely love to know when his plane tickets were purchased.

The Red Sox lost tonight to the Blue Jays as Toronto's ace, Roy Halladay, won his 14th straight decision. Sure wish the Red Sox had somebody like that. When the score was 5-2 in the ninth inning, Halladay didn't leave it up to his shaky bullpen. He stayed in the game and finished strong. I hope Pedro was watching.

Pedro admitted he didn't stick around to speak to reporters on the Saturday before the All-Star break because he said he was "a little bit mad after the game. It's so difficult to win a ball game. You know what I mean? Too much difficulty every time when I pitch."

Again, he'd win more often if he'd go the distance when the game is on the line. Halladay had a three-run lead after eight innings, and had thrown more than 100 pitches. What do you think the odds would be that Pedro would pitch the ninth inning under those exact same conditions? That's why Halladay is 14-2, and Pedro is 6-2.

And don't even get me started on the fact that Halladay was pitching on the first day back, while Pedro still has two more days off. This is a pennant race, and it sure would have been nice to see Pedro go head to head with Halladay—and *beat him*! Instead, Pedro goes on Sunday against John "Way Back" Wasdin and his ERA of 45.00. Wasdin, who pitched for the Red Sox from 1996 to 2000, earned his nickname because of his propensity to give up the long ball, and he's only pitched one inning this year—giving up five runs on eight hits. Let's hope Pedro doesn't have difficulty winning that ball game.

Meanwhile, Hideki Matsui hit a game-winning solo blast in the ninth inning to lift the Yankees over the Cleveland Indians, 5-4. The Yankees scored three runs in the final two innings to take a three-game lead over the Red Sox. It's never too early to look at the wild-card race, and the Red Sox still lead the Oakland A's by a game. Basically, if the season ended today, the Red Sox would be in the playoffs (and it would be a very short season).

JULY 18

If you've ever gone over to someone's house and they've pulled out the old projector to show you slides of their trip to the Grand Canyon or Aunt Mimi's electrolysis treatments, you have an idea of how bad the Red Sox "slide" show has been. Three games. Three runs. Three losses. Tonight, they managed just one run against Toronto's Kelvim Escobar. The Red Sox haven't won since Manny and Pedro left early. Coincidence? Most likely.

And Jason Giambi better stop, drop, and roll. The man is on fire. Two more home runs tonight give him five in his last five games and tie him with Carlos Delgado for the American League lead with 28. Yanks win, 10-4. The Sox are four games back.

Fortunately, the A's have lost both of their games since the All-Star break as well. So, the Sox still lead the wild-card race by a game.

Also today, the Red Sox activated both Casey Fossum and Jeremy Giambi from the disabled list and sent Freddy Sanchez and Jason Shiell down to the minors.

JULY 19

Now I know what it feels like to be a Yankee fan. Feels good. Really good. Even though the Red Sox were carrying the weight of a three-game losing streak and the uncharacteristically sleepy-eyed offense had only managed two runs in the first five innings, *and* even though the Blue Jays scored three times in the sixth inning off Ramiro "the Hero" Mendoza to take a 4-2 lead, I never doubted the Red Sox were going to win this game. If I had that kind of confidence in my everyday life, I'd be unstoppable. Alas, I'm not good enough to be so confident. But the Red Sox are.

It started when Kevin Millar homered in the second inning. He ripped it down the line in left—one of those "if it's fair, it's gone" moon shots. Well, it grazed the outside of the foul pole for a home run, and that confident feeling started to rise.

Ramiro the Hero kept putting up zeroes except for a lone run in the third. He got the first two batters in the sixth inning, then walked Vernon Wells and hit Carlos Delgado smack-dab in the middle of his rear end. That put runners on first and second with two outs. He got two strikes on Bobby Kielty and just missed getting a called third strike that would have ended the inning. Instead, Kielty ripped a two-run double, and Tom Wilson followed with an RBI single. The Blue Jays had grabbed a 4-2 lead. It was the kind of turn of events that can cost a team a ball game. But not a team with so many last-at-bat victories, and certainly not a team of destiny.

Bill Mueller homered in the sixth to make it 4-3 Toronto. It stayed that way into the eighth inning when Carlos Delgado—the big leagues' RBI leader—came to bat with runners on second and third and nobody out. Time to walk him? Apparently not. With southpaw Alan Embree on the hill, Grady Little brought the infield in and pitched to Delgado. I couldn't believe it!

"You can't pitch to Delgado," I screamed.

First pitch, ground ball to short, runners hold, throw to first, one out. That whole pitching to Delgado thing? Good idea.

Now, the Sox intentionally walk Kielty to load the bases, and bring Todd Jones in to face the right-handed-hitting Tom Wilson. But the Jays send up left-handed-hitting Greg Myers. Grady Little must have known that would happen, so this must have been the matchup he wanted.

Jones falls behind, 3-1, to Myers. There's still only one out, and the bases are loaded. Here it is—the pitch that could decide the game. Jones delivers. Crack!

Not a loud crack, mind you. Just the sound of the bat meeting the ball. It's another ground ball—4-6-3 double play. Inning over.

Now, could there be any doubt about who was going to win this game? Only when the Red Sox were down to their last out, still trailing 4-3 with nobody on base in the ninth inning did I begin to wonder what was going on.

"Wait a minute," I thought. "This had the feeling of a Red Sox victory written all over it. Millar's home run. The 4-6-3 double play. Those things happened for a reason. I can't believe the Red Sox are going to lose this game. What good is it to feel like a Yankees fan if it's not supported by Yankees results?"

Nomar Garciaparra walked. All right. Fate is back in business. Nomar almost never walks. It's only the 23rd time all season that he's taken a free pass, and it's the first time in 50 at bats. So, something was up. The first three pitches to Manny Ramirez were off the plate. It appeared the Blue Jays weren't going to let Ramirez beat them with a home run. Strike!

OK, so they don't want to put the winning run on base either. Then, on the 3-1 pitch, Nomar takes off for second. The thinking had to be: if it was ball four, he'd get to second anyway, and if it was a strike, Manny would be swinging, and Nomar might have a better chance to score on a ball in the gap. The pitch was a strike, but Manny didn't swing. Instead, he thought it was ball four and started toward first base. The catcher, Greg Myers, fired the ball to second, but Nomar slid in safely. That was not only odd, but it also figured to be unproductive. Now, with the count 3-and-2 and the tying run in scoring position, the Blue Jays would most certainly walk Manny Ramirez and pitch to David Ortiz.

Base hit to right. The Jays decided to pitch to one of the game's best RBI men, and it came back to bite them. Didn't anybody watch the way Tony LaRussa managed against the Red Sox? There's no way he would have pitched to Manny in that situation.

Nomar scored. Ortiz made the final out. And we headed into extra innings. The game was, in theory, still in doubt. But it was almost a guaranteed Red Sox win. Nomar walks? Then he steals second and they pitch to Manny? C'mon, this was too easy.

In the 10th, the Fates had a laugh at Toronto's expense. Jeremy Giambi, back from the disabled list, got an infield single. Now, if they ever had a competition to determine the slowest player in Major League Baseball, Giambi might actually win by coming in last. I don't think he'll get another infield single until Celine Dion stops loving herself too much.

Gabe Kapler pinch ran for Giambi, stole second, went to third on a throwing error, and scored when Trot Nixon squibbed a hit through the drawn-in infield. Game over. As you'd expect, Sox win, 5-4.

Really now, the Red Sox win by stealing two bases in the ninth and 10th innings? That's not your normal, everyday, run-of-the-mill Red Sox victory. But when Fate takes over, you don't know *how* it will happen, only that it *will* happen.

The Yankees also won, but the A's lost. So, the Red Sox are four back and two up in the respective playoff races.

JULY 20

And on the seventh day, Pedro Martinez pitched. And he looked around at all the offense the Red Sox had created, and he thought, "This is good." After seven full days of rest, Pedro finally got back on the hill, and the Red Sox welcomed him back from his fun-filled trip to the Dominican Republic by giving him nine runs to work with. The Sox earned a split with the Blue Jays, 9-4. And now, in the 27 games the Red Sox have played against the Blue Jays and the Yankees, Pedro is 1-0. Nice to have him contributing to the pennant race for a change.

Apparently, Pedro pitches quite well on seven days rest. He went seven innings, striking out eight and giving up three harmless singles to a powerful Toronto lineup.

The Yankees completed a four-game sweep of the Indians, while the A's were swept by the Twins. It's nice to have some breathing room on the A's, because the Red Sox will go head-to-head with them six times in August.

JULY 21–22

The Red Sox easily swept a two-game series from the Detroit Tigers, and simultaneously beat the Yankees—beat them to the punch, that is.

Both of the American League East front-runners were interested in adding a left-hander to their bullpen. Both targeted Scott Sauerbeck of the Pittsburgh Pirates. The Red Sox got him. The Yankees went to Plan B (or was it Plan AARP?) and picked up 46-year-old Jesse Orosco from the San Diego Padres. Advantage: Boston.

"We've wanted another really good left-hander in the pen for some time," Red Sox GM Theo Epstein said. "This was the top left-hander available, one of the top left-handers in the game in the bullpen. Sauerbeck is just about everything we're looking for in a left-handed reliever."

Yankees GM Brian Cashman conceded, "He's a good pitcher," Cashman said, "and we'd have liked to have had him, but it wasn't going to happen with them."

The Red Sox did have to give up Brandon Lyon to get Sauerbeck, and that's not an insignificant loss. But Lyon's role with the team has been greatly diminished. He stepped up big-time when the Red Sox were in desperate need of a closer, but once the Sox traded for Byung-Hyun Kim, and then Todd Jones, Lyon wasn't just no longer the closer, he wasn't even the setup guy. So, if you've already got Jones, Mike Timlin, and Chad Fox as your right-handers, then adding a lefty to support Alan Embree and Casey Fossum is the way to go. The Red Sox got Lyon last year for nothing and not only did he contribute greatly, he may have just brought the Sox a very important missing piece to a championship puzzle.

Sauerbeck is what you'd consider a left-handed specialist. Left-handed hitters are only hitting .175 against him over the past two seasons. Righties, by the way, only hit him at a .203 clip. So, he's good. And he's been very good lately. His ERA over his last 13 appearances with the Pirates is 1.74. If destiny is working weekends, Sauerbeck will be able to neutralize the Yankees' Jason Giambi or Nick Johnson in a couple of key situations when the Yankees come to Fenway Park this coming Friday, Saturday, and

Sunday.

The Red Sox will also get a chance to see Orosco, who carries a 7.56 ERA and some anti-Red Sox history of his own. Orosco helped the Mets beat the Red Sox in the 1986 World Series. In fact, he was on the mound when the final out of Game Seven was recorded. Of course, that was 17 years ago, and he was only 29 years old then.

"We're an equal-opportunity employer," GM Brian Cashman quipped. "We don't discriminate for age if he can get people out."

That remains to be seen.

And even though there are still eight days before the trading deadline, the Red Sox say they're ready to go as far as the team currently constituted can take them.

"We're not looking to make a trade for the sake of making a trade. Our goal is to try to win the World Series," Epstein said. "We have a lot of confidence in the guys in that clubhouse. This could be it unless there is a deal out there we feel really makes us better. Otherwise we're going to stay with what we have."

The Yankees are less likely to stand pat, because they didn't really get what they wanted, and because they always go out and get more.

JULY 23

Happy Birthday, Nomar! Last year on his 29th birthday, Nomar Garciaparra hit three home runs, including a grand slam, and drove in eight runs. This year he went 0-for-4. But Trot Nixon celebrated Nomar's birthday with two home runs, including a grand slam, and he drove in five runs. It's been a pretty easy week for the Red Sox so far. They beat the Tigers, 14-5 and 7-4, and dropped the Devil Rays, 10-4, tonight. During their current five-game winning streak, they've outscored their opponents 44-21.

It was a good day to be Trot Nixon, considering he was 1-for-12 with the bases loaded this year, and he's more likely to be remembered for the "12 Angry Men" he left on base against the Cardinals on June 12. But it was soon after that day that his mediocre season started to become quite a bit more. Nixon's batting average dipped to .295 on June 23. In the 22 games he's played in since then, he's 32-for-83 with seven home runs, 19 RBI, and 21 runs scored. He's now batting .320 for the season, with 16 homers and 61 RBI. Not bad for a guy who spends plenty of time in the middle of trade rumors. Too often fans seem too ready to get rid of

Nixon, as if he could be so easily replaced. Yet Peter Gammons of ESPN wrote just last month that "six years after being the eighth pick in the nation, (Nixon) is now one of the two or three best right fielders in the American League."

The Red Sox reached the century mark with their 100th game of the season, and at 60-40, they're 20 games above .500 for the first time this year. Since the Yankees were rained out last night, but beat the Baltimore Orioles tonight, the Sox remain 2 1/2 games out of first place. But the Oakland A's have lost five of seven games since the All-Star break and have fallen four games behind Boston in the wild-card race.

It's also my birthday. Turned 40. If the team of destiny does its part, I could be down to just four more years of walking around on earth. I wonder if the dinosaurs saw it coming like this.

JULY 24

The wheels came off for Ramiro Mendoza. His four starts this year have all gotten gradually worse, finally bottoming out tonight when he was charged with seven runs in 4 1/3 innings against the Tampa Bay Devil Rays. His performance might just have been bad enough to inspire the Red Sox to increase their efforts to find another starting pitcher. When Mendoza was surprisingly good, the Sox might have thought they could get away with him in the rotation for the next 2 1/2 months. But when he is predictably bad, Sox management may see it as an impetus to go after someone more consistent and proven.

Chad Fox wasn't any better than Mendoza. He entered the game and proceeded to give up a single, a walk, a homer, and a double. That wasn't enough to convince Grady Little that he just might not have his best stuff today, so after a fly ball out, he gave up another RBI single. Tampa Bay scored seven runs in the fifth inning and took an 11-2 lead. Managers don't get questioned as often in blowouts as they do in tight ball games, but the Red Sox lost this game 15-9. Couldn't Little have made pitching changes a little sooner to keep the light-hitting Rays from scoring more than nine runs?

It's a shame, because the Yankees also lost today, so the Red Sox missed a chance to be 1 1/2 games out with the Yankees coming to Fenway Park for a three-game series.

Pedro Martinez—Red Sox Nation turns its lonely eyes to you. Little judiciously, albeit belatedly, altered his pitching rotation to make sure Pedro threw in Game One of the Yankees series. And here it comes. Pedro really needs to come up big in this one. Remember, he missed his first scheduled start against the Yankees when he hurt his oblique. And he was outpitched by Mike Mussina the last time he faced New York. The general thinking the first 10 times the Red Sox and Yankees faced each other was that the games weren't all that important because it was too early in the season. Now, it's important. And it's important to the Red Sox that they know they can count on Pedro to beat the Yankees. He's only 7-7 in 20 career starts against New York. Even if he can't be a horse who goes the distance, he can at least be a bull—fiercely determined, snorting, growling, unwilling to surrender—at least until some little dance man in tight pants sticks a handful of swords into him. Love that bullfighting! Almost as good as horse racing, the "sport of kings." Because apparently kings have always liked to see horses saddled, hoofed, reigned in, and whipped for their gambling pleasure.

8

Instant Classics

JULY 25

I'll do my best not to criticize Pedro again, and instead just call Game One of this series an "instant classic." Yankees manager Joe Torre agreed.

"That's a classic automatically, right now," said Torre. "That was incredible. Two pitchers pitched their tail off."

It seemed like the first time in a very long time that Pedro Martinez finished a game without his tail. But Torre was right. He did pitch his tail off. He left his heart out on the field, and if you'll forgive me one more cliché, he gave it everything he had.

So did the portly David Wells. He was pitching with the kind of back pain that would have kept him out of just about any other start. But as a true indication of the importance of this game, Wells went out there anyway, and also pitched his rather substantial tail off.

The Red Sox got things started in the first inning when Nomar Garciaparra walked with two outs, and Manny Ramirez drove the ball to deep center field for a run-scoring double. In the second, Jorge Posada blasted a solo shot to tie the game. Posada was 5-for-39 lifetime against Martinez, a .128 average, and had never hit a home run off the Red Sox ace. It was the first of many oddities in this game.

For instance, all of the Red Sox runs were scored on two-out base hits. Wells, who entered the game having given up just seven walks in 135 innings this year, walked five batters, including three in a row with two outs in the sixth inning. (That, by the way, means that Wells has walked 12 batters all year, and eight of those walks have been against the Red Sox.) Enrique Wilson, who was given a chance to start and play third base because of the two doubles he hit off Pedro on July 7, stole his first base of the year—and then stole another one. Both times he went on to score the go-ahead run.

The Red Sox regained the lead in the home half of the second when Johnny Damon stroked a two-out base hit, scoring Bill Mueller. The next 17 batters in the game were retired until Damon slapped another base hit in the fifth inning. Pedro had retired the Yankees in order in the third, fourth, and fifth innings. But because it took him 50 pitches to retire 12 Yankees in the first two innings, along with his seven strikeouts and two walks, his pitch count was already annoyingly high.

In the sixth, Pedro gave up a couple of bleeders through the right side of the infield. Both base hits by Bernie Williams and Jorge Posada were just beyond Todd Walker's diving reach. Then Nick Johnson, off the disabled list just in time for this game, grounded a 3-1 pitch to second base. Instead of it being a double play to end the inning, Posada was running on the pitch, so the only play was to first base. Williams scored the tying run. At the end of 5 1/2, the score was tied, and Pedro had thrown 100 pitches. It's the secret of the Yankees' success against Pedro. They've won 12 of the 20 games Pedro has started against them by keeping the game close and forcing him to throw a lot of pitches. Then they go after the Red Sox bullpen. Once again they were following the formula perfectly.

But the Red Sox were looking to break the game open in their half of the sixth. With two outs, Wells walked Mueller, Nixon, and Varitek. His loss of control came suddenly, but Torre had seen enough. With Johnny Damon, who had already had three hits off Wells, coming up, Torre summoned newly acquired Jesse Orosco. Pitching in a major-league record 1,230th game—his first with the Yankees—Orosco struck out Damon. Nice pickup that was for New York.

So, the game remained tied and tense into the seventh. That "Pedro killer" Enrique Wilson led off with a single and moved to second on a wild pitch that went behind Alfonso Soriano. The go-ahead run was on second with nobody out. Pedro was undoubtedly pitching his last inning. The questions were, what did he have left, and would he get out of the inning with the lead? Pedro went to his sixth full count of the night, and struck out Soriano for the third time.

But Wilson had only just begun to continue his torment of Pedro and the Red Sox. With no stolen bases since the previous September, and with no great need to steal a base in this situation, he took off for third base and made it without a throw. Now the go-ahead run was on third with only one out and Derek Jeter at the plate. Jeter walked.

Now it was decision time. Would Red Sox manager Grady Little leave Pedro in to pitch to the Yankees' most dangerous hitter, Jason Giambi? Sox lefties Alan Embree, Scott Sauerbeck, and Casey Fossum were available. Pedro was up to 119 pitches, and he was already in a bit of a foul mood because of the home plate umpire's incredibly shrinking strike zone. Little's decision? He kept Pedro in, and Pedro proceeded to strike out Giambi for the third time. He got him with 95- mile-an-hour high heat. It was his 10th strikeout of the game.

So it was up to Bernie Williams, who entered the game in an 8-for-45 slump since coming off the disabled list earlier this month. Pedro had gotten Giambi with plenty of hard stuff. He obviously knew this was his last inning, and he was leaving it all out on the field. He kept the heat coming to Bernie Williams, and the count went to 2-2.

A curveball. Pedro went with a breaking pitch. Why would he try to trick him when the fastball was working so well? He was one blistering fastball away from getting out of the inning. Instead, the curve hung up in the zone, and Williams rapped it for a base hit to right. Wilson scored the go-ahead run. It was 3-2 Yankees, and Pedro's night was over.

"(Martinez) pitched his heart out there tonight," Little said. "And he did a heck of a job. He just got that curveball up a little bit to Bernie there in his last hitter and he hit it for a base hit."

Pedro finished with 128 pitches, the most he's thrown in three years. On July 23, 2000, Pedro struck out 15 White Sox, beating them 1-0. Tonight, he struck out 10 Yankees, walked four, and gave up seven hits and three runs. He's now gone seven innings in five of his last seven starts, and in the other two games, he went 6 2/3. He's only gone past the seventh inning twice this year. I think he was a bulldog tonight. He was tenacious and gutsy, but he didn't do what he was supposed to do.

But the Red Sox did what they've done all year. They bounced right back. Down 3-2 in the eighth inning and facing Armando Benitez, David Ortiz delivered a one-out single. Damian Jackson pinch ran for Ortiz and immediately stole second base. Jackson has done that so often this year, he reminds me of Herb Washington of the 1974 Oakland A's. After the American League adopted the designated hitter rule in 1973, A's owner Charles O. Finley decided to use a roster spot on a world-class sprinter. At that time, Washington was the world indoor record holder in both the 50-yard dash and the 60-yard dash. The A's used him exclusively as a pinch runner. In 1974, Washington played in 92 games and *never* batted. He stole 29 bases in 45 attempts, which proves stealing bases isn't all about speed. Washington only played in 13 games in 1975, and ended his career with 105 games played—*zero* at bats.

After Bill Mueller popped up for the second out, Jackson moved to third on a passed ball. Benitez went to 2-0 on Trot Nixon when Torre sprung from the dugout. He touched his right arm, signaling for Mariano Rivera. This was merely more evidence of this game's subtext. Torre wasn't managing as if this were a normal regular-season game. He had to get Nixon out. And he wasn't about to watch Benitez mess around when he had Rivera loose and ready.

Nixon walked. Jason Varitek soft-served a single over shortstop. Jackson scored, and the game was tied at 3. Amazing stuff! Varitek gets my vote for Mr. Clutch.

The game moved into the ninth still tied. Byung-Hyun Kim, whose record of misfortune against the Yankees has been well documented, gave up a leadoff single to whom else but Enrique Wilson? What does he do? He steals second. Kim throws a slider in on Soriano's fists, but Soriano fights it off and grounds weakly to second base. He's out, but Wilson ambles over to third base. There was one out, and the go-ahead run was on third.

Jeter delivered the sacrifice fly to center field. The Yankees were back in front, 4-3.

"I think that anybody that watched that game tonight had to enjoy it," Little said. "We would have enjoyed it much more had we won. But that was a well-played, well-pitched game there, and I think anyone who saw it would be proud to say they saw the game."

Varitek added, "It was a good game but we were on the short end. We are always on the short end."

Certainly, they were in this case. But this exciting game with all its built-in drama, intrigue, and pivotal managerial maneuvering still had a few more thrills in it. Nomar Garciaparra ripped a one-out double off the Monster. He represented the tying run at second base, with Manny Ramirez coming up. There was a good chance that Rivera would pitch to him, because Manny was just 3-for-24 lifetime (.125) against the Yankees closer. But Manny walked on five pitches. It was evident that Rivera wasn't going to let Manny see anything hittable.

Now with runners on first and second, Kevin Millar jumped in the box and was a bit overanxious. He ended up striking out on a high fastball that zipped past him at eye level. Two down. Damian Jackson was the scheduled hitter, but Little went with Jeremy Giambi instead. When it comes to Giambi, Little has more faith than a bus full of nuns.

Giambi hit a soft line drive to Soriano. Game over.

"That's the way it's going to go all season long," Sox center fielder Johnny Damon said. "We both respect each other; we both fear each other. We know they're capable of putting together a great game, and they know we are. Unfortunately, we couldn't get those extra key hits."

Very unfortunate. Almost calamitous. Boston slips 3 1/2 games back and faces the improbable task of beating Mike Mussina tomorrow. John Burkett will enter the game 0-6 with a 9.66 ERA in nine regular season starts against the Yankees. Yikes!

JULY 26

Back-to-back classics! As good as yesterday's game was, this one was better—and not just because the Red Sox won this time (although that helps). This one had higher ups and lower downs. Yesterday was all about Pedro—watching his pitch count and wondering if the Red Sox could give him enough runs. The anxiety level for Game Two of the series began with the first batter and never relented.

Alfonso Soriano led off the game with a double. Uh-oh. They're going to pound Burkett today. Jeter lifted a ball high and deep to left—an out—but another well-hit ball. This could get ugly. Jason Giambi grounded to second. Hey, this might not be as bad as it initially looked. Bernie Williams bounces to short to end the inning. This will certainly be a long and fretful afternoon of survival.

Now, it's Mike Mussina's turn to take the hill. He walks Johnny Damon, and one out later, Nomar Garciaparra absolutely crushes one to straightaway center field. His 16th home run of the year gave the Red Sox a 2-0 lead. The Red Sox would add another run before the inning was over, when Trot Nixon doubled home Kevin Millar. All right, Burkett's got three runs to work with. So, even if the Yankees start spraying the ball all over the ballpark, the Sox are sure to stay in this thing for a while.

My apologies to Mr. Burkett. He was phenomenal. As he left the mound with runners on first and second and two outs, he tipped his hat to the crowd, which was giving him a standing ovation. Burkett went 5 2/3 innings, allowing just three hits, and a "can-you-believe-it?" *zero* runs.

"I believe in myself and that's really all it is, plain and simple," Burkett said. "I've had people questioning my ability all my life. I've always been the underdog. So, it's comfortable for me for people to doubt me."

It also can't be denied, however, that all the doubt is justified. Consider the two-inning, eight-run performance against Toronto on May 30. Consider that each of Burkett's last three wins was against Detroit, which is challenging the 1962 Mets for the dubious distinction of "worst team ever." Consider that this is a guy who went 22-7 for the San Francisco Giants in 1993 but has never won more than 14 games in any other season in his 16-year, big-league career. Consider that every scribe, sports announcer, or would-be journalist was pounding out the fact that Burkett had never beaten the Yankees. Never.

Well, never say never. Because Burkett had beaten the Yankees before. It was Game One of the 1996 American League Divisional Series when he was pitching for the Texas Rangers. Burkett threw a complete game, beating David Cone and the Yankees, 6-2. All the reports saying he'd never beaten the Yankees were erroneous, or at the very least, incomplete. He had never beaten them during the regular season.

Burkett is now 21-12 pitching for the Red Sox, but fans will still be riddled with doubt every time he pitches. But that's OK; he's comfortable with doubt.

Back to the game. Burkett had just left with runners on first and second. Manny Ramirez's 25th home run of the year in the fourth inning had given the Red Sox a 4-0 lead. Alan Embree came in to face Hideki Matsui, and Godzilla grounded out to second. Another lefty versus lefty move that worked perfectly.

The Red Sox had a chance to break the game wide open in their half of the sixth. With runners on first and second, Bill Mueller put a line drive into the left-center-field gap. Bernie Williams ran gracefully to the spot where the ball was about to make contact with the grass. Then, with a full extension dive, he slid his glove under the ball and made a sensational catch. He saved two runs, at least. The Red Sox bullpen would be required to get the final nine outs, and the momentum had just swung to the New York dugout.

The Yankees got two runs in the seventh off Embree and Todd Jones. Then, Scott Sauerbeck started the eighth and got Jason Giambi to fly out, but Bernie Williams rolled a ball 30 feet up the third base line. Sauerbeck gloved it, and in one motion, turned and fired the ball in the general direction of first base. He rushed it unnecessarily, and the ball went past Kevin Millar at first. Williams ended up on second base. A pair of lefties was due up for the Yankees, so Sauerbeck continued.

He got Hideki Matsui to pop up to left field, but Nick Johnson tagged him for a run-scoring double. Time for Byung-Hyun Kim. He's frequently asked to get anywhere from three to six outs. This time, he'd need to get four.

Instead of Kim facing right-hander Raul Mondesi, Torre sent up lefty Karim Garcia to pinch hit. Not exactly the kind of move that strikes fear in a Red Sox fan. Garcia is a .245 hitter without a lot of power. Kim should have been able to handle this and get the Sox out of the inning still holding that slim lead.

But it didn't happen. Garcia promptly rapped a single to right. The game was tied at 4-4.

Now it appeared all the work that Burkett had done would be for naught. What a shame. You could smell a 4 1/2-game Yankees lead, and it stunk.

Todd Walker led off the Red Sox eighth with a double to deep left. Nomar, Manny, and Millar were due up—the heart of the Red Sox order. Three clutch guys, each with a chance to drive home the go-ahead run. Nomar bunted. Read that again—*Nomar bunted*!

It wasn't until after the game that we learned it was Nomar's decision to try to sacrifice Jackson (pinch running for Walker) over to third. He'd done it against the Astros in the 14th inning on June 15, and even though it had worked, not too many people had thought it was a good idea then—and nobody thought it was a good idea now. Against the Astros, he got the bunt down, and Manny Ramirez won the game with a single. Against the Yankees, he popped the ball up to Mussina.

"We will advise him against it. But we can't guarantee that he won't do it again," Little said. "If he has a feeling up there that we don't have, there's no telling what might happen. The kid is just doing whatever he can to help us win a game."

That's true. And if it had worked, the potential winning run would have been on third with one out. Manny might have been intentionally walked, leaving it up to Millar. It's not the world's worst strategy, but I'd rather have three .300 hitters taking their hacks, instead of one—and no offense to Millar—the worst one.

As it turned out, Manny was intentionally walked anyway, and Millar flied out to right. It would have been deep enough to score Jackson, somewhat validating what Nomar had done. Then, with two outs and Trot Nixon stepping up, Torre pulled Mussina and brought in his lefty specialist, Jesse Orosco. This was a bad move on Torre's part, because he had to expect Little would bring Nixon back to the dugout and put Gabe Kapler up to bat. Orosco against Kapler couldn't be the matchup Torre considered his best option, could it?

Well, it worked out fine for New York. Kapler struck out swinging. I swear, Orosco might pitch until he's 50 before he gets another right-handed hitter out. But the game went into the ninth, still tied at 4.

After failing to get his ill-advised sacrifice bunt down, Nomar trotted out to shortstop and began the ninth with a sensational play. Enrique Wilson (again!) shot a ball up the middle. Nomar, ranging far to his left, got to the ball, spun around, and fired a strike to first base. That was clutch! We usually reserve the word "clutch" for offense, but that was a play that changed the rest of the inning, and therefore, the game.

After Soriano struck out, Jeter singled. Again, I maintain, Nomar's acrobatic play was immense. But so was Johnny Damon. Jason Giambi lifted the ball into shallow center field. Damon got a good jump on it, but he was playing Giambi very deep. The ball hung up forever, and Damon churned along. Finally, as gravity did its job bringing the ball down, Damon dove awkwardly toward the ground. The glove was on his right hand, but the ball was on the left side of his body. Managing somehow to avoid twisting his wrist in a way it was never meant to go, Damon plucked the ball out of the air, as it was about to fall safely for a hit. Inning over. Two great defensive plays gave the Red Sox a chance to win it in their final at bat.

Joe Torre doesn't like to use Mariano Rivera in non-save situations, so he handed the ball and the responsibility to Armando Benitez. I couldn't have been happier about that. The odds of the Red Sox squeezing a run across against Benitez are far greater than they would be of getting to Rivera. This would be the Red Sox last best chance, however. Because once the Yankees scored in the top half of an extra inning, Rivera would be summoned to close the door.

And if you don't think the Red Sox are a team of destiny, consider how they scored the game-winning run. With one out, Jeremy Giambi got a base hit. And that's not the strange part. That didn't happen until Giambi, who appeared to be running through water, stole second base.

"It was close, but he was out," said Jeter.

It matters not. He was called safe. Jason Varitek struck out on the pitch. So the game-winning run was at second with two outs and Johnny Damon coming up. This is where I think Torre made his biggest mistake. Why not bring Rivera in now? He can get four outs and take you through the 10th, and you can worry about the 11th inning when you get there. Instead, Torre stayed with Benitez *and* chose to intentionally walk Damon. Torre must have known that David Ortiz would be sent up to pinch hit for Jackson, so he basically chose Ortiz over Damon as the lefty most likely to make an out in this situation. Wrong decision.

"Let's try to win this thing right here," Little told his team. And then he turned to Ortiz and said, "Go hit the Green Monster."

Ortiz was just following orders when he stroked a 1-2 pitch off the left-field wall. The Red Sox, who nearly blew a 4-0 lead, were instead rushing onto the field to celebrate a 5-4 victory over the Yankees. Instead of being 4 1/2 games back, they returned to where they had been when the series started, 2 1/2 back.

Sometimes it takes a David to beat Goliath. And there's no doubt that the Yankees are Goliath. But when David slung that rock high up off the wall, the result was a Red Sox win of biblical proportions. Do I exaggerate? Talk to me in

October.

Games like that are season-savers.
—Red Sox second baseman Todd Walker

JULY 27

When this year is over, there will be moments to cherish, memories to hold on to, and musings to carry us through long winter months. Some of them are already known, like Trot Nixon and Jason Varitek hitting back-to-back homers on June 7 to complete a comeback against Milwaukee, or Ramiro the Hero's five zeros in his first start against the Yankees, or the Blue Jays' deciding not to intentionally walk Manny Ramirez in the ninth inning on July 19, and Manny delivering a game tying single. Personally, I'll never forget Nomar Garciaparra's 11-pitch at bat leading to his 11th triple of the year, albeit in a loss to the Cardinals on June 12. Some of the most treasured memories have yet to unfold. Certainly, David Ortiz's wall ball to beat the Yankees yesterday is near the top of the list, but it was bumped today by Varitek's three-run bomb. That's the one that will be passed down for generations. Grandpa will say something like this: "Sonny, let me tell you about one of the biggest home runs I've ever seen in a regular season game…"

The Yankees began as they so often do, by jumping out in front early. Jason Giambi's home run in the first gave the Boys from the Bronx a 1-0 lead. They'd add solo runs in the third and in the sixth. Meanwhile, Jeff Weaver was shutting down the Red Sox. Weaver entered the game with a 5.40 ERA and only two wins in his last 10 starts. He's the Yankees' weakest link, but he was at his sharpest on this day.

Finally, with one out in the Red Sox seventh, Weaver walked Trot Nixon and hit Bill Mueller around the ankle. That was Weaver's 113th pitch, and Joe Torre came out to get him. Keep in mind, Weaver had only given up two hits to this point, and he was working with a 3-0 lead. Also keep in mind that Varitek, a switch-hitter, was the next batter. When Torre summoned lefty Chris Hammond, it meant that Varitek would turn around and swing from the right side, where he's more comfortable. Torre was asked after the game why he didn't let Weaver try to work his way out of trouble.

"I like the question," Torre said. "All year, I've been asked 'Why is he [still] starting?' So I like being asked, 'Why did you take him out?'"

Ever the diplomat, but there's no way Torre "liked" being asked that question. That question was only asked because Varitek took the third pitch he saw from Hammond and drove it high, deep, and gone—over everything in left! It was a three-run homer that tied the game and sucked the life right out of the Yankees, at least for the moment.

And oh, by the way, Johnny Damon followed that up with a home run of his own. Amazing! Only a matter of moments had passed and the Red Sox were suddenly in front, 4-3. It's interesting that Damon's home run may have been as important as Varitek's in the scope of this one game, but it was merely a continuation of the magic spun by Varitek's bat. Varitek's home run soared in a mythical kind of flight. It brought people to life, and put hope where there had been despair. Damon's came while the ballpark was still buzzing. I would bet a lot of people missed it while they remained lost in the gaze of seeing Varitek's ball fly through the summer night sky and disappear over the Monster seats. That's why, I think, Varitek's home run was so wonderfully special, while Damon's might be lost in the telling and retelling of this story.

Even fewer will remember David Ortiz slapping a three-bagger into the right-field corner to plate two more. The Red Sox scored six times in the inning and held on to beat the Yankees, 6-4. The most dramatic series in recent memory (and that St. Louis series in June was pretty darn good) ended when Jorge Posada popped a shallow fly to left field, dangerously close to the foul line. Manny Ramirez went full bore after it, and just at the point where the grass stops and the dirt begins around the foul line, Manny slid feet first like a base runner, extended his glove beyond his shoe tops and plucked the ball out of the air as it was about to make contact with the ground. A sensational catch to end the game with the Yankees threatening! Manny lay on the ground for a moment, soaking it all in with a wide grin across his face.

"It felt unbelievable to make that catch," Ramirez said. "It was like the first catch I ever made, and I was very happy."

Good times, baby! These are very good times. It even began with the Red Sox poking the big bear with a stick. Having called the Yankees the "Evil Empire," Sox president Larry Lucchino got actor James Earl Jones—the voice of Darth Vader in the *Star Wars* movies—to recite the national anthem before the game. The Red Sox are certainly enjoying this, and well they should. The Yankees have won the division each of the last five years, but they have to know that this year they're getting their biggest challenge from the Red Sox.

"It's going to be a dogfight all the way to the end," Torre said. "I'm not sure who's going to win. It's going to come down to pitching. Whoever pitches the best the rest of the way is going to have the advantage."

He might be right. And if he is, I like the Red Sox chances. The addition of Kim and Sauerbeck, plus the return of Pedro Martinez, give the Red Sox a very formidable pitching staff.

Right now, everything's moving in the right direction for the Red Sox. They've picked up 2 1/2 games this month while the Yankees have stumbled back to mediocrity with an 11-10 record so far in July. The Yankees also just lost their first game this year in which they had a three-run lead at any time. And if they bother to look back on this series, they'll have to admit they were a few steps away from sweeping the series, but they blew it! I guess they better not look back, because somebody's gaining on them.

JULY 28

> It was as great a three-game series as I've ever seen.
> —Red Sox president Larry Lucchino

That it was. It was like Muhammad Ali and Joe Frazier I, II, and III. Two heavyweights slugging away, earning each other's respect while the loathing increases.

Probably more than any other sport, baseball is like a chess game. Managers study the field as if it were a large square comprised of 64 little squares, and are always thinking several moves ahead. And the object of the game when the Red Sox play the Yankees is to get the king to topple over on his side. The Yankees are the kings. The Red Sox are the knights—limited in their movement, yet they can be very dangerous when used effectively. The fans are mere pawns—disposable pieces whose broken hearts and devastation are seen as means to an end. And of course, first-year players are known as rooks. Base runners could be bishops, because they're always moving diagonally. And George Steinbrenner is the queen—because he holds the most power.

When it comes to highly competent managers, the Red Sox have been "searching for Bobby Fischer" since the days of Dick Williams. And to date, no one has suggested that Grady Little could ever be matched up with Big Blue the supercomputer. But this weekend, Little seemed to stand up to the great Boris Spassky, a.k.a. Joe Torre.

Consider the three-game series as one long chess game. Torre comes out with the classic Brazilian Defense. It's a 2-2 game in the sixth on Friday night, and Torre brings in Jesse Orosco to pitch to Johnny Damon with the bases loaded. Solid move. And it works. Damon strikes out.

But Torre had made a far more subtle move in the top half of that inning. With runners on first and third, he sent slow-footed Jorge Posada from first base with Nick Johnson at the plate. Johnson grounded out to second. It would have been a double-play ball, if Posada hadn't been running. Instead, Bernie Williams scored the tying run.

Indeed, Torre was the grand master in this one. He started Enrique Wilson, primarily because Wilson had had a pair of doubles off Pedro Martinez 18 days earlier. Wilson ended up stealing his first two bases of the season, and both times those steals led to him scoring the go-ahead run.

By the time Jeremy Giambi floated a soft parabola toward second base, and the Yankees had survived another Pedro Martinez game, it looked like Torre was on his way to a convincing victory.

Ah, but as Field Marshall Count Helmuth von Moltke liked to say, "No plan survives contact with the opposition."

On Saturday, it was Little's turn to make "all the right moves." Recognizing that John Burkett had just pitched a marvelous 5 2/3 innings, Little called on Alan Embree to pitch to Hideki Matsui with runners on first and second. Clearly, the lefty versus lefty play is as old as the Levenstien Defense. It worked for Little just as it had worked for Torre the day before.

Little's next move of import was to bring Scott Sauerbeck in to start the eighth. And it would have worked, except that someone appeared to shake the board. An off-balance Sauerbeck threw the ball away, and Bernie Williams ended up on second base. After left-handed-swinging Nick Johnson brought Williams home with a double, Little went with what has become his standard move—he brought in Byung-Hyun Kim to pitch to Raul Mondesi.

But Torre must have seen it coming. He countered with Karim Garcia who, despite his .245 average, promptly won the battle and tied the game.

Little lost control of one of his best pieces when Nomar Garciaparra tried to sacrifice in the eighth inning. But Torre appeared to momentarily falter. With runners on first and second, he brought Orosco in again to face another lefty, Trot Nixon. But obviously, Little had the option of pinch hitting with Gabe Kapler. True, Kapler was in an 0-for-17 funk, but it was hard to imagine that Torre's best possible matchup was Orosco versus Kapler. But even ill-advised moves sometimes work. Kapler struck out.

Then Torre made his fatal mistake. Unwilling to sacrifice a piece too early, he failed at the game's most critical juncture. The game was tied in the ninth inning. Torre had to get out of that inning, but he was unwilling to make his best move—Mariano Rivera.

Instead, he went with the inconsistent Armando Benitez. Even as Benitez began to falter, Torre left him out there. Then he made the curious decision to walk Damon and pitch to David Ortiz. All right, but how about bringing in Rivera at that point? Rivera can get four outs, so Torre could still have had him for the 10th inning. And I can't believe Torre was thinking about the 11th inning when Benitez was pitching to Ortiz with the winning run on second base in the ninth. That's thinking a little too far ahead.

By Sunday, you could see that these two managers had studied the same masters. They were using their new lefties out of the pen in similar ways, pinch hitting, pinch running, stealing bases—trying to use every piece remaining on the board. Then just as Little had lifted a near-flawless Burkett at the first sign of trouble the day before, Torre walked out to get Jeff Weaver on Sunday. Weaver had only given up two hits, but after he walked Trot Nixon and hit Bill Mueller, Torre decided it was time to get him out of there. It turned out to be the worst move either manager made all weekend.

Back-to-back homers gave the Red Sox the lead. Later, Torre did something I've never understood. He brought in Orosco, who intentionally walked the first man he faced, Manny Ramirez. Torre must have feared Benitez would uncork a wild pitch trying to issue an intentional walk, but it forced a new pitcher to potentially get out of whatever rhythm he was gaining in the bullpen.

David Ortiz punctuated a six-run seventh with a two-run triple. Check and mate! Sure the game wasn't officially over, but the Ortiz triple was like taking the other guy's queen with your pawn. You don't recover from that.

The king has been toppled. The good knights had a great weekend. The pawns are excited. And the queen can cry if he wants to.

And in fact, the queen did cry a little. George Steinbrenner issued a statement today saying, "We didn't play well in Boston, but I'm not getting down on anyone, It's a long season and a long way to go. They haven't won anything yet."

I like his use of the word "yet," saying it hasn't happened, but that it will. And I disagree with him to this extent: the Red Sox have won something. They've won George's undying love and respect. He doesn't want to admit it, but he loves this Red Sox team. He just wishes his Yankees were this good. I would bet Steinbrenner is feeling some compunction right about now after issuing a statement through his publicist Howard Rubenstein. If he had been asked a question, sure, go ahead and answer it. But to volunteer your own sniveling seems either unnecessary or narcissistic.

This was a good day to be off. Coming off an emotionally draining series, the Red Sox are fortunate to have a moment to exhale before they begin a six-game road trip through Texas and Baltimore.

JULY 29

And to think, Red Sox GM Theo Epstein had some doubts about signing Bill Mueller. Sometime after he signed Mueller to a two-year, $4.5 million contract, Epstein popped a tape into his VCR to watch Mueller's scouting reel. Epstein said there wasn't one line drive on the tape. It was all a bunch of broken bats and bleeders. He wondered at that time what he had gotten himself into. But tonight's game reaffirmed that he made a pretty sound judgment call when it came to Mueller, both in character and ability.

First—the character. Mueller said, "I am very humbled. But I was just trying to do my job getting good at bats and driving in some runs. I don't worry about individual numbers. We're in a big race, and I try to focus on winning baseball games. I'm not a big stats guy or records guy. My foundation is to go out and help my club get the victory."

Sounds like a guy who might have just knocked in a winning run with a sacrifice fly or something. But Mueller had just become the first player in the history of baseball to hit grand slams from both sides of the plate in the same game.

"From what I've been hearing, it didn't turn out to be an ordinary night," Mueller said.

No, it was extraordinary. Three home runs, two of them grannies, one lefty, one righty, and nine RBI. "It's just a night I went out and tried to do what the guys in front of me did, have a good approach, battle, play for nine innings," added Mueller. "That's what I was trying to do. Just trying to do my job at the time. Have good at bats and drive some runs in. I was just fortunate that I got some balls up and they carried out."

He's never going to become an arrogant ballplayer if he keeps talking like this. Mueller is the 12th player to hit two grand slams in the same game. Nomar Garciaparra had been the most recent when he did it on May 10, 1999.

The Red Sox beat the Rangers tonight, 14-7. And the news just keeps getting better. Today, they acquired hard-throwing, right-handed reliever Scott Williamson from the Cincinnati Reds. The Yankees were actively involved in trying to get Williamson for themselves. One major-league executive said, "They were competing with the Red Sox all the way. They just lost out."

The Red Sox got him for minor-league left-handed pitcher Phil Dumatrait, a minor-league player to be named later, and cash considerations. The addition of Byung-Hyun Kim, Todd Jones, Scott Sauerbeck, and now Williamson—all acquired since May 29—allows the Red Sox to say good-bye to the likes of

Rudy Seanez, Ryan Rupe, Steve Woodard, and Brandon Lyon. The Red Sox bullpen was once the team's greatest weakness, but it has since become an overwhelming strength.

Williamson is a 27-year-old flamethrower with an average of 11.3 strikeouts per nine innings. He's a legitimate closer in his own right, having converted 21 saves this season. But it looks like he'll be used as more of a setup man for Kim—although there is always the option of returning Kim to the starting rotation and making Williamson the closer. Epstein and Grady Little called that a remote possibility at this time. We'll see.

Williamson was the National League Rookie of the Year in 1999. He backed that up with a solid sophomore season, striking out 136 batters in 112 innings. But he appeared in only two games in 2001 after undergoing "Tommy John" surgery. He came back strong last year and just kept getting stronger. After the All-Star break, he posted a 1.33 ERA. In his big-league career, he's made 217 appearances and has a marvelously low 2.93 ERA.

"He's a very hard thrower," Epstein said. "His stuff is among the top handful of stuff you'll see. He has a fastball that is 95 to 96 with explosive life, real nasty slider, devastating split-finger as well. It's really a potent combination coming out of the bullpen."

Right now, the Red Sox are "scary good." And how did the Yankees respond? By making themselves weaker, and taking care of what was eating Raul.

They dumped outfielder Raul Mondesi, who basically signed his release papers when he left Fenway Park before the game was over Sunday night. He was apparently in a snit over being pinch-hit for in the eighth inning.

"He didn't do the worst thing anybody has ever done, but I wasn't comfortable with it," Yankees manager Joe Torre said. "It's not acceptable, what he did."

Yankees GM Brian Cashman tells it like it is: "Sunday night, after he was pinch hit for, he decided that he was going to shut it down, shower up, and leave. Before that game was concluded, he had left the clubhouse and took off. That's what motivated me and Joe Torre to pursue a change of venue for Raul."

The Yankees traded Mondesi and about $2 million to the Arizona Diamondbacks for outfielder David Dellucci and two minor-leaguers. To their credit, the Yankees got rid of a bad apple, but they didn't make their team any stronger. And the Red Sox did.

JULY 30

With the trading deadline looming at 4:00 p.m. EST tomorrow, Yankees owner George Steinbrenner summoned his management team to Tampa, Florida. There he's expected to give his GM, Brian Cashman, a stern talking-to for somehow being outmaneuvered by Theo Epstein—not once, but twice. Getting George nervous and upset is extremely gratifying. Losing 9-2 to the Texas Rangers was not.

Ramiro Mendoza may have just pitched his way out of the starting rotation while simultaneously forcing the Red Sox hand. For the second time in a row, Mendoza failed to make it out of the fifth inning while giving up seven runs. He can't be trusted as a starter, and he no longer fits in the bullpen. The Red Sox have a tough decision to make where he's concerned.

Meanwhile, they made the tough decision regarding Chad Fox. They released him. The Red Sox certainly had high hopes for Fox at the start of this season. Grady Little even designated him as the de facto closer during the old "committee" days. But he was inconsistent before he was injured, and he's given up five runs in his last two outings. Scott Williamson will be with the team in two days, and in the meantime, the Sox have called Jason Shiell back up.

JULY 31

For we are always what our situations hand us...
It's either sadness or euphoria.

—Billy Joel, *Summer, Highland Falls*

Let's start with the euphoria. Red Sox Nation spent most of this day celebrating the second coming of Jeff Suppan. After making another deal with the Pittsburgh Pirates, GM Theo Epstein said emphatically, "We were going to get a starter today."

The one they got is one who began his career with the Red Sox way back in 1995 as a 20-year-old. Suppan is enjoying his best season in the big leagues—on pace to have his fifth straight 200-inning season, and currently 10-7 with a 3.57 ERA—but he's primarily been a mediocre journeyman. He's pitched for four teams in nine years, compiling a 59-71 career record with a 4.86 ERA. He pitched three years for the Red Sox before being left available in the expansion draft in 1998, when he was scooped up with the third pick by the Arizona Diamondbacks. On the upside, Suppan is a significant improvement over Ramiro Mendoza.

Today's trade also closes the book on the Brandon Lyon for Scott Sauerbeck deal. The Pirates were balking at the trade almost since the day they got Lyon, because they did an MRI on his right elbow and noticed some inflammation. Lyon admitted to being on anti-inflammatory medication, and when the Pirates determined they needed to put him on the disabled list, they began renegotiating with the Red Sox in search of a different player to complete the Sauerbeck deal. In today's trade, Lyon comes back to the Red Sox along with the minor-leaguers in the original deal. So that trade is effectively washed away. The end result is the Red Sox gave up Freddy Sanchez for Suppan and Sauerbeck. That is the kind of wheeling and dealing that can create a certain amount of euphoria.

The Red Sox end up with an incredibly strong bullpen and a legitimate third starter who can bump the ineffective Ramiro Mendoza out of the rotation. It looks like the Red Sox, absent a waiver wire pickup in August, will go the rest of the season with Pedro, Lowe, Suppan, Wakefield, and Burkett as their starters. And they'll have Mendoza ready for long relief, Embree and Sauerbeck as left-handers, Jones and Timlin as their primary middlemen, and Williamson setting up Kim. That's a 12-man pitching staff that doesn't have too many weaknesses. The Red Sox, who managed to contend despite a dozen late-inning collapses in the first half, have gotten significantly better over the past week.

The Yankees didn't fare quite as well, though they did help themselves where they needed it most. In two separate deals with the Cincinnati Reds, they gave $3 million in cash, along with their top prospect Brandon Clausen, for third baseman Aaron Boone and relief pitcher Gabe White. (I told you the "do-nothing kings" would end up with White.) Boone replaces Robin Ventura at the hot corner, while Ventura was jettisoned off to the Dodgers for outfielder Bubba Crosby and right-hander Scott Proctor. Ventura was only hitting .251, with nine homers and 42 RBI. Meanwhile, Boone made his first All-Star team this season, and is hitting .273 with 18 homers and 65 RBI. It's a definite upgrade at third, but the Yankees had to give up an awful lot to get the deals done.

Now for the sadness: Alex Rodriguez hit a walk-off grand slam off Todd Jones in the 11th inning. Pedro Martinez was once again victimized by poor run support, or you could say he was once again outpitched. He went six innings, giving up three runs. Texas starter Colby Lewis, making his second start since being recalled from the minors last Saturday, went six innings, giving up just two runs. Yep, Pedro Martinez was outpitched by Colby Lewis.

But once again, the only known strategy to beat Pedro was employed.

Rangers manager Buck Showalter said, "We were grinding it out. We got him up to 100 pitches by the sixth inning."

It's obvious that teams know that Pedro is all about pitch counts. The opposition is then in the enviable position of being able to make effective outs. If a batter gets Pedro to throw six or seven pitches before striking out, he'll be high-fived back in the dugout. The other team just has to think, "Stay close and get Pedro to throw at least 15 pitches an inning. He'll be out by the seventh, and then we can take our chances with whoever the next guy is."

It's working. Since coming off the disabled list on June 11, Martinez has three wins and seven no-decisions.

By the way, Trot Nixon hit his 20th home run, his 10th in July.

Overall, it was a good day. The work of Theo Epstein trumps the disappointing loss, probably because Red Sox fans are more accustomed to the latter than the former. But it's been a good, albeit short, run for young Theo Epstein.

A lot of ink and breath were wasted commenting on Epstein's age, 28, when he was hired to be the Red Sox 11th GM since 1933. His grandfather Phillip and granduncle Julius Epstein wrote the movie *Casablanca*, which included the line, "Here's looking at you, kid." And everybody's been looking incredulously at this kid ever since he became the youngest GM in history.

But the kid's got a resume. He graduated from Yale, went to work for the San Diego Padres, got himself a law degree, and has been groomed for great things. After working as an intern with Larry Lucchino in Baltimore, Epstein followed Lucchino to the San Diego Padres. He spent two years in their media relations department, and two more years as an assistant in baseball operations, all the while getting his law degree. He ultimately became the Padres' director of baseball operations.

Combine all that with the fact that he's been a Red Sox fan all his life, and I'd say he was ready for the position. I don't know how many other 29-year-olds (now) could handle prolonged negotiations with the Chunichi Dragons, or who could repeatedly outmaneuver the Yankees for midseason pitching help. But by all accounts, Epstein has done a superb job. The Red Sox are now positioned to make a serious run at making the playoffs, and once there, they have a team that will match up against any team they'll face. It's a team of destiny to be sure, but even destiny needs a human touch from time to time.

9

Dog Days

AUGUST 1

Nobody needs to panic just because the Red Sox have lost three in a row. Nobody needs to overreact just because the A's beat the Yankees last night to move to within half a game of the Red Sox in the wild-card race. Nobody needs to have an anxiety attack over the fact that Oakland won with a 10th-inning home run by last year's American League MVP, Miguel Tejada. Nobody needs to assume that just because the A's have been the best team in baseball in the second half of the season three years in a row that they're automatically going to do it again. And nobody needs to perseverate over the fact that the A's had a 20-game winning streak last August when Tejada batted .375 and drove in 25 runs, many of them with late-inning heroics like tonight's.

Nobody needs to do any of that stuff—because I've got it covered.

So far on this road trip, the Red Sox offense has been slowed down by the likes of Robert Ellis, Colby Lewis, and now Pat Hentgen. Their ERAs before pitching against the Red Sox were, respectively, 18.00, 8.33, and 4.92. No matter how much better the Red Sox appear to be "on paper," they have to start getting it done on the field—especially against these low-level pitchers on sub-.500 teams.

AUGUST 2

Derek Lowe put up another stinker on the road. I thought this problem had gone away when he won two of three road starts and posted a road ERA of 1.89. Then he beat the Yankees at their stadium in the Bronx. But his last two road starts have been awful—11.2 IP, 12 runs against Toronto and Baltimore.

Today, he didn't make it out of the sixth inning. After cruising along, allowing just one run in the first five innings, Lowe fell apart, and the Orioles wound up scoring seven times in the sixth. Sox lose, 11-2. Add the name of Rodrigo Lopez to the list of guys with ERA's over *six* who have been able to shut the Red Sox down this year!

Again, the Red Sox hitters were stymied. During the four-game losing streak, the Red Sox have been outscored 29-8. Nomar, Manny, Ortiz, and Millar are a combined 9-for-48.

Meanwhile, the Yankees pounded Oakland's Barry Zito for eight runs, taking the second game of their series, 11-7. I have no idea if that's good news or not. It really depends on whether you think the Red Sox have a better chance of catching the Yankees or fending off the A's.

AUGUST 3

Suddenly, whenever someone mentions the greatest Red Sox pitchers of all time, Tim Wakefield's name has to be included. Only nine pitchers have won 100 games for the Red Sox. Roger Clemens and Cy Young are tied with 192. Sixty-nine wins behind is Mel Parnell, followed by Luis Tiant, Joe Wood, Bob Stanley, Joe Dobson, and Lefty Grove. And now Tim Wakefield.

When the Red Sox needed it most, Wakefield came up with a solid performance—three runs in 5 2/3 innings. The Red Sox had to wait out two major thunderstorms, but finally earned themselves a 7-5 win. All of Boston's runs were scored by way of the home-run ball. And 14 of the last 15 runs the Red Sox have scored have come on long balls.

And again, the Yankees-A's series is confusing enough to make a Red Sox fan's head explode. The Yankees lost for the first time in 58 games this season when they were leading after eight innings. Yankees manager Joe Torre went to his most reliable weapon in the bullpen, Mariano Rivera, for a fourth straight day. It was the first time in his career that Rivera was used on four consecutive days. And he responded by blowing his fourth save opportunity in 25 chances. It shows that Torre has very little faith in the rest of his bullpen, and it elucidates a glaring Yankees weakness.

It was also another example of Torre making a very questionable move. Yankees starter Andy Pettitte was throwing a one-hit shutout through eight innings when he walked the leadoff hitter in the ninth. Torre gave him the hook and brought Rivera in. Rivera promptly gave up a single to Eric Chavez and a two-run double to Miguel Tejada. Oakland won, 2-1. Rivera blew two games in the series, and had three blown saves on the Yankees' nine-game road trip.

But—and it's a pretty big "but"—the A's look to be getting some of their magic back. Tejada, who beat the Yankees with a home run in the 10th inning two days earlier, was running up and down the dugout tonight telling everyone, "I'm gonna get him"—meaning Rivera.

"I just said, 'I'm going to do it,' because that's all you can do," Tejada said. "I told everybody in the dugout that we could win this thing. It's not going to get any better than today."

Boy, do I hope he's right! I'd hate for it to get any better for the A's. They're still just half a game back in the wild-card race, and the Red Sox trail the Yankees now by 3 1/2 games.

AUGUST 5

Trot Nixon is carrying this team. Granted this team is only 19-14 in its last 33 games, but during that stretch, Nixon has had 12 homers and 26 RBI and has raised his batting average from .297 to .322.

"This is the year Trot's established himself as one of the best right fielders in the game," said Kevin Millar. "He's been as consistent as can be."

Nixon's previous career high for batting was .280 in 2001 when he also established a career high in homers with 27. Teams that win the World Series always seem to have a few guys having "career years." For the Red Sox, it's Nixon, Millar, Mueller, Varitek, and Ortiz. Those guys, plus Manny Ramirez and Nomar Garciaparra, who have been maintaining their health and normal standard of excellence, have given the Red Sox the kind of offense that doesn't panic when it falls five runs behind—as it did tonight.

That's because Jeff Suppan was awful in his return to Fenway. In his first start for the Red Sox since September 17, 1997, Suppan gave up seven runs in five innings. Boston was in a 5-0 hole after three innings. But then they exploded.

"It is becoming a situation where it doesn't really surprise us that much anymore," Little said. "But those seven runs tonight came as quickly as any seven I have ever seen in my life."

The Red Sox got a pair of three-run homers from Nomar and Millar in a seven-run third inning. The Red Sox have now scored seven or more runs in an inning *nine* times, six runs twice, and five runs 10 times.

For Millar, it was his first home run *and* his first RBI since July 22. He's been frigid lately. After driving in 24 runs in June, he only knocked home seven in July, and his batting average, which was at .319 on July 1, is down to .286.

Nomar has reached safely in 50 of the 51 home games this year.

The Red Sox finished the third inning with a 7-5 lead, but Suppan gave that up. Then the Sox led 9-7, but Todd Jones gave that up. It came down to a battle of the bullpens, and the Red Sox won. After scoring in every inning from the second through the sixth, the Angels were held scoreless over the final three innings. The Angels bullpen—probably considered the best in the league—was outdone by the new guys in the Boston pen.

Tied 9-9 in the sixth, Nixon delivered what proved to be the decisive run with a base hit against Anaheim's Brandon Donnelly. Donnelly, the best reliever in baseball this year, saw his ERA rise to 0.82. He's now given up five earned runs in 54 2/3 innings this year.

Meanwhile, the Yankees and A's both won, so the races are unchanged. Oakland got its third great performance from rookie right-hander Rich Harden. He's made four starts, winning three of them, striking out 22 in 27 innings, and posting a 1.33 ERA. I will say this, however. His four starts have been against Kansas City, Anaheim, Cleveland, and Detroit who rank fifth, 10th, 13th, and 14th in the American League in runs scored. If Harden is for real, he gives the A's four excellent starters, which will be tough to beat. But I'd say the jury is still out on the young fellow.

Also today, the Red Sox put Jeremy Giambi back on the disabled list with shoulder tendinitis, and replaced him on the roster with David McCarty, a first baseman/outfielder who was put on waivers by the Oakland A's.

AUGUST 6

If "friendly Fenway" were any friendlier to the Red Sox, they'd have to get a room. After a rare complete-game victory from Pedro Martinez, the Red Sox are now 18-3 in their last 21 home games. But this night was all about Pedro—the suddenly and surprisingly *muy macho* Pedro. The biggest knock on Pedro (and believe me I've knocked to the point where I ought to just use the bell) is that he leaves too early—too often when the game is on the line.

Tonight, he wouldn't relinquish the ball. He did exactly what I've been wanting him to do. He pitched like an ace, a horse, a stud, and a leader. And I can't help but wonder why.

Let's start with this comparison. On June 21 against Philadelphia, Pedro left after the seventh inning with the Red Sox leading 2-1. He had thrown 92 pitches. Tonight, he had thrown 93 pitches through seven innings, and the Red Sox led Anaheim 3-1. And even though the bullpen is far more trustworthy now than it was in June, Pedro came out for the eighth inning. To me, it was absolutely the right move. We're talking about the staff ace who has had to endure 10 no-decisions throughout the course of the season. Let him get through the eighth inning, and then give the ball to your closer. It all makes sense.

But after Pedro struck out the side in the eighth inning, raising his pitch count to 108, he came back out for the ninth. Meanwhile, the Red Sox had added a run in the bottom of the eighth, so the score was now 4-1. With a three-run lead and a new and improved bullpen, Sox manager Grady Little did a one-eighty in what has been the institutionalized babying of Pedro Martinez. He didn't even have anyone warming up in the bullpen when he sent Pedro out to finish what he'd started.

Pedro was doing exactly what staff studs are supposed to do during a pennant race, and I wanted him out of there! I couldn't believe they were using him unnecessarily. Yes, he had 10 strikeouts through eight innings, but he'd also given up eight hits. Yes, he'd struck out the side in the eighth inning, but he gave up a run in the sixth and labored through the seventh. In fact, if it weren't for an incredible leaping catch up against the center field wall by Johnny Damon, Pedro might not have escaped the seventh. Adam Kennedy lined a shot deep and to Damon's right. In full stride, Damon leaped. Crashing his knees and shoulder into the wall, he snared the ball with the back of his glove just inches away from the Monster. The play ended with Damon sitting on the warning track and the crowd erupting in applause, not once, but twice, because the fans started up again when the catch was shown on the big screen.

The next batter singled, and one out later, David Eckstein scraped the left-field wall, narrowly missing a home run. Pedro got out of the jam, but it's safe to say Damon's catch saved at least one run, and probably more.

Still, Pedro was sharp, and I haven't seen him this into a game in a long time. When he got out of that seventh inning on a comebacker, he sprinted off the field with the hint of a smile on his face. And when he struck out Scott Spiezio to close out the eighth, he pumped his fist and looked skyward. He wanted this game—badly. And it appeared his night was over, especially when the Red Sox made it a three-run lead.

But there was Pedro to start the ninth. The first batter bounced back to the mound. One out. Then Adam Kennedy reached on an error to David McCarty—ironically, a defensive replacement at first. Kennedy moved to second on the ever-popular "defensive indifference," and he scored on a base hit by Robb Quinlan. It was 4-2 with a runner on first.

Two pitches later, all I could think of was David "Bleeping" Eckstein. The little shortstop for the Angels who had had just three home runs this year connected and sent the ball high and deep to left-center field. Immediately, there were memories of Bucky "Bleeping" Dent in the 1978 playoff game between the Sox and Yankees at Fenway Park. Dent's home run propelled the Yankees into the postseason and on to their 22nd World Series title. Eckstein's shot obviously couldn't have had the exact same impact, but it looked like it was destined to tie the game. The ball sailed through the night sky. Hearts sank in chests across New England. Nobody breathed for the few seconds it took the ball to reach the left-field wall. Bang!

The ball slammed into the wall, missing the Monster seats by Eckstein's height—5 1/2 feet. Quinlan moved to third, and Eckstein stopped at second.

"I got it as much as I could get it," Eckstein said, "but in this ballpark I don't hit the ball that high, that far."

Still, the tying run had moved into scoring position with two outs. Pitching coach Dave Wallace walked to the mound to talk with Pedro, but there was no way he was going to take him out. The die had already been cast. The look Pedro shot Wallace confirmed it.

"You could see it in his eyes—he wanted to go out and get it for himself," said Little. "The kid's in good condition right now, as good as he's been in a long time—we're proud of what he's doing."

With the next pitch, Pedro hit Darren Erstad in the foot. Bases loaded. All season long, the consensus opinion has been that Pedro either hasn't gotten enough run support, or the bullpen has blown too many leads. The run support issue is more myth than fact. In Pedro's seven wins, the Red Sox have scored 6, 5, 12, 9, 6, 5, and 9. That's an average of 7.42 runs per game. To be fair, though, it's in his 10 no-decisions that he's gotten minimal offensive support. In five of those games, the Red Sox have scored three or fewer runs. Plus, he was the pitcher of record when the Red Sox were shut out by Minnesota in May. The simple fact is that since losing that game to the Twins on May 9, Pedro is 5-0 in 12 starts. And in the seven games in which he didn't get a decision, he allowed a total of only 10 earned runs.

So, this was it. Time for Pedro to bear the burden on his own shoulders. He was given four runs to work with, and there would be no bullpen help. Tim Salmon, clubber of 283 career home runs, is the batter. Strike one. Strike two. Both swinging. Salmon has also struck out 1,252 times. The crowd was on its feet waiting for the final punch-out. They would have to wait. Ball one. Ball two. The fifth pitch was fouled off. All five pitches were fastballs. Pedro was going out with his best stuff. Strriiike *three*! Salmon looked at a 96-mile-an-hour fastball that appeared to be high and quite possibly outside. No matter. Game over.

All's well that ends well, they say, but I have to wonder if keeping Pedro in to throw 128 pitches for the second time in 12 days was the right thing. I've never liked the fact that he's so coddled or that his health is such a concern, but I assumed it was necessary. Was it? Could he have finished more games earlier this year when the bullpen was so horrible? Or have things changed now that the pennant race is so hot? Is Pedro angry about the criticism he hears? Did he demand or merely agree to pitch the ninth inning? Is he prepared to pitch like this again and again down the stretch? Is he strong enough to? How much will the 20 extra pitches he threw in the ninth inning affect him in his next start—which just happens to be against Oakland? He'll be matched with Tim Hudson in that one. Hudson is having a similar year to Pedro's in that he's 10-4 with 11 no-decisions, despite a 2.64 ERA. That could be a game in which Pedro needs to go the distance. Will he be able to? Will the Red Sox let him?

It was a great game from Pedro, but it's left me wondering about the consequences.

Also tonight, Nomar Garciaparra hit his 20th home run—his 14th at

Fenway Park.

The Yankees completed a post-trading-deadline trade with the Seattle Mariners. The Yankees got rid of Armando Benitez only three weeks after they got him. In return, they got Jeff Nelson *back*. Nelson pitched for the Yankees from 1996 to 2000, winning four World Series rings. His return further exposes the myth of the Yankees' never making mistakes. Since letting Nelson walk as a free agent, the Yankees have tried to replace him with guys like Jay Witasick, Dan Micelli, and Mark Wohlers—all ineffective. The Yankees even gave the oft-injured Steve Karsay $22.5 million, and he's been injured all year. Believe me, the Yankees make plenty of mistakes, and letting Nelson go was one of them. Now, they've got him back.

New York has lost five games since July 26, each loss going to a member of the bullpen. And after going 145-1 over the past two years when leading after eight innings—a simply amazing record—the Yankees have lost two such games in the past four days.

The Red Sox now trail in the East by 2 1/2 games and continue to lead the A's by half a game in the wild-card race.

AUGUST 7

When David Ortiz homered off Ramon Ortiz (no relation) to lead off the second inning, it was his 11th straight extra base hit. Therefore, when he homered again to lead off the third inning, it gave him 12 straight extra base hits. And it would be 13 except that his last single was the game-winning hit off the wall against the Yankees on July 26. That would have been a double if the game hadn't ended as he touched first base. Both his home runs tonight were solo shots. It was the fourth time this year Ortiz has homered twice in the same game.

Not bad for a guy who was unceremoniously released by the Minnesota Twins after banging out 20 home runs in 125 games last year at the age of 26. That's when most guys are considered to be entering their prime, and it might very well be true for Ortiz. Minnesota hasn't made a lot of mistakes recently, but how could they let this guy go and get nothing in return? He's not only a capable and clutch hitter, he's a great clubhouse guy.

Ortiz was signed as a non-drafted free agent by the Seattle Mariners in 1992. Four years later, he was the proverbial "player to be named later" who sent Dave Hollins to Seattle and Ortiz to Minnesota. After relative success with the Twins, he was dumped and scooped up by the Red Sox in January. That's worked out pretty well so far.

By the way, Nomar Garciaparra's second-inning blast was a two-run homer, his 21st of the season, and his sixth in his last 10 games. Ho-hum! The Red Sox had another six-run inning in the second, and rolled to a 9-3 victory, completing a three-game sweep of the Angels.

Boston, which picked up a game on the Yankees yesterday, picked up a game on the A's today. Oakland, a bad road team, lost 3-2 to the Tigers. Barry Zito, last year's Cy Young Award winner, fell to 8-10.

AUGUST 8

The Red Sox had a bad day. Grady Little had a bad day. Derek Lowe's day wasn't any better. Consequently, I am depressed. When opportunity knocked today, the Red Sox acted like it was a cop coming to a crack house and hid under the bed. Instead of taking advantage of a double header with the Orioles, the Red Sox lost both games. I blame Grady. And I'm concerned about D-Lowe.

Game One: After the Red Sox erased a 3-1 deficit with home runs from Trot Nixon and Doug Mirabelli in the sixth—taking a 4-3 lead— Grady had a chance to turn to his bullpen for the final nine outs. Granted, this was a day-night double header, and Casey Fossum was pitching in the nightcap. So, if Grady called to the pen in the seventh inning of Game One, he might reasonably expect that he'd need a good seven innings out of his bullpen today (assuming only five innings from Fossum). So be it. Lowe had given up six hits and three runs through the first six innings. He wasn't having a dominating day. He was having a day very much like his previous seven starts, which is to say, mediocre to bad. He gave six innings. Now get him out of there.

Nope. Grady sent him back out to give up a single, a walk, and a game-tying double. Then he brought in Scott Williamson and allowed him to give up three consecutive singles before deftly determining that Williamson didn't have his best stuff on this afternoon. By the time the inning was over, the Orioles had scored seven times, and they went on to win, 10-4. Over and out. Missed opportunity.

Game Two: After the Orioles scored four unearned runs off Fossum in the second inning (an error by Bill Mueller opened the floodgates), Fossum settled in, and the Red Sox tried to battle back. In the eighth inning, the Red Sox scored one run on a bases-loaded walk to Jason Varitek. That made the score 4-2, Baltimore. Orioles pitcher Kerry Ligtenberg had just given up a single and the bases-loaded walk. He hadn't retired a batter, and the bases were still loaded with one out. Gabe Kapler was due up, but Little decided to send Trot Nixon up as a pinch hitter. Little had to know that the Orioles would bring in left-hander Buddy Groom to face Nixon, whose ineptness against left-handers is legendary. Instead of letting Kapler bat against a struggling Ligtenberg, Little *chose* the matchup of Nixon versus Groom.

Nixon struck out swinging. Oooh, somebody shock me! But here's the even more curious part of Little's decision. The next batter, Todd Walker, was also left-handed. So, he actually chose to bat back-to-back lefties against a left-handed specialist. Solid thinking, no? *No!* Walker grounded out, and the Sox lost, 4-2. Bad day for Grady.

About Lowe's night? He's now given up 36 earned runs in his last 49 innings, covering eight starts. His ERA is a shade over *five*, and he's supposed to be the team's number two starter. Not even Fossum was this bad when he was struggling at the start of the season. And based on tonight's performance, you'd have to say that Fossum is currently pitching better than Lowe. So, would it be lunacy to pluck Lowe from the starting rotation for a while and give Fossum another chance? Sure, we're talking about demoting a guy who won 21 games last year and is 11-6 this year, but he's been nothing short of awful for the better part of two months. That's a long time to stink. Lowe's the equivalent of egg salad that's been left out in the sun for too long.

I doubt the Red Sox would even consider dumping him in the pen for a while, probably because of some misplaced loyalty. Grady is definitely the kind of manager who likes to show his players that he has faith in them. Sometimes it works. Sometimes it's blind faith. And it may be time for Little to open his eyes about D-Lowe.

The Yankees won and the A's lost, so the Red Sox are four down and one up in the playoff races.

AUGUST 9

Some home-run history was made at the old ballpark tonight. Manny Ramirez hit his 100th home run in a Red Sox uniform, reaching that milestone faster than any other Red Sox player. He hadn't homered in 43 at bats, but he was still able to reach the century mark in two fewer at bats than Jimmie Foxx, 1,388 to 1,390. Trot Nixon hit his 100th home run two days ago. It took him 2,252 at bats.

Kevin Millar's two-run homer in the eighth inning—that proved to be the difference in the game—was the 10,000th home run hit at Fenway Park. Fenway, built in 1912, joins Yankee Stadium, Wrigley Field, and the old Tiger Stadium as the only ballparks where 10,000 or more home runs have been hit.

In the ninth inning, Brook Fordyce hit the 10,001st home run at Fenway, a solo shot to cut into a 6-3 Red Sox lead. But Byung-Hyun Kim picked up his ninth save in 10 chances, and the Red Sox won, 6-4.

The Yankees lost, 2-1, as Seattle's Gil Meche outpitched Andy Pettitte and kept Pettitte from winning his ninth straight decision. The A's, however, won.

AUGUST 10

Everybody's a loser today. The Red Sox, Yankees, and A's all lost. And it's been a series of lost opportunities for all three. So far this month, the Red Sox are 5-5, while both the A's and Yankees are just 5-4. At some point, one of these teams is going to get hot. Let's hope it's the Red Sox, and let's hope it's soon.

Today's game had all the earmarks of a Red Sox comeback victory. Down 5-1, the Red Sox got a run in the sixth and another in the seventh on a solo blast from Jason Varitek. The bullpen was shutting the Orioles down, and it looked like the Red Sox would chip away and pull this one out. The Sox loaded the bases in the ninth inning for Nomar Garciaparra. He put together an eight-pitch at bat, but finally struck out on a breaking ball in the dirt. The Red Sox lost, 5-3.

The Yankees suffered from a case of Red Sox-itis when their bullpen imploded in relief of Roger Clemens. Sometime after Clemens signed a jersey for Seattle center fielder Mike Cameron that read, "To Mike: All the best! Rocket," Clemens went out and gave up three runs in six innings. He left with a 4-3 lead, but the Yankees lost 8-6. Four relievers followed Clemens, each giving up at least one run. Prodigal son Jeff Nelson, pitching against the team that had just traded him the previous week, gave up two runs in 2/3 of an inning.

The A's lost their second of three games in Chicago, and now they'll fly out to Oakland to meet the Red Sox for four games. Pedro Martinez will start the opener against Tim Hudson. In many respects, these two guys are having very similar years. They're second and third in ERA, respectively (2.32 and 2.64). Hudson is 10-4, Pedro 8-2. Hudson has 11 no-decisions, Pedro 10. And they both have suffered to some extent from a lack of run support. But the difference between the two is that the A's are 20-5 in games started by Hudson, while the Red Sox are only 11-9 in games started by Pedro.

The Yankees are clearly the bigger rival, but these four games against the A's will be HUUUUGE!

10

Wild Card, Wild Ride

AUGUST 11

Another big series began with Pedro Martinez on the mound, and when it was over, his manager said, "That was about as good a performance as you'll see out there by any pitcher against anybody. He was pinpoint perfect with his control and his stuff is good too, so that's a tough combination."

Unfortunately, Grady Little was talking about A's starter, Tim Hudson, who threw a two-hit shutout against the league's most potent offense. The Sox were impotent when it was most important. Both hits were infield singles (by Manny and Nomar). Only five balls made it to the outfield, and Hudson needed only 93 pitches to finish the job.

Pedro, on the other hand, threw 101 pitches—*in five innings*! Five innings? That's all we get from the ace? Mister "pick up my contract extension or I'll walk" only has five innings in him at the start of a Fortnight of Fortitude (14 games against Oakland and Seattle)? Martinez's unbeaten streak ended at 12 starts.

I'm not going to pile on Pedro again. He's pitched extremely, if not exceptionally, well this year. This was his first loss since May 9, a string of 13 starts during which he won five. But he's no Tim Hudson. Hudson said he can't remember when he's pitched a better game. And Johnny Damon said Hudson "pitched well enough to pitch a perfect game almost." Somehow Hudson came up with his best game when it really mattered, which is what I've been waiting for Pedro to do all season long. I'm still waiting.

Nomar Garciaparra was the American League Pepsi Player of the Week. He earned the honor by hitting .438 with four homers and eight RBI. He's a legitimate MVP candidate this year, especially if the Red Sox make it to the playoffs, as they are destined to do. Nomar leads the Red Sox in runs (92), hits (157), and RBI (82).

As Hall of Famer Ted Williams once said of Nomar, "The kid plays like he's been here before."

And Nomar certainly looked like someone who'd been around for a few years when he burst onto the scene in 1997. As the sixth unanimous selection for the American League Rookie of the Year Award, Nomar set major-league records for runs batted in by a leadoff hitter with 98, and home runs by a rookie shortstop with 30.

He also set a rookie record with a 30-game hitting streak, shattering the mark of 26 games established by Guy Curtright of the 1943 Chicago White Sox. He led the American League in hits with 209, and he broke the Red Sox rookie record for total bases (365) set by Williams himself.

There's little argument that Nomar began his career with the *two* best offensive seasons ever by a shortstop. Alex Rodriguez had already played in parts of two seasons when he broke out with 36 homers in 1996. So, his first two seasons wouldn't be compared to Nomar's. But even if they were, Nomar put up better numbers. In his first two seasons, A-Rod hit .329, with 59 homers and 207 RBI. Nomar hit .313, with 65 homers, and 220 RBI. So, Nomar had more homers, hits (404-391), and RBI than A-Rod. Then he followed those first two seasons with back-to-back batting titles. He hit .357 in 1999, and his .372 batting average in 2000 was the highest batting average by a right-handed hitter since Joe DiMaggio hit .381 in 1939.

Knowing what they had in Nomar, the Red Sox locked him up with a five-year, $23.5 million contract extension before the start of the 1998 season. That means his contract expires at the end of next season. The same is true for Pedro, Derek Lowe, and Jason Varitek. So the Red Sox have to decide whom to trade and whom to keep. I hope they keep Nomar. He's still in the early stages of a Hall of Fame career, and it would be nice to see him one day reside in the pantheon of Boston sports legends, along with the likes of Bobby Orr and Larry Bird. Of course, to reach that rarified air, he'll have to bring a world championship to a starving city.

Nomar has tired of the Boston media, but he's appreciative of the fans, and he's consistently been a clutch performer. In his first postseason in

1998, Nomar hit three homers and drove in 11 runs in four games against the Indians. Only Bobby Richardson of the Yankees had more RBI in a series, with 12 against the Giants in 1960. And that was a seven-game series.

When that series was over, Nomar stood on the first base dugout at Fenway Park and applauded the fans. They, in turn, applauded him. Standing on the field, disappointed that the season had ended, I couldn't help but get caught up in the pure emotion of the love fest unfolding before me.

In 13 postseason games, Nomar has had seven home runs with 20 RBI and is batting .383. Those are the kind of numbers legends are made of, and a big performance in the World Series this year would most assuredly put Nomar at or near the top of the list of Boston sports legends.

The only knock against Nomar in the past has been his health. His nickname in the minor leagues was "Glass," because he was so breakable. And he's been on the disabled list four times in seven big-league seasons. He missed all but 17 games in 2000 after undergoing wrist surgery. But you can't help getting hit by a pitch on the wrist, which is what caused all his problems. I don't think Nomar is injury prone at all. After heading to Georgia Tech as a 135-pound freshman, Nomar has worked out obsessively and bulked up to 190 pounds. He played in 153 games last year, and he's played in all but three games this year, and those were simply to give him some rest.

As for the name Nomar, it's his dad's name spelled backwards. His father, Ramon, wanted to come up with a name for his son that incorporated all the letters of his own name. Nomar already had a cousin named Roman, so that choice was eliminated from consideration.

Nomar says, "When you think of the other possibilities, like Manro or Omnar, it's a good thing he stopped."

Moran? Maron? Ramno?

AUGUST 12

I thought John Burkett had this whole "first inning thing" figured out. He had that little stretch of seven starts where he gave up 15 first-inning runs, and then he went five starts without giving up a run in the first inning. Tonight? "And after one full inning of play, it's the Oakland A's *five*, and the Red Sox nothing."

Facing last year's Cy Young Award winner, Barry Zito—who, despite his 8-10 record, ranks fifth in the American League in ERA—Burkett gave up a pair of two-run homers to Terrance Long and Eric Chavez. Game over, right? Not exactly.

Burkett retired 15 of the next 17 Oakland batters, and the bullpen got the final nine outs. Oakland finished with just the five runs.

The Red Sox got a three-run double by Jason Varitek in the fifth inning to make it a 5-3 game. It stayed that way until the eighth inning when the Red Sox put runners on second and third with nobody out.

A's manager Ken Macha called on his closer, Keith Foulke. Foulke has thrown two innings nine times this year, and he was being asked to do it again. As he walked to the hill, Macha said, "Just try to minimize the damage."

Everyone knew the Red Sox were going to score. It was just a matter of how many times. Well, how about zero?

Foulke struck out Bill Mueller, Nomar Garciaparra lined hard to third, and Manny Ramirez grounded back to the pitcher. The Red Sox three best hitters had failed. And the Red Sox lost, 5-3.

If the season were to end today, not only would it have been an unexpectedly short season, but the Red Sox would not be in the playoffs. They're now a game behind Oakland, and four behind the Yankees, who beat Kansas City.

All seems dire right now, but really, who cares if the Red Sox go 2-5 on this road trip? If they come home and go 5-2, there's no blood, no foul. I'll take 7-7 during this tough stretch and take my chances from there.

Of course, I don't like what I heard from Derek Lowe today. A guy sporting a 5.07 ERA should probably keep the sarcasm to a minimum.

"Apparently I'm the only way we're going to make the playoffs, even though Pedro and I won 41 games last year and we didn't make it," said Lowe. "It's up to me, apparently. The whole season depends on my 10 starts the rest of the year. That's what I understand."

If he meant it, I'd love it. If he truly believed the fate of this team rests on his ability to make 10 quality starts and had expressed his determination to do that, then I'd applaud his willingness to bear the burden of being one of the team's most important players. But he's disinclined to accept that responsibility. He's reluctant to speak with confidence. And I believe that's because he has doubts, and he wants us all to know that even if he pitches poorly and the Red Sox don't make the playoffs that it's not his fault. Well, excuse me Derek—but *yes, it is*!

It wouldn't be 100 percent his fault, but clearly he would be one of a very few players on the team who didn't live up to expectations. So, when the "blame pie" is passed around, Derek Lowe would get the biggest slice. He's 2-3 with a 6.43 ERA in his last seven starts. He should either vow to turn things around or just shut his pie hole.

AUGUST 13

Baseball's a funny game. Not "ha-ha" funny but funny in the way it produces ulcers, fingernails bitten down to the nub, and dangerously high blood pressure. But every so often, it's worth it. Like tonight.

If there can be a must-win situation in August, this was it for the Red Sox. They needed to stop the bleeding. And they needed to do it against the best home team in the American League, and against a pitcher with a 10-1 home record. And they needed it to come from Derek Lowe.

"We needed somebody to cowboy up tonight, and Lowe did," Millar said. "He went out and pitched a great game and battled his butt off."

Even pitching without a butt, Lowe seemed to get better as the game went on. But the A's got a single and a pair of walks in the fifth inning to load the bases with two outs. Lowe's been taking a walk on the wild side all year. He's walked 52 batters in 150 innings, compared to only 48 walks all of last season in 219 innings.

Now, with the bases loaded, Lowe fell behind 3-0 on Erubiel Durazo. Another walk would have cut the Red Sox lead to 4-3. It would have ended Lowe's night, and potentially opened the floodgates. Strike one. Strike two. Strike three. Quite possibly, the three biggest pitches of the year.

Lowe bounded off the mound, pumping his fist, and releasing his own "barbaric *yawp* over the roofs of the world" (with apologies to Walt Whitman). This was a fantastic moment. It might very well have been the biggest out of the year for the Red Sox.

"That's the biggest out I've got in a long time," Lowe said. "The emotion is directed to nobody, but to get that out after throwing three balls is something I'm proud of."

As it turned out, that was Lowe's last pitch of the evening. Four different relievers pitched an inning apiece. Meanwhile, Manny Ramirez hit a two-run homer in the seventh inning, chasing A's ace Mark Mulder, who fell to 15-9. Kevin Millar followed Ramirez by greeting Chad Harville with a solo home run. It was Millar's 20th home run of the year, matching his career high and giving the Red Sox five players with at least 20 homers. It was also the 10th time this year that the Sox have hit back-to-back home runs.

That put the game out of reach, and the Red Sox held on to win, 7-3. Millar called it the biggest win of the year—*so far*—and Grady Little concurred.

"It'll rank up there as one of our bigger wins this season, and doing it against a pitcher the quality of Mulder is even bigger," Little said. "It was big for us to come out of here with a win tonight after the first two games. Doing it against a pitcher the quality of Mulder is saying a lot. These guys battled out there, and we were able to come out of it in good shape."

Later, Millar dismissed the preposterous notion that because the Red Sox have historically experienced late-season swoons, this year's edition will do the same.

"We have about 15 new guys on this team. I don't know any better. Billy Mueller doesn't know any better. Todd Walker doesn't know any better. David Ortiz doesn't know any better. We're here to win. We don't care what happened to the old Sox. We're here to win."

Yes, the sky fell yesterday, but all the cumulous clouds are right back where they belong as the Red Sox pull back even in the wild-card race and return to three games behind the Yankees.

New York's Jeff Weaver got pummeled again. The Yankees lost to the Royals, 11-0, dropping two of the three games at Kansas City. The Yanks have gone 0-4-1 in their last five series against teams with winning records. They are so eminently "catchable" this year. Yet the Red Sox can't seem to catch them.

AUGUST 14

Anyone who jumped off the bandwagon is welcome to climb back on as long as they understand they'll have to buckle up. It's going to be a bumpy ride. From this point forward, no one is allowed to get off the ride until it comes to a complete stop. Please make sure the safety bar is secure, and keep your hands and feet inside the ride at all times.

Tonight's wild ride didn't really begin until the eighth inning. Tim Wakefield had pitched a beautiful game, allowing just two runs, but Oakland's Ted Lilly did him one better. The Red Sox trailed 2-1 in the eighth when Alan Embree came on. He quickly put runners on second and third with nobody out. Just as A's manager Ken Macha had said to closer Keith Foulke two nights earlier, Sox fans were just hoping Embree could "keep the damage to a minimum." But certainly, another run or two for the A's would have put this game out of reach.

Embree bore down and got the next batter to ground out to third. The runners held their positions. Then Embree struck out Eric Byrnes on three pitches. It was now quite possible that Embree could get out of the inning without giving up a run. Embree had abandoned any attempt to mix in a breaking ball. He was firing nothing but 96-mile-an-hour gas. Billy McMillon flailed away at strike three. If there's such a thing as momentum from one inning to the next, Embree had just swung it hard to the Red Sox side.

Meanwhile, Foulke had entered the game to record the final two outs of the eighth inning, and he was back out there to close it out in the ninth. Taking a page out of Embree's book, Foulke got two strikes on Manny Ramirez leading off the ninth, then threw nothing but fastballs. The problem for him is that his fastball only clocks at around 92, and he was throwing them to Manny Ramirez, not Billy "the Kid" McMillon. Ramirez spoiled four pitches until he got one he liked. On the 10th pitch of the at bat, Ramirez smoked one over the wall in left. His 28th home run of the year had just tied the game! Ramirez looks to be about ready to start carrying this team. He is officially in a groove.

Foulke, angered by the blown save, blew away the next three Sox hitters, striking out the side. But the damage had already been done.

Solid move from Grady Little to bring his closer, Byung-Hyun Kim, into a tie ball game. He brought in his best pitcher at the most crucial time. The Sox had to get out of the ninth, and Kim had to be prepared to go at least two innings.

But Kim came about two feet from blowing it. A's third baseman Eric Chavez took him deep to right. Gabe Kapler was on a dead run as he and the ball arrived at the wall at the same time. Kapler reached up and plucked the ball out of the air. It didn't look as if it would have cleared the wall, but it certainly would have gone for extra bases. Big play! Potentially, a game-saving play!

Kapler led off the next inning with an infield single. Damian Jackson bunted him over to second. Johnny Damon laced a single so hard to right that Kapler couldn't even try to score, but Bill Mueller brought him home with a sacrifice fly. The Red Sox led 3-2. An error by Chavez made it a two-run lead, and Kim closed it out. The Red Sox came and left the Bay Area with a one-game lead over the A's. That makes it a very successful "business" trip, so far.

The Red Sox now travel to Seattle, still trailing the Yankees by three games in the East.

AUGUST 15

When people talk about the worst trades in Red Sox history, there are a couple that fly to the top of the list. Trading reliever Sparky Lyle to the Yankees in 1972 for first baseman Danny Cater is often cited. While Lyle made the greater impact on his new team, the Yankees didn't make the postseason in Lyle's first four seasons with them. That deal had a shelf life of six years before the Yankees won the World Series in 1977, and it certainly couldn't be singled out as the reason the Yankees won—or that the Red Sox didn't.

But generally, the deal considered to be the worst is the one that sent Jeff Bagwell to the Houston Astros in 1990 for Larry Andersen. What's conveniently overlooked by critics when they routinely roast former GM Lou Gorman for trading a future Hall of Famer for an aging reliever is that Bagwell was in Double-A at the time. He hadn't displayed any signs of power. He was 180 pounds and playing third base. That meant he was behind Wade Boggs and Scott Cooper in the organization's depth chart. Even if the Sox had projected him as a first baseman, they already had Mo Vaughn in Triple-A. I defend the deal, because without Andersen, the Red Sox might not have made it to the postseason that year.

Furthermore, anybody who tells you they knew Bagwell would hit over 400 home runs and win an MVP Award is full of donkey dust. Bagwell played in 205 minor-league games—none above the Double-A level—and he hit a grand total of six home runs. Then he hit 15 in his Rookie of the Year season of 1991. Who knew?

Yes, he was the Eastern League MVP in 1990 and led the league with 220 total bases, but he wasn't a power hitter. He was a good hitter who could have been projected as a potential batting champion someday, but he didn't even hit .300 his first three years in the big leagues. Then in year four, he hit .368 with 47 homers, on his way to winning the National League MVP Award. Again, who can project that kind of sudden offensive explosion?

Meanwhile, it's true that Andersen only threw 22 innings for the Red Sox before leaving as a free agent following the 1990 season, but he only gave up three runs in those 22 innings for a 1.23 ERA. It can't be denied that Andersen was instrumental in getting the Red Sox to the postseason. Unfortunately, they were then swept by the Oakland A's. But trading a player who wasn't likely to help you for several years for a player who helped you get to the postseason can't be *the worst trade in Red Sox history*.

However, Andersen was a significant loss when he left as a free agent, because he was baseball's funnyman for a while. Andersen is credited with saying things like: "How does a fly, flying right-side up, land on the ceiling upside down?"

Or: "If Americans throw rice at weddings, do Chinese throw hot dogs?"

And: "Why does sour cream have an expiration date?"

Andersen also had this to say after his friend Jon Kruk had surgery to remove a cancerous testicle: "I sent Kruk one of those fruit and nut baskets at the hospital. I don't know if he likes fruit, but I know he'll appreciate the nuts."

But a trade that seldom gets mentioned among the Red Sox worst blunders may have actually been worse than either the Lyle or Bagwell deals. What about the deal that sent Jamie Moyer to the Mariners in 1996 for utility outfielder Darren Bragg? Since the trade, Moyer has won 113 games. Care to guess who has more wins since the start of the 1999 season, Pedro Martinez or Jamie Moyer? It's Moyer, 75-74. And think about this: since the trade, Pedro Martinez, Moyer, and Roger Clemens are first, third, and fourth in winning percentage in the major leagues—and the Red Sox could have had them all at the same time.

Today, the Red Sox battled Moyer, a 15-game winner this year, and knocked him out in the sixth inning. At the time, the score was tied 4-4. That's because newcomer Jeff Suppan was awful for a third straight game.

In his three starts with the Red Sox, Suppan has given up 20 hits, and amazingly, 16 of them have been for extra bases—10 doubles, one triple, and five home runs. Opponents are slugging .662 against him. It's a deadline deal that is killing the Red Sox so far.

But despite Suppan's continued struggles, the Red Sox were still in this game, until the fates conspired to work against them. In the seventh inning, Todd Walker pulled Nomar Garciaparra off the bag with a bad throw on a potential double-play ball. Then, a grounder to Nomar took a wicked hop and hit him in the clavicle. That loaded the bases for Ichiro Suzuki. He popped a foul ball off third that Bill Mueller slid for unnecessarily and dropped. Four outs were possible. Instead, after Mueller's drop, Ichiro turned on one and hit a grand slam. The game was effectively over. Sox lose, 10-5.

The A's also lost, but the Yankees won when they scored four runs in the ninth. Three of those runs scored on an Aaron Boone home run that was initially called foul, but the umpires huddled together and decided the Yankees should win the game. Actually, the ball was 10 feet fair, but the idea of a conspiracy theory makes me feel better sometimes.

AUGUST 16

If Pedro Martinez doesn't own the Mariners, he at least leases them with an option to buy. He brought a 0.94 ERA against the Mariners into the game, then went out and dominated for seven innings, allowing one run and striking out seven. The Red Sox won, 5-1, as Pedro improved to 11-0 lifetime against the Mariners, 6-0 at Safeco with a 0.68 ERA. Surprisingly, the 11 wins are the most Pedro has against any team. It's surprising, because you'd think his most wins would come against a bad team in the same division—like Baltimore or Tampa Bay. And since Pedro's been in the American League, the Mariners have won 455 games in five full seasons, the third most in the American League behind only the Yankees (497) and the A's (457). The Red Sox, by the way, have only won 446 games since the start of the 1998 season.

Still, Martinez does his best work against the division with the best teams. He's now 32-4 lifetime against the AL West, including a 17-3 mark on the road.

As for the Yankees, Joe Torre said it best, "We lucked out. I don't even want to see a replay. I'd just as soon go home, go to sleep, and wake up tomorrow."

That's right. One day after the Yankees win with a "fair is foul, foul is fair" home run, they win when Baltimore's Jack Cust was tripped by the devil—*twice*. There can be no other explanation for it. In the top of the 12th inning, Jason Giambi hit his league-leading 35th home run to give the Yankees a 5-4 lead, but the Orioles had a chance to tie it in the bottom half.

Cust was on first base when Larry Bigbie rapped a two-out double into the right-center-field gap. As Cust rounded third base, he tripped and fell. When he got back up, he found himself in a rundown between third and home. Suddenly, he realized there was nobody covering home plate. He was running ahead of Yankees third baseman Aaron Boone with nothing to stop him from scoring the tying run. That is, until he tripped and fell— *again*. Boone tagged him for the final out of the game.

Said Boone, "It was bizarre, certainly."

No it wasn't. It was the Yankee way!

Said Orioles manager, Mike Hargrove, "Those things happen."
Yeah? When?

Meanwhile, right after the Orioles took three of four from the Red Sox, they went out and lost seven straight, including four in a row at home to the Yankees.

AUGUST 17

The Mariners scare me. Their bullpen is an absolute mortal lock. When their closer Kazuhiro Sasaki went on the disabled list with broken ribs, they turned to another "secret Asian man," Shigetoshi Hasagawa, from Kobe, Japan. He threw a scoreless inning today, running his streak of consecutive scoreless innings to 27 2/3. He hasn't given up a run since June 1 against the Twins. He's pitched in 49 games this year for the Mariners and has given up *four* runs, for an ERA of 0.62. Meanwhile, he's converted 13 straight save opportunities. Now the Mariners have Sasaki back, and whether he gets the closer's job back remains to be seen, but he's still a dominant pitcher. And the Mariners have another "untouchable." Rafael Soriano has only given up three runs in 28 1/3 innings since July 1. Overall, his ERA is 1.24.

Basically, if the Mariners have the lead after six innings, they're going to win. Today, they led 3-1 in the eighth inning. The Red Sox put runners on second and third with two outs against revitalized starter Freddy Garcia. So, M's manager Bob Melvin called for the first of two sure things. Soriano came in and got Nomar Garciaparra flailing away at a breaking ball in the dirt to end the threat. Then Hasagawa closed it out. The Red Sox lost, 3-1.

They went 3-4 on the trip and are just 8-9 this month. The Yankees got a three-hit shutout from Mike Mussina, and the A's thumped Toronto. So, the Red Sox fell five games behind New York and will return home to face Oakland—with whom the Red Sox are tied for first place in the wild-card race.

If the Red Sox come home and take care of business against the A's and M's, then I'd say it was a good trip. These 14 games against the best of the West really should be judged in their entirety.

AUGUST 18

The Red Sox were off, but the Yankees won their fifth straight. Say good-bye to the East Division title. Let's go, wild card!

Once again the Red Sox enter a pivotal series in a dead heat with their primary opponent. As they wave good-bye to the race against the Yankees, the Red Sox welcome the A's to Fenway Park for a three-game set beginning tomorrow night. As it was when the Red Sox and Yankees faced each other on May 18 with identical records, the Red Sox and A's will square off with identical 71-53 records.

The Red Sox will be leaning on the advantage, either real or imagined, of playing at home. Not only do the Sox play much better at home (their winning percentage is .661 at home, .484 on the road), but the A's are also a much better home team. And it shows in the pitching stats of two of the three pitchers the Red Sox will face in this series.

When pitching in the expansive Network Associates Coliseum with so much friendly foul ground, Tim Hudson has a 2.16 ERA. On the road, his ERA is 3.02. He's an excellent pitcher wherever he is, but he's at his very best at home. It's even more disparate for Mark Mulder, who starts tomorrow night. Mulder's home ERA this year is 2.18, while on the road it's 4.23. That's a difference of more than two runs. Combine that with a Red Sox home batting average of .292, and there's at least reason to hope the Sox can get to these guys.

August 19

Abigail Van Buren said, "If you want a place in the sun, you've got to put up with a few blisters." That happy place in the sun is the playoffs, and tonight the Red Sox had to put up with a painful and woefully ill-timed blister.

Derek Lowe was pitching his finest game of the year, but after six innings of two-hit shutout baseball, he walked off the mound staring at his right thumb. When he didn't come out for the seventh after throwing only 78 pitches and holding on to a 2-0 lead, there could be little doubt about what had happened.

"Derek has that pop on him every once in a while," Grady Little said. "Until he just can't go, we are not totally aware of it each inning and each minute. But we do know he has it, he's had it, and when they come out and said he couldn't go, he can't go, and that is it."

Lowe had a blister on his thumb. It was now up to the much improved bullpen to get the final nine outs. But you know how you sometimes hear, "The names have been changed to protect the innocent"? Well, the names in the Red Sox bullpen have been changed to protect some leads, but it's not working. In fact, none of the three acquisitions made before the trading deadline has worked out so far. Jeff Suppan has been awful, and both Scott Sauerbeck and Scott Williamson have been inconsistent. Neither Scott throws enough strikes when coming into a tight ball game. Sauerbeck issued a pair of walks in the seventh inning, giving him six walks in six innings with the Red Sox. Then Williamson came in and, after paying way too much attention to Eric Chavez at second base (as if he was going to steal third base with his team two runs down. C'mon!), threw a splitter that didn't dip to Ramon Hernandez. Two seconds later the ball was in the Green Monster seats—a three-run homer that put the Sox in a 3-2 hole they would never climb out of. A great game by Derek Lowe was wasted as the bullpen picked up its 23rd loss of the season, two more than last year's pen absorbed.

Sauerbeck now has a 4.50 ERA, and Williamson, who also walked a batter and now has three in 8.1 innings, has a 5.40 ERA. Sure sounds a lot like Bobby Howry and Chad Fox to me. A nice promotional idea might be to pass out Scott Tissues when those guys come in the game, and fans can cry and blow their noses.

Of course, the fact that the Red Sox only scored two runs can't be overlooked. They got those runs early off Mark Mulder but also hit into three double plays in the first four innings—two of them by Manny Ramirez. So they certainly squandered some decent opportunities. Also, Mulder had to leave after the third inning because of a recurring hip problem. He said he hasn't been able to cover first base or back up home plate in some of his more recent starts, and tonight the problem was exacerbated. But with the 15-game winner suddenly out, the Red Sox could still only manage *one* hit in six innings against four Oakland relievers.

That's not what you call making a stand on your homestand.

AUGUST 20

I still believe in this team. This is the team that bounced back from a dozen or more so-called devastating defeats in the first half of the season. This is the team that lost the first two games in Oakland last week, then roared back to split the series. And that team still exists. However, tonight's game has a lot of Red Sox fans scurrying off the bandwagon like rats from a sinking ship, or moviegoers watching *Gigli*.

The Red Sox left 17 men on base—in a nine-inning game. They left the bases loaded twice. They left 13 men in scoring position. They were zero for their last 10 with men in scoring position. Their top five guys in the order came up with 19 men on base (not at all at once), and despite combining for eight hits, they only managed to drive in one run. If it's not yet clear that the Red Sox lost this game, let me drive the point home by pointing out that Byung-Hyun Kim gave up four runs on four hits while recording just one out.

The Sox lost, 8-6. I would have cried, but I didn't want my makeup to run (I was getting ready for my TV anchor gig).

These are two games the Red Sox really should have had. The strength of the A's is their starting pitching, but due to injury last night and total ineffectiveness tonight, the A's starters have only gone a total of 6 1/3 innings in this series. The Red Sox jumped on Ted Lilly for four runs in the second inning, and when he put two runners on with one out in the fourth, he was yanked. The Red Sox scored once that inning to take a 6-3 lead, but it was already evident that too many squandered chances could be their undoing. And it was. It was also the Kim implosion *and* the Sox inability to get to the A's bullpen.

In the battle of the bullpens over the first two games, it's been all A's. Oakland's pen has thrown 11 2/3 innings of shutout baseball, while the Red Sox pen has given up seven runs in six innings. This is the way it was early in the year when the "committee" faltered. This isn't supposed to be happening anymore.

But Kim, facing a lineup with a .251 batting average—second lowest in the American League—gave up three straight hits to start the eighth inning. Bringing Kim in to start the eighth was a curious move by Grady Little. Feeling this is a game he had to have, Little asked the best guy in his pen to get the final six outs instead of three—just as Ken Macha did eight days ago with Keith Foulke in Oakland. It worked for Macha, but not for Little. Macha made his move out of necessity, because the Red Sox had put two runners in scoring position with nobody out. Tonight, Little panicked. He showed too little faith in his setup guys and too much faith in Kim. Kim is good, but he's not automatic, and bringing in the closer is a major commitment. If a setup guy puts a couple of runners on, you pull him, but if the closer does that, you're stuck with him. When Kim gave up three line-drive hits to start the inning, it was pretty obvious he didn't have it tonight. But Little stayed with him until the damage had already been done.

Not that I'm blaming Little. If he had brought Kim in to start the ninth with a two-run lead, Kim would have been just as likely to blow it. If he didn't have his best stuff in the eighth, he wouldn't have had it in the ninth either. No, this loss rests squarely on Kim and the 17 men left on base.

Combined with the Yankees' seventh straight win, the Red Sox are now 7 1/2 games behind New York and two games behind Oakland in their respective races. The Yankees have put the Red Sox in their rearview mirror, and objects in that mirror are even further away than they appear. Even I've given up on that race. But a few too many Sox fans have given up entirely. That I can't understand. Some fans seem to think there's a prize that goes to the first person to kick dirt on the Red Sox grave. This team may be on life support, but they're not dead yet. And nobody needs to sign a "do not resuscitate" order.

Here we go, folks. As Johnny Damon said, "It's crunch time now, and we have to start winning a lot of games."

All right. Now do it!

AUGUST 21

I walked into the Red Sox clubhouse before today's game and noted that Todd Walker was back in the lineup in the two spot. Scanning a bit further down, I read that David Ortiz was in as the designated hitter. "Good," I thought. "Grady Little is trying to let Ortiz hit his way out of his 4-for-39 slump." Then, scanning still further down the oversized lineup card posted outside the manager's office, I saw the name "Casey Fossum" in the pitcher's slot.

What? Pedro Martinez was scheduled to start what had become arguably the biggest game of the year. What gives?

I walked into Little's office as he was in the middle of the explanation. Pedro had called in sick. No lie. The ace was taking a sick day. Little said Pedro had called the team trainer at 7:30 a.m. and had been at the doctor's office from 8:30 a.m. until 2:00 p.m.. There had been no official diagnosis yet, but Little said it was something "flu- like." Nobody knew if Pedro would be at the ballpark that night or not, but Little said he would recommend against it, if it turned out that Pedro had something contagious.

We learned about an hour later that Pedro has "severe pharyngitis" and an abnormally high fever, which turned out to be 101—and that he had intestinal discomfort.

Textbooks tell us that pharyngitis is the inflammation of the pharynx, often causing a sore throat. In severe cases it can cause strep throat. Treatments include warm saltwater gargles, pain relievers, and fluids.

Antibiotics are needed if strep throat is diagnosed. Most cases of pharyngitis go away on their own, without complications.

You know, it really doesn't sound all that bad. But since there's no possibility that Pedro begged out of a crucial game, I'll assume that he was in no condition to pitch. Still, this is yet another Pedro story that involves disappointment and frustration. It's also the second time this year that Pedro has stunned Red Sox Nation with his disappearance from a big game. The first time was on May 20 when he was supposed to start against the Yankees. Instead, we learned a few hours before game time that he had a problem with his latissimus dorsi. Bruce Chen started that game, and despite his rather weak effort, the Red Sox won by scoring 10 runs.

They would need another assist from their offense tonight, and they got it in a big way. Perhaps the biggest hit of the game came in the first inning. After the Red Sox had left 17 men on base the night before, David Ortiz stepped up to the plate with runners on first and second and two out. If he didn't come through, it might just be the beginning of another frustrating night. Instead, Ortiz blasted a three-run homer, and the Sox were on their way to beating the A's 14-5.

It turned out to be a good night after all. The Red Sox won without Pedro, and he'll be well rested and ready when he returns. Plus, the wild-card lead is down to one game instead of what could have been three.

AUGUST 22

The Red Sox have more lives than Shirley MacLaine's cat. They were left for dead after losing the first two games in Oakland last week, but they bounced back to win the next two. They were having dirt kicked on their graves this week after losing two more to the A's, but they've been born again. A nail-biting victory over the Mariners tonight, combined with an A's loss to the Jays, puts the Red Sox back into a tie for the wild-card lead. The next 34 games are going to make for quite a race.

Jeff Suppan could have a huge bearing on the pennant race, so his start tonight carried considerable significance. "Soup" has been "meat" in his first three starts for the Red Sox, lugging around an ERA just under nine. That dropped precipitously tonight when he pitched into the seventh inning, allowing just two runs. The Red Sox got a solo home run from Manny Ramirez in the seventh, and one from Jason Varitek in the eighth to take a 6-3 lead. In the ninth, Grady Little went to his closer, Byung-Hyun Kim. That's when the real excitement began.

Pitching with a three-run lead, Kim walked the leadoff hitter. (I hate that!) His next pitch to Ben Davis was rocketed high and deep to right field. Trot Nixon was still going full speed as he got to the wall. Reaching over the wall, Nixon caught the ball while leaning into the Red Sox bullpen. He had taken a two-run homer away! It was a remarkable catch, made even more so because of the circumstance. Ichiro Suzuki grounded into a force play, then took second base on "defensive indifference." (It's strange they won't give a guy credit for a stolen base just because the other team was apathetic about it. I'd like the catcher to tell the umpire, "I wasn't indifferent about it. I was merely ambivalent.") Ichiro scored on a base hit, which put the potential tying run at the plate in the person of Edgar Martinez.

Martinez is the best designated hitter to ever play the game. He's a lifetime .316 hitter approaching his 300th home run and his 1,200th RBI. He is not the guy you want to see in this situation. Martinez fouled off the first two pitches; neither swing was particularly good. He seemed to be having trouble with Kim's underhand delivery, but he fouled off three more pitches and worked the count full. Finally, Kim got him to pop meekly foul of first base. The Red Sox had the game, 6-4.

Ramirez's home run was his second in two nights and his fifth in his last nine games, but he still doesn't seem to be locked in as the RBI machine he's been at times in the past. In fact, he's gotten gradually worse over the summer. Manny hit .351 with nine homers and 27 RBI in June, then dropped to .337, eight and 18 in July. And so far this month, he's at .282 with six homers and 11 RBI.

Also today, the Red Sox sent Casey Fossum back down to the minor leagues. After Fossum stepped in to fill Pedro Martinez's rather sizable shoes, the Red Sox realized they couldn't use him again for at least four days. Not wanting to enter the series with Seattle without a long man in their pen, the Sox called up right-hander Bronson Arroyo, who had thrown a perfect game for the Pawtucket Red Sox two weeks ago.

As for Pedro, he's feeling better and is likely to pitch against the Blue Jays on Tuesday. I asked Little if Pedro's return hinged at all on the team's desire to have him pitch against the Yankees in both of the upcoming series, or if they were just going to get Pedro back in the rotation as soon as possible. His response was noncommittal, but I got the sense they're going to wait until Tuesday, so Pedro can pitch the final game of the Yankees series on Sunday, and then the series opener in New York on Friday. I like the thinking, because it means the team still hasn't given up on catching the Yankees.

Meanwhile, the Yankees gave up on left-hander Sterling Hitchcock and traded him to the St. Louis Cardinals for two minor-league pitchers. The Yankees, of course, will continue to pay most of what's left on Hitchcock's $6 million salary.

Today's other big news: A's lefty Mark Mulder could be out for the entire season. He's got a stress fracture in his hip. His last outing of the year may have been his poor start at Fenway Park three days ago. This is a huge blow to Oakland, because they haven't gotten much out of their fourth and fifth starters, and now they've lost a third of their "big three." Y'know, I almost feel bad for Oakland. Almost—but not quite.

AUGUST 23

This one was extra special—extra long—but well worth the wait. Byung-Hyun Kim, pitching for the fourth straight day, had his third shaky outing of the week. Still, it's beginning to feel like the magic is back!

Once the Red Sox fell behind 5-4 in the fourth inning, and it stayed that way through the sixth, I figured they were cooked. That Seattle bullpen just scares me. But David Ortiz came through in the clutch once again. Batting against Seattle's Rafael Soriano, who hadn't given up a run in his last 11 1/3 innings and who's sporting a 1.18 ERA, Ortiz lifted his second home run of the homestand into the bleachers. That tied the game at 5-5.

After Kevin Millar singled and Bill Mueller walked, Seattle manager Bob Melvin brought in Armando Benitez to pitch to Jason Varitek. Thank you, Mr. Melvin. In his short time in the American League this year, Benitez has given up 15 hits and 11 walks in 17 innings. I liked Varitek's chances, and he came through with a base hit to bring home the go-ahead run.

Todd Jones and Alan Embree took the Red Sox through the eighth inning. In the ninth, Little left Embree in to face Ichiro Suzuki (lefty versus lefty), and Embree got him to ground out to short. That's when Little made the move to bring in Kim. It's a textbook move, but 35,000 hearts started beating a little faster in the Fenway stands.

Kim quickly got the second out, but then Ben Davis lifted a high fly ball to right field. Trot Nixon went back to get it, but the afternoon sun was especially difficult, and he appeared to lose the ball for a moment. He flailed toward it with his glove, but it landed over his head, one-hopping the wall. Davis stopped at second base. He was the potential tying run.

Kim put Mike Cameron in an 0-2 hole, then threw him one right down the heart of the plate. Cameron didn't miss it. He stroked it about two feet to the left of Kim's ear—a sharp base hit to center, and the game was tied.

The Red Sox got runners to second and third with two outs in the home half of the ninth, but Gabe Kapler hit a high-hopper to short. He was out at first by less than half a step, and we headed for extra innings.

This is when Little made a strong, authoritative move. He took Kim out in the 10th. In most cases, Little would stick with Kim because he has the ability to go a few innings, but Little may have determined his best chance to win this game was to get Kim out of there. Mike Timlin retired the middle of the M's lineup in order in the tenth.

Nomar Garciaparra led off for the Sox and finished his day 0-for-6. Damian Jackson followed with a single, and M's left-hander Arthur Rhodes was called upon to get David Ortiz out—which he did.

With two outs, Kevin Millar jumped on the first pitch he saw and sent it to the 379-foot mark on the left-center-field wall. Mike Cameron leaped. The ball hit his glove, but bounced out.

"I thought I had it, and when I hit the Monster it probably just popped out," Cameron said.

Actually, it fell out before he hit the wall—not that it matters. Damian Jackson scored from first base, and the Red Sox won, 7-6.

Oakland won. New York lost. The wild card is tied. The Sox are five back in the East.

AUGUST 24

Again, Pedro? I'm just asking. Again? In the middle of an important series with the Seattle Mariners, just days after he was unable to pitch against the A's, this is the day he chooses to tell a local beat reporter that after he gets his $17.5 million next year, he's outta here! So, instead of focusing on the Mariners, the Yankees, or the wild card, we're focusing on Pedro—a positively negative story about Pedro—*again!*

Apparently, after spending the better part of six hours at the doctor's office on Thursday, Pedro Martinez went home to curl up inside his own misery—*and listen to sports talk radio.* That's the only place he could have heard any criticism regarding his inability to pitch against Oakland. The local newspapers and television outlets simply reported the facts spoon-fed to them by the Red Sox—that Pedro's a warrior, so for him to be unable to pitch, he must be extremely sick.

However, after the news broke, fans were rather bitter and upset, and they and a couple of talk show hosts aired their views on WEEI. There were some who outwardly questioned whether Pedro was faking an illness, or who said that he should have pitched no matter how sick he was. That anger subsided after the first hour or so, once more details were available about Pedro's illness, and the fury was replaced by frustration and disappointment. Still, Pedro had heard enough, or the lackeys who report to Pedro had heard enough. Stung by New England negativity yet again, Pedro no longer wants to stick around where he feels underappreciated. He has been one giant energy drain on an otherwise exhilarating season. When he pitches, he pitches extremely well. When he's not pitching, he's bitching. And unfortunately, he's done a lot more of the latter this year.

Anyway, after two days of rest, and two more days of light workouts, Pedro will take the ball in the series finale against Seattle tomorrow.

"We just want to get him on the mound as soon as possible," Sox manager Grady Little said. "We have to win games. We feel like we're in better shape when he's on the mound to do that. He wants to get back out there."

Regarding tonight's game, Derek Lowe showed continuing evidence that he might be back to his form of a year ago. Another 7 1/3 strong innings from him tonight in a 6-1 win over Seattle. Lowe has now given up a total of three runs in his last three starts.

David Ortiz hit another three-run homer in a five-run fourth inning, and the Red Sox have magnetically pulled the Mariners back to the pack in the wild-card race. Seattle has lost five in a row, and now leads both the Red Sox and the A's by only one game.

AUGUST 25

Well, when the series began, I dared to dream. The Mariners, leaders of the West, also had a four-game lead on the Red Sox, with the teams scheduled to play four games at Fenway Park. What if the Red Sox swept them? I only said it aloud in trusted company, because it had an air of ridiculousness. Seattle is too good. They're "Yankees good." Winning three of four would be a real accomplishment. A split would be satisfactory. Worse might be more likely. Still, I dreamed about the possibility. And then it happened.

It was almost a lock when Pedro returned to health and it was announced that he'd pitch today. Of course, I didn't expect the residual hangover from his illness to affect him as much as it did. Pedro's fastball was in the upper 80s, but nowhere near his more customary 92 to 95 miles per hour. He fooled the Mariners with his off-speed stuff, especially his change-up, and kept them off balance enough to be extremely effective, even if he wasn't dominant. Pedro went six innings, allowing just one run and striking out four.

"He's not even close to being 100 percent. He's sick for real and he still comes out and gives us his best," David Ortiz said. "I hope the people here in Boston appreciate what he's done for the ball club. We get to be around one of the greatest in the game."

Some spin-doctoring there, as there has been most of the week. Several players and management types have made the rounds, telling every microphone they could find that Pedro's heart is the biggest in the game, etc. His heart may be big, but it's his arm that continues to get the job done. Pedro improved to 12-0 against Seattle, and his ERA actually rose to 1.00 against them.

The Red Sox won, 8-1, improving to a season-high 21 games over .500. With the win, the Sox, M's, and A's all have identical 76-55 records. Thirty-one games to go! The marathon that is the baseball season has officially become a sprint. The Red Sox survived the tough 14-game stretch with the best of the West by going 8-6.

By the way, David Ortiz homered for the fourth time in five games, giving him 20 home runs for the year. He's the sixth Red Sox player with at least 20 homers, which is a club record. The major-league record is seven, held by the 1996 Orioles and the 2000 Blue Jays. Bill Mueller has 16 home runs.

AUGUST 26

These are the games when Sox manager Grady Little loses some of my support. The Red Sox five-game winning streak was snapped when they lost to the Toronto Blue Jays, 12-9. I'm not saying this Red Sox pitching staff is going to remind anyone of the 1970's Baltimore Orioles, or that the bullpen doesn't still have a few problems, but I *am* claiming that this Red Sox pitching staff is too good to be giving up 12 runs. Somewhere in the course of that game, the manager has to make a few moves—and much quicker moves—to prevent the other team from running it up like that.

Instead, Little kept Tim Wakefield in the game long enough to give up seven runs, as the Red Sox fell behind 7-1. Then, after the Red Sox came back to tie it with the help of a five-run fourth inning, Little went to the "not-so-great Scott" tandem of Sauerbeck and Williamson. With the game tied at 7 in the eighth, the two combined to give up five runs. After another gutsy comeback, the Red Sox lost for the 19th time when they've scored five runs.

"It was a tough way to lose after we battled back the way we did," said Sox manager Grady Little. "It was admirable the way we kept coming back and were able to tie the game. It was a shame it got away from us there in the top of the eighth inning."

It's time to turn that record over. How many times have we heard that song this year? It's true enough, and it says a lot about the team's character. But what it really says is that our offense is killer, and our bullpen is killing us, because the only time you can battle back is when you're in a deep hole.

Kevin Millar hit his second career inside-the-park home run. Oddly enough, his first big-league homer was an inside-the-parker when Sammy Sosa lost the ball in the Wrigley Field ivy in 1999.

Meanwhile, the Yankees, Seattle, and Oakland all won. This was a bad day.

AUGUST 27

Let's just say this was not the kind of game you'd expect the Red Sox to win. First of all, John Burkett was on the hill making his fourth start of the year against Toronto. In his first three games against the Jays, he was 0-2 with a 14.73 ERA. Also, Burkett was pitching on three days' rest—something he hadn't done in five years—and the last time he went on three days' rest, he gave up four runs on 18 pitches and was pulled from the game.

Combine all that with the fact that the Red Sox were facing Cy Young candidate Roy Halladay, who was looking for his 18th win. In baseball, though, and especially with this year's Red Sox, you should expect the unexpected. The Red Sox hit three home runs off Halladay, and Burkett went six innings, allowing just three runs. The Red Sox won, 6-3.

The first big blow came with the Sox trailing 3-0 in the fifth. Jason Varitek came through with a three-run blast to tie the game. Then in the seventh, Todd Walker took an 0-2 pitch off his shoe tops and dropped it into the right-field bullpen. It was a two-run shot that gave the Sox a 5-3 lead. David Ortiz added a solo blast in the eighth, and the bullpen closed it out.

Walker's home run was his 10th, giving the Sox nine players with 10 or more homers, a new club record. The home run by Ortiz was his fifth home run in his last six games, giving him a career high 21. When you consider that Ortiz had only two home runs and 19 RBI at the end of May when Shea Hillenbrand was traded, it's clear that Ortiz is the reason why Hillenbrand hasn't been missed at all.

Since the trade, Ortiz has had a chance to play regularly, and he's responded. In the last 2 1/2 months, he's ripped 19 homers and driven in 56 runs. His overall slugging percentage is .572. Hillenbrand has hit 11 homers and driven in 40 runs for the Diamondbacks. That's better than I thought he'd do, but not as well as Ortiz has done.

The Yankees lost again tonight, so the AL East lead is cut to four games. Keep in mind, it was 7 1/2 games just seven days ago, and the Red Sox will host the Yankees for three games beginning the day after tomorrow.

Meanwhile, Oakland took over the lead in the West. So, the Red Sox are now tied for the wild-card lead with Seattle. Both teams are a game behind the A's.

AUGUST 28

On a day the Red Sox were off and the Yankees won, I had some time to reconsider all the grousing I've done about Pedro this year. I'm still frustrated by what he does off the field, but there's no doubt he continues to get it done *on* the field. In 23 starts, he's allowed 38 earned runs. Take away his abysmal start against Baltimore in April, and it's 22 starts, 28 runs. That's truly remarkable. He's currently leading the American League in ERA and winning percentage, and is second in batting average against opposing hitters. And through his injury and illness, he's also second in strikeouts, five behind Roger Clemens.

Sometime earlier, I attempted to make the case that Clemens just might be the best pitcher of all time. For that analysis, I considered only 300-game winners. But if you open up the debate to include *all* pitchers, Pedro Martinez—at this point in his career—might be the best ever.

Selecting from the top of the non-300-game winners, let's consider Sandy Koufax, Bob Gibson, Whitey Ford, and Greg Maddux.

Let's start with the truth about Koufax. From 1955 to 1960, the Dodgers southpaw was 36-40 with an ERA of 4.09. It wasn't until well into his career that he became the game's premier pitcher. From 1961 to 1966,

Koufax won 129 games, lost 47, and had an ERA of 2.19. That's an amazing six-year run! But it was only six years. His career numbers don't measure up quite as well.

Gibson's best years were from 1963 to 1970, when he went 156-81 with a 2.62 ERA. The league ERA during those years was about 3.70. So, he was a run per game better than everybody else's average. Gibson was also a 20-game winner five times.

From 1953 to 1964, the Yankees were "Ford driven." Whitey Ford won 207 games in those 12 years, and his ERA was 2.33. He finished with a career ERA of 2.75 and 236 wins.

Still, Maddux may be the best of the lot, and since he's pitching within roughly the same time frame as Pedro, it's easier to compare them. Maddux is a model of consistency and excellence. With 13 wins already this year, he's almost certain to have his 16th straight season with 15 or more wins, breaking the record he shares with Cy Young. His best stretch was from 1992 to 1998, during which time he went 127-53 with a 2.15 ERA. The 1994 and 1995 seasons were particularly outstanding. He went a combined 35-8 with a 1.59 ERA. That's just sick!

Maddux has had 10 seasons with an ERA of 3.00 or better, while the league ERA has been 4.12. He's been the league leader in ERA four times and in the top three nine times. The only knock on Maddux is his 11-13 postseason record.

Now, let's look at Pedro. His lifetime ERA is 2.60, the lowest among these greats. In 10 full seasons, Pedro has won 152 games. That's fewer than Maddux's 165, but it would have been about even if not for Pedro's injury-plagued 2001 season, when he won only seven games in 18 starts. Still, health matters, so the edge goes to Maddux.

Remember Koufax's awesome six-year run? Well, from 1997 to 2002, Pedro went 104-32 with a 2.19 ERA. That's 25 wins and 15 losses fewer than Koufax, with an identical ERA. Attribute the 40 additional decisions by Koufax to the four-man rotations of the 1960s, and you could call that a wash. But consider the offensive production in today's game, and Pedro's ERA is actually much more impressive. In fact, the league ERA during that stretch was 2.5 runs higher than Pedro's 2.19.

Furthermore, the Web site baseball-reference.com includes a statistical category that ranks pitchers of all generations in what is called "adjusted ERA." Pedro is ranked number one. Maddux is tied for third. Ford is 25th, Koufax 30th, and Gibson 39th.

I believe the best way to gauge a pitcher's performance is by ERA and wins. Pedro has the best ERA, and his winning percentage of .707 is third on the all-time list behind Al Spalding and Spud Chandler. Who? That's what I said. Ford is fourth in winning percentage at .690. By comparison, Koufax won just over 65 percent of his decisions.

Pedro is also second on the all-time list in strikeouts per nine innings. Randy Johnson is first at 11.2, and Pedro is next at 10.6. Koufax, the only other guy up for discussion who recorded more than a strikeout per inning, is fifth at 9.27.

And in 2000, during a time of tremendous offensive production, Martinez established a single-season record for the lowest combined number of hits and walks per nine innings. The record he beat had stood for 118 years.

So, it looks to me like the numbers suggest that Pedro's current run is the best stretch of pitching the game has ever seen. He's tops in ERA, tops in winning percentage, and his strikeout totals indicate a kind of dominance and "unhittability" the others never had. However, Pedro will have to maintain his current level for several more years to have a career that measures up to Ford's or Maddux's. Ford won 236 games with a .690 winning percentage and a 2.75 ERA. Pedro needs to win 74 more games to equal Ford's total, and he doesn't have much margin for error regarding his winning percentage or ERA.

Maddux's lifetime ERA is 2.83, and he's won 64 percent of his decisions, but he's 14 wins shy of 300. When he gets there, and he will, his numbers will be superior to Clemens's. At that time, Maddux could be considered the greatest of all time.

But the one thing you can't take away from Pedro is: he's included in this discussion. And that makes him pretty special.

"Boom-a-rang" Lou Merloni has returned. The Red Sox sent a minor-league pitcher to the San Diego Padres for Merloni, who was waived in March after five years with the Red Sox. Merloni can play a little bit—in 65 games this year with the Padres, he hit .272, one point higher than his career average. The fact that he can do a respectable job at three infield positions could make him a valuable asset down the stretch.

The three-game series with the Yankees at Fenway starts tomorrow!

AUGUST 29

As I sat at the ballpark some 4 1/2 hours before game time, there was a calm broken only by the humming of three lawnmowers working simultaneously. The field crew, working under a cloudless sky, was cutting those "shadow-light" stripes across the infield and outfield—the ones that look so nice on a ball field but would probably make your own lawn look ridiculous.

I noted that it takes four guys to hold the hose to water down the infield. It made me wonder if any of those guys uses his job as a pick-up line: "Hi there. I'm hose guy number three over at Fenway Park! Impressed?"

This could have been any day at the ballpark, but it wasn't. And as I was thinking this, a teenage boy sat down next to me and confirmed it.

"You can always tell when the Yankees are in town," he said.

"Why's that?" I replied.

"Can't you feel it?"

Yes, I could. And it was nice to know I wasn't alone. There were five guys holding the hose now. And a batboy, no more than 12 years old, was standing in the deep part of center field, trying to hit balls over the Green Monster with a blue aluminum bat. Got one!

At least two hours had passed by the time I heard that Manny Ramirez, as Pedro Martinez had done eight days earlier, had called in sick. Manny had some of the same symptoms Pedro had, and he would not be in tonight's lineup against the Yankees. Manny's played in 131 of the Red Sox 133 games this year, so he's entitled to a day off. I just wish it wasn't tonight. Pharyngitis is no friend of mine.

But who needs Manny? For the ninth straight game, the Red Sox banged out at least 10 hits. They jumped on Jose Contreras for seven runs in three innings. (Contreras is one example of losing out to the Yankees that doesn't hurt so bad). Then they got three more off Jeff Weaver and rolled to a 10-5 victory.

It was a game that showed some of the character and resiliency of the Red Sox this year. After the Yankees scored two in the first, the Red Sox answered back with three in their half of the inning. Then, after the Yankees took the lead with three in the fourth, the Red Sox came right back with four in the bottom of the frame. The Yankees still hold a 3 1/2 game lead over the Red Sox, and you wouldn't expect the New Yorkers to fold, but it's worth noting that they've been outscored 39-16 in their last four games. The Yankees are a team with holes. But I must repeat, it's a shame the Red Sox haven't been able to exploit those holes enough to catch them this year—at least not yet.

The hitting star in this one was Bill Mueller, who's become a kind of "Yankee Kueller." With three more hits today, including a home run and four RBI, Mueller's batting .380 with four homers and nine RBI in 14 games against the Yankees this year. Also, since Seattle's Ichiro Suzuki is in a 7-for-40 slump, dropping his batting average to .324, Mueller leads the American League with a .330 average. Maybe Dusty Baker was right. There could be a batting title in this kid's future.

Nomar Garciaparra and David Ortiz also homered for the Sox. Ortiz has now homered in each of his last five starts.

Derek Lowe was less than spectacular in this one, but he stuck around long enough to pick up his 14th win. Fourteen wins and a 4.76 ERA tell you all you need to know about this Red Sox offense.

Seattle and Oakland both won. The A's are putting together another spectacular August. They've won seven in a row, 11 of their last 13, and have a major-league best record this month of 18-9.

Tomorrow, it's Pedro against Andy Pettitte. Definitely good times!

AUGUST 30

I crapped the bed.

—Red Sox pitcher Alan Embree

That's what Embree accurately stated following today's game, but those words could just as easily have been spoken in Spanish by Pedro Martinez, or in Korean by Byung-Hyun Kim. It's a pretty big bed each of those pitchers made, and the Red Sox had to lie in it.

Let's start with what Grady Little said before the game when asked about Pedro's overall health following his bout with pharyngitis.

Question: "Is he at full strength?"

Answer: "Yes, we feel like he is. He's ready to go today."

Then in the postgame, Little said, "He wasn't 100 percent out there. He's still a little bit affected by the sickness he had last week, and it caught up with him pretty good there about the fourth inning. We were hoping that it would all be behind him, but it wasn't totally."

No, I guess it wasn't. Pedro only lasted four innings and left with the Red Sox trailing 5-4. He gave up nine hits, including four in a row to start the fourth. He gave up two more hits against the Hall of Fame bound, Enrique Wilson, whose batting averages the past three years have been .211,

.181, and .237—but he's hitting .444 (8-for-18) against Pedro. How do you figure that?

So far this year, the Red Sox and Yankees have played each other in five series. Pedro was injured for the first two, and the Red Sox lost all three of the games he did start against New York. Since coming to the Red Sox, Pedro is a mere 8-8 with seven no-decisions against the Yankees. New York has won seven of the last 10 games, and 12 of the last 16 games that Pedro has started against them. He needs to do better.

So does this bullpen. With the help of Nomar Garciaparra's league-leading 13th triple, another home run by David Ortiz, and a solid relief effort from Bronson Arroyo, the Red Sox were still in this game—trailing 5-4 in the eighth. But when Arroyo gave up a one-out double to Aaron Boone, Little called for the recently reliable Alan Embree. And we know what he did to the bed.

Embree allowed the inherited runner to score, then two more of his own. By the time he escaped the eighth, the Sox were down by four. It was especially unfortunate, because the Red Sox rallied for three runs in their half of the eighth. David McCarty delivered a key two-run double off Mariano Rivera. The Yankees' lead was back down to one, and Rivera had thrown 27 pitches. This one wasn't over yet.

At least not until Kim gave up Jorge Posada's second home run of the game. That poke was too deflating even for this Red Sox team. They lost 10-7. Kim is 1-2 in six appearances against the Yankees this year with a 5.40 ERA. He also needs to do a lot better.

"This could be the biggest game of the year," Yankees manager Joe Torre said. A curious thought coming from a manager who, even if his team had lost, would have still had a 2 1/2 game lead. It seems to me the Yankees are atypically worried about themselves this year. They've lost a bit of their swagger, but they haven't lost their stranglehold on first place.

Meanwhile, the A's and Mariners both won again. The Sox have slipped half a game behind Seattle in the wild-card race.

Tim Wakefield goes against Roger Clemens tomorrow. It could very likely be Clemens's final start at Fenway Park.

AUGUST 31

I am a wee, little man. It took 34,000 people at Fenway Park to finally convince me that I have the maturity of a green banana and about as much class as a substitute teacher. Because it cannot be denied that what a sellout crowd at Fenway did today was a wonderful and classy thing. Nor can I deny that I just couldn't have done it. They gave Roger Clemens a standing ovation, and they extended it until he finally popped out of the dugout and waved his cap to all corners of the ballpark. It was a magnificently special moment. The Boston fans let Roger know some seven years after he left that they appreciate and respect what he did for the Red Sox and what his career has meant to the game of baseball. He's an awesome pitcher, a genuine family man, a devoted teammate, and a disciplined perfectionist. And he deserved that moment. He earned those cheers. And I know, deep in my heart, that had I been among those who paid to see his Fenway farewell, I could not have stood and applauded. I would have sat as a wee, little man on my wee, little hands. I wouldn't have booed, but I couldn't have cheered.

"It was very special," Clemens said. "It gave me the opportunity to say thank you."

I would have much preferred he said "thank you" while on the other end of an 8-2 game. But as I said, I'm a wee, little man.

The Red Sox actually had a chance to prevent Clemens from winning his 100th game at Fenway Park. They loaded the bases in the ninth inning, trailing 8-4, but Mariano Rivera struck out Nomar Garciaparra to end the game.

This was the third straight game that Manny Ramirez missed because of a sore throat. Hey Manny, suck on a lozenge and get back out there!

Complicating matters are reports that Manny was at a hotel bar Saturday night, visiting with Yankees infielder Enrique Wilson. Considering the contagious nature of pharyngitis, I hope he at least kissed Enrique on the lips.

It's unclear if those reports are true, and I'm not sure what to make of them even if they are. He's not bedridden, and nobody's accusing him of having drunk alcohol that night. So, it's plausible that he's too weak to play effectively, but still able to sit with a friend for a while. There are just too many questions at this time to assess the situation fairly. It sure would help if Manny actually spoke to the media—which, by the way, I find ironic. The two guys on the team who refuse to speak are the ones who came down with throat ailments.

The Red Sox also fell 1 1/2 games behind the Mariners in the wild-card race.

11

September to Remember

SEPTEMBER 1

After going out to visit a friend Saturday night, flying to Philadelphia with the team on Sunday, bouncing around the clubhouse laughing with his teammates before today's game, and taking batting practice, Manny Ramirez was asked to pinch hit in today's game, and he said no. He is dead to me.

That may be a tad strong, but, apart from illegal and immoral activities off the field, this may be the most appalling and contemptible behavior I have ever witnessed by a professional athlete. Again that may be a bit overstated, but it's difficult to tone down this overwhelming sense of betrayal. Manny is not sick. His butt is not dragging, he's not vomiting, and his tummy does not ache. About the most I'd believe at this point is that he may feel a bit logy. He was asked to pinch hit, and he declined. I can't even begin to comprehend that level of selfishness, indifference, and irresponsibility. His teammates, who have battled back countless times and who now find themselves in the midst of a pennant race, needed him, and he abandoned them. How can they even look him in the eye? How can even his closest friends, Pedro Martinez and David Ortiz, defend him?

Eighteen players went into the game for the Red Sox, and not one of them was Manny. But while the guy with the eight-year, $160 million contract sat and watched, the Red Sox won anyway.

"This says a lot about the team and guys who are on it and guys who went into the game today," Trot Nixon said. "You can look at that any way you want. I'm sure a lot of people would like to have seen Manny up there. Well, I'm just as confident with the people who went to the plate. Those guys are the MVP's of this game. I'm not talking about Manny, just those guys."

"Those guys" include Lou Merloni, who delivered an infield single with the bases loaded in the ninth inning and with the Red Sox trailing the Phillies, 9-7. "Those guys" also include David McCarty, who drew a walk when he pinch hit for Todd Walker in the eighth inning, with the Red Sox trailing, 6-5. And "those guys" certainly include Johnny Damon, who was banged up pretty good on Saturday when he crashed first into Gabe Kapler and then into the center field wall while chasing down a fly ball. Kapler is a serious weightlifter, and Damon said it hurt more running into him than into the wall, because at least the wall gave a little bit.

Those guys all played, but Manny refused to so much as grab a bat and walk to the plate. Even if he were too weak to hit a home run, his presence or ability to simply put the bat on the ball could have made a difference, but he wouldn't even try. I can't believe his teammates mean so little to him that he could let them down so obviously and unapologetically!

His teammates are now aware of the truth about Saturday night. Enrique Wilson told the New York newspapers that he met Manny at the Ritz-Carlton on Avery Street (where Manny lives), and the two of them went to the Ritz-Carlton on Arlington Street, where the Yankees were staying.

"He came to my room, we went to the lobby, and he left," Wilson said. "He didn't go to the bar. After he left, I don't know if he went home. He told me that he was sick. He didn't want to play [Saturday] because he didn't feel so good."

His teammates also know that Manny blew off an appointment to see a doctor on Sunday morning, and that he sure hasn't looked or acted too sick to pinch hit for the past couple of days. His teammates know he quit on them. How could he be so oblivious and so callous? I have no idea how he'll be able to ingratiate himself back into the fold.

Just as he did last year when he embarrassed himself by failing to run out a ground ball against Tampa Bay, Manny may have shown his true character today—but so did the team. After Mike Timlin did a masterful job getting out of a bases-loaded jam in the Philly seventh, the Red Sox came to bat in the eighth trailing 6-5. David Ortiz delivered a two-run double to put the Red Sox up by a run.

But after Timlin gave up a leadoff homer to Ricky Ledee, then walked two batters and hit a third, Alan Embree came in and gave up a two-run single to Jim Thome. This one was starting to look a lot like the June 21 game—the one in which Thome tied the game twice with home runs, and the Phillies won it with a Todd Pratt homer in the 13th inning.

Instead, the Red Sox rallied with a six-run ninth inning—capped by Trot Nixon's seventh career grand slam, his second this season.

"This is a really big win for us," Nixon said after driving in a career-high six runs. "It gives us momentum, and that's something we hope to carry through the rest of the road trip."

Nixon's numbers are worth noting at this time, and it may help to compare them to Nomar Garciaparra's. Nomar, who just yesterday struck out with the bases loaded, is hitting .322, with 23 homers and 91 RBI. Trot is at .312, 25, and 84. The production levels are very similar, even though Nixon has had 155 fewer at bats and 54 fewer hits. It's also remarkable that Manny is at .317, 31, and 90. Very quietly, Nixon is producing on a fairly even level with the team's two superstars.

No thanks to Manny, the Red Sox moved a game behind the Mariners, who were off today, and 4 1/2 behind the Yankees, who were utterly dominated by Toronto's Roy Halladay. Yankees first baseman Jason Giambi is 0-for-his-last-24.

SEPTEMBER 2

Manny Ramirez sat on the bench again tonight, but this time it was not of his own choosing. In this instance, he was a healthy scratch. Now, I'm a guy who enjoys a nice healthy scratch from time to time, but this was the most satisfying one ever. Grady Little made the hard decision and benched Manny in the middle of a pennant race.

"He's available to DH today, but I like the way our club has responded the last few days, and we're trying to win the game," Little said. "I'm putting the team out there that I think gives us the best chance to win tonight."

Grady Little lied, and the Red Sox swore to it. Theo Epstein issued a statement, an uncommon method of communication for him, that said, "Grady's going with a lineup that gives us the best chance to win as a team, and tonight, that does not include Manny, despite his availability to DH."

It's clear the Red Sox wanted everyone to know that Manny was healthy enough to play, and that he wouldn't be playing. But they were careful not to characterize it as a benching or suspension. That would essentially keep the Players Association out of it. For acting like a spoiled brat the day before, Manny was being given a time-out, a public scolding—with pay.

The decision was greeted warmly by the Red Sox players, who concurred that a statement needed to be delivered. Whether or not Manny actually "got" the message is open for debate, but it was sent nonetheless. And that was important.

The beauty was in the irony. Taking Manny's spot in left field was Gabe Kapler, and what does he do? He hits a homer. The game-winning homer. Undoubtedly, the baseball gods approved of Little's decision.

The Red Sox only managed two hits against Bartolo Colon, a home run by Trot Nixon in the second and Kapler's shot in the sixth. The only other Red Sox hitter to reach base was Kevin Millar, who walked in the fifth inning, only to be erased on a double play. So, the Red Sox didn't leave a runner on base.

Meanwhile, John Burkett pitched his best game of the year, allowing just one run in six innings. Scott Williamson induced a double-play ball in the seventh inning with White Sox on the corners and one out. And Byung-Hyun Kim picked up his 12th save by pitching a perfect ninth, although Paul Konerko just missed hitting a home run down the left-field line. The ball was 10 feet foul. The Red Sox won for just the fifth time this year when they've scored three runs or fewer.

Imagine—the Sox winning with just two hits. The only thing more unbelievable would be if Manny actually grasped the depth of his wrongdoing.

SEPTEMBER 3

David Ortiz is a monster—a huggable, lovable, unbelievable monster! In his last 13 games, Ortiz has had 22 hits, nine homers, 17 runs, and 21 runs batted in. The team's "dominating Dominican" is not Manny Ramirez (making $17 million), or Pedro Martinez (making $15.5 million); it's Ortiz (making $1.25 million). Can you say baseball bargain? After his two-run homer in the eighth inning that gave the Red Sox a 4-3 lead tonight wasn't enough to secure the Red Sox third-straight victory, Ortiz hit another home run in the 10th inning. It was the fifth time this year Ortiz has homered twice in a game. It was the Red Sox 21st victory in their final at bat, and their 38th comeback win.

Manny was back in the lineup and contributed a base hit in the first inning that moved Nomar Garciaparra to second base. Nomar eventually scored on an Ortiz bloop to left, and in the eighth, Manny walked in front of Ortiz's two-run blast. But Manny's greatest contribution came on defense. With the score tied 4-4 in the ninth inning, Chicago's Magglio Ordonez ripped a double down the left-field line. Pinch runner Aaron Rowand got on his horse and galloped around from first base. Manny hustled into the corner. Like a third baseman fielding a bunt, he bare-handed the ball and, in one motion, sidearmed an accurate throw to Nomar, who fired a BB to the plate where Jason Varitek applied the tag. Nomar's throw was awesome, but the play would never have been made—and the game would have been over—if Manny hadn't gotten the ball to him as quickly as he did. The Red Sox won the previous night without Manny when a statement needed to be made, but it's nice to have him back. It'll be a lot easier to forgive his transgression if he's a difference-maker down the stretch.

Byung-Hyun Kim pitched the ninth and tenth innings to pick up the win, but he's been told he won't be the closer for the upcoming weekend series against the Yankees. In 4 2/3 innings against the Yankees this year, Kim has given up four runs on six hits, with one loss and one blown save.

The Yankees lost tonight to narrow their East division lead to three games. It's the closest the Red Sox have been since August 14. The A's and M's were both shut out. So the Sox are tied with Seattle, and two games behind Oakland. The A's 10-game winning streak received a lot of attention and praise, but since August 21, the Red Sox and A's have both gone 10-3. The Yankees are 5-7, and the Mariners are 5-8. It's a trend I'd like to see continue.

SEPTEMBER 4

There's no chance the Red Sox will come out of this weekend in a tie with the Yankees. New York won today to take a 3 1/2 game lead. But I dared to dream about a sweep against Seattle, and I'm double daring to dream about another one in the Bronx. It all starts with Pedro tomorrow night, and there are about fifteen-and-a-half million reasons why he needs to finally beat the Yankees again. I expect him to come up big. I've even got a good feeling about Tim Wakefield on Saturday, and I've got my fingers crossed about Jeff Suppan on Sunday. The Red Sox are playing so well right now, a sweep is very possible. But so, of course, is getting swept.

Meanwhile, Seattle may be in the tank. They were shut out for a second straight day by the lowly Devil Rays. Oakland lost as well. "Tank you" again, Baltimore.

This should be an interesting weekend for Manny Ramirez. He and the team have managed to put "pharyngitis-gate" behind them, but there's still the matter of a little ESPN interview Manny did last week. In a conversation with Joe Morgan—during the series with the Yankees in which Manny wasn't playing—he said that it was his dream to one day play for the Yankees. Granted, that's the dream of a lot of people, especially those who grew up in the shadows of Yankee Stadium, but the timing of such a statement was regrettable. It's like a Hatfield telling ESPN that he'd one day like to live with the McCoys. Go ahead and dream your little dream, Manny, but keep it to yourself—especially during a pennant race.

The phrase around Boston is, "that's just Manny being Manny," but nobody really knows what that means, or who he is. *Sports Illustrated* once wrote that Manny is "tougher to read than Sanskrit." He's been a mystery inside a riddle, wrapped around an incredible amount of talent, ever since he got to the big leagues.

He was drafted with the 13th pick in June of 1991 by the Cleveland Indians. He was 19 years old at the time and had been living in New York's Washington Heights for only six years. After moving from Santa Domingo, the capital of the Dominican Republic, when he was 13, Manny didn't do well in school and was slow to pick up English. He never graduated from high school, but riches weren't far away, because he could always swing a bat.

Manny's 1994 rookie year was a strike-shortened season, but he still managed to hit .269 with 17 homers and 60 RBI. He finished second in the Rookie of the Year voting to Bob Hamelin, who played only four more years and never again matched the production of his first year.

Ramirez, meanwhile, went on to become one of the preeminent sluggers in the game. In his final two years in Cleveland, he hit 82 home runs and drove in 287 runs while batting .341. Those are the kinds of numbers that made him the most coveted free agent on the market at the end of the 2000 season, but he may also have become available because of a growing concern over his lack of intensity.

He missed 44 games during his final year in Cleveland, primarily because of a strained left hamstring, which management didn't think he was working as hard as he could to come back from. Indians owner Larry Dolan said, "It doesn't look like he wants to help us."

Which is exactly how it looked recently when Manny returned rather slowly from his sore throat. But following the criticism in Cleveland, he returned that year to drive in 75 runs in his final 71 games. He also homered in his last at bat at Jacobs Field.

Then he signed with the Red Sox and homered in his first at bat at Fenway Park. In fact, it was the first pitch he ever saw while wearing a Red Sox uniform. It was exactly what fans were looking for and what management was paying him for.

It was on December 12, 2000, that Manny signed an eight-year deal worth $160 million. His contract breaks down like this:

$13 million in 2001.
$15.5 million in 2002.
$18 million in 2003.
$20.5 million in 2004.
$20 million in 2005.
$19 million in 2006.
$18 million in 2007.
$20 million in 2008.

There are also award bonuses, such as $200,000 for winning an MVP award, $75,000 for making an All-Star team, and $150,000 for being the World Series MVP.

Add it all up and you've got yourself an RBI machine that can sometimes say brilliant things like, "I'm just tired of seeing New York always win"—which is what he said at his first press conference after signing with the Red Sox. You've also got someone who can leave two weeks' pay inside a cowboy boot, or forget to cash five consecutive paychecks, prompting a call from Cleveland's bean counters.

He's done those things. He's failed to run out a ground ball. He's stolen a base only to be tagged out when he started running back to first because he thought it was a foul ball. Most recently, he stepped off second base to pick up his helmet without calling time out and was tagged out. It's all just "Manny being Manny," and you have to take the good with the idiosyncratic.

"I don't like too many things in my head," Manny has said. "I don't care who is pitching. All I need to see is the ball. My mind is always clean.

Empty, empty, empty."

Words to live by, and apparently he does.

SEPTEMBER 5

They say it's never over till it's over, or until the fat lady sings, or until an actor appears in an Old Navy commercial. Well, how about this one: it's never over until you give Pedro Martinez an eight-run lead in the third inning. Game over.

The Yankees were on their back in this one from beginning to end. It's as if they were "the English patient." Andy Pettitte, a viable Cy Young candidate looking for his 18th victory, pitched as if he was trying out for the Red Sox bullpen. It was that bad!

Johnny Damon got the night started innocently enough with a bunt down the first base line. Nobody covered first base, and Damon was on board. With one out, Nomar Garciaparra got an infield single. Manny Ramirez followed with a base hit to right, scoring the first run. A David Ortiz base hit scored the second run. None of the balls were hit hard, but the Red Sox were up 2-0. Jason Varitek singled to make it three runs in the Red Sox first.

The Sox had given Pedro his second straight three-run lead, but this time he held it. Pedro came out sporting a brand new red glove and threw 10 of 14 pitches for strikes, retiring the Yankees in order in the first. The Red Sox added another run in the second. Then Pedro threw just nine pitches in the second inning while picking up strikeouts numbers three and four. A three-run triple by Johnny Damon in the third chased Pettitte, who gave up eight runs and nine hits. Oddly enough, he struck out five.

The game turned into a laugher, especially in the fourth inning, when Manny made a great catch at the wall to rob Bernie Williams of extra bases. He had his back to the plate and was on a dead run when he grabbed the ball about two feet from the fence. Quite pleased with himself, Manny tossed the ball into the stands and ran toward the dugout—only to find out, as Trot Nixon had before him, that there were only two outs. Pedro stood on the mound with his red glove covering a big grin. Manny being Manny was funny this time. No pressure. No anxiety. The Red Sox won, 9-3.

Pedro's pitches were exploding once again. With such a big lead, he was able to leave after striking out nine in six innings. His only problem continues to be with Manny's buddy, Enrique Wilson. That guy, playing for the injured Derek Jeter (rib), smacked a pair of doubles and is now 10-for-

20 lifetime against one of the best pitchers the game has ever seen. Explain that phenomenon!

That was the easy one. Tomorrow it's Tim Wakefield matched up against Roger Clemens. A Red Sox win would close the gap to 1 1/2 games.

SEPTEMBER 6

It's about time. It's about time Tim Wakefield gave the Red Sox this kind of performance. It's about time he got his 10th win, considering he got his ninth win seven starts and 34 days ago. And it's all about time for the Sox, and whether they have enough of it to catch the Yankees. Talent isn't an issue. They have enough of that. But after a second consecutive Bronx blowout, the Red Sox still remain 1 1/2 games behind the Yankees. The Red Sox are on a roll, but it's one that could end tomorrow, or it's a wave they could ride right into the postseason. Who knows what tomorrow will bring? Right now, it's all about time. In this moment in time, life is good.

"We're not getting too high," said Sox first baseman Kevin Millar. "I think that's the thing you're seeing. You're starting to see some eye of the tigers in here. Everybody has that look, that it's business now."

This one was easier than yesterday's game. This time it was a six-run fourth inning that drove Clemens out of the game. Forget the weakness of the Yankees bullpen, the Red Sox have been pressing the pound key against the Yankees starters. The first eight batters in the Sox fourth reached base. The onslaught included two walks, an error, and five hits. The only out recorded came when Kevin Millar singled and tried to move to second while Manny Ramirez was scoring. Nomar Garciaparra, Todd Walker, and Millar all homered in the game, and the Red Sox rolled to an 11-0 victory.

"We're good," said Sox manager Grady Little, "and we're getting hot at the right time."

"Our offense is scary," said Johnny Damon. "It's someone different every day."

The offense has been scary plenty of times this year, but we haven't seen this kind of performance from Tim Wakefield all year. He threw seven shutout innings, allowed just four hits, and finished the year 2-2 against Clemens. He also contributed to the continuing plunge of Yankees slugger Jason Giambi, who has hit a 3-for-54 skid. With his average down to .246, he's starting to hear some boos.

The Red Sox have won five games in a row—on the road against playoff contenders. They've won 12 of their last 15 games and are now just

1 1/2 games behind the Yankees. It's worth noting that the Sox were 7 1/2 games back on August 20, and they were 5 1/2 games back seven days ago after losing to the Yankees at Fenway Park. I couldn't be happier—though I did lose a gray hair today. I'm kind of conflicted about that. I mean, I'm not happy about losing a hair, but at least it was a gray one.

SEPTEMBER 7

Poof! It can all disappear as with a magician's sleight of hand. We thought we saw the Red Sox ready to overtake the Yankees, but they pulled a rabbit out of a hat (or more accurately, David Wells pulled a fantastic performance out of his butt). It doesn't exactly feel like the magic is gone for the Red Sox, but this game serves as a reminder of how resilient the Yankees are, and that they have the survival skills of an Outback hunter.

Truly, a remarkable effort was made by both of today's starting pitchers. Jeff Suppan, who had a career record of 0-4 against the Yankees entering the game, took a one-hitter into the seventh. David Wells, who had been winless in seven starts since July 19, was better. Wells, who had given up 24 runs in his last 22 innings, pitched 7 1/3 shutout innings. He was both portly and amazing on his way to picking up a 3-1 victory.

"Boomer responds to challenges," Joe Torre said. "There's no bigger challenge since he's been back here than this game today. He certainly restored order."

In an outstanding and wholly unexpected standoff, Suppan was the first to blink. And in the blink of an eye, Bernie Williams's first home run in 65 at bats cleared the wall in the seventh inning, giving the Yankees a 2-0 lead. Williams's big blow came with two strikes and two outs. The Red Sox were just about that close to a clean sweep. But the lead that was once insurmountable, and then quite mountable, might be out of reach again.

The Yankees received some inspiration from their shortstop, Derek Jeter, who fought his way back into the lineup despite a rib cage injury that kept him out of the last five games.

"I would have kept talking to (Torre), over and over," Jeter said. "Eventually, he'd have to cave in."

That's what you want to see. Are you listening, Manny?

In the West, Oakland was thumped for a second straight day by Tampa Bay, and Seattle lost a second straight game to Baltimore. The Mariners have only scored eight runs in their last five games—against Tampa Bay and

Baltimore, not exactly the cream of the crop. The Mariners have also lost 11 of their last 17 games, but trail the Red Sox in the wild-card race by only 1 1/2 games. It's frustrating to see the Red Sox playing so well, yet be unable to either catch the Yankees or create more of a cushion in the wild-card race.

SEPTEMBER 8

I feel like I could spit. But first I'd want to eat peanut butter and drink orange juice so I could hork up a great big loogie. This was the absolute worst game of the year. It was "coyote ugly," meaning baseball fans would rather gnaw off their own arm than watch this kind of mockery of the game. Forget the four Red Sox errors! That's just the beginning.

I mean, I can handle a ground ball going through somebody's legs from time to time, or an errant throw, but the Red Sox were downright stupid tonight. It was the 143rd game of the season, and it looked like the first day of spring training. Mike Timlin fielded a comebacker with Luis Matos on second base. He had Matos trapped in a rundown, but instead of running right at him, Timlin fired the ball to second base. Matos took off for third and was safe when Bill Mueller was screened on the throw to third.

Byung-Hyun Kim fielded a sacrifice bunt and should have known it was too good a bunt to get the runner at second base. But he took the time to look that way anyway, then hurried his throw to first and threw wildly.

Scott Williamson walked the first batter he faced to load the bases in the seventh, then gave up a bases-clearing double.

Johnny Damon made his first error of the year, because Todd Walker wouldn't get out of his way on a shallow fly ball. Dumb!

The Red Sox banged out four more home runs and 16 hits, but still lost the game, 13-10. Baltimore scored four times in the seventh, and four more *un*earned runs in the eighth off Kim. The four home runs brought the Red Sox season total to 213, which ties the single-season record set by the club in 1977.

Still, this game leaves a taste in your mouth as bad as a Cheerios burp. This was the 11th game the Sox have lost this year when they've scored at least seven runs. Yet, they're still very much alive in the pennant race. Boy, can they hit!

SEPTEMBER 9

It's now a record-setting offense for the Red Sox. A franchise known for its powerful teams has never had this much power before. In the second inning of the Red Sox 9-2 victory over the Orioles, David Ortiz hit the team's 214th home run.

"I hit that one good," Ortiz said about the ball that traveled 430 feet, becoming the 33rd drive in Camden Yards' 12-year history to land on Eutaw Street.

Bill Mueller and Jason Varitek also homered for the Sox. For Mueller, it was his 19th, putting him one shy of joining six other Sox with at least 20 home runs. And that's what's so remarkable about this team. It's all about depth.

The 1977 Red Sox, who for 25 years had held the franchise record for home runs, also had power throughout their lineup. Jim Rice led the squad with 39 homers, followed by George Scott and Butch Hobson, who had 33 and 30 respectively. Then there were Carl Yastrzemski (28), Carlton Fisk (26), and Fred Lynn (18). Bernie Carbo and Dwight Evans combined for 29 more. But that team finished second in the American League in runs scored that year. The 2003 Red Sox lead the major leagues in runs, home runs, batting average, slugging percentage, and on-base percentage—and they've struck out the eighth fewest times. In case you haven't noticed, this team can flat-out hit.

The major-league record for home runs in a season by a team is 264, set by the 1997 Seattle Mariners. That team was led by Ken Griffey Jr., with 56 home runs, and Jay Buhner with 40. The Red Sox, meanwhile, have Mueller with 19 and Manny Ramirez with 32. In between, there are five guys with 23 to 26 home runs apiece. This Red Sox lineup routinely has Mueller, the league leader in batting average, hitting eighth, and Jason Varitek, who has 24 home runs, batting ninth. That Mariner team only hit .280, while the 2003 Red Sox are hitting .292.

The Red Sox have scored 881 runs this year, an average of 6.15 per game. So they don't have a chance of catching the 1931 Yankees, who scored 1,067 runs, averaging 6.92 per game. Still, this is the best-hitting team in Red Sox history, and it ranks among the best of all time.

The Ortiz rocket launch was the team's 591st extra base hit, also establishing a new team record. And the major-league mark is well within reach. It was set by the 1996 Mariners, who rattled 607 extra base hits.

Concerning tonight's game, there's some concern concerning Trot Nixon, who limped off the field with a strained left calf muscle. Grady Little said after the game that Nixon won't play tomorrow. Meanwhile, Derek Lowe pitched in and out of trouble, picking up his 15th win, and Ramiro Mendoza, making his first appearance since August 2, pitched a scoreless ninth with a seven-run lead.

SEPTEMBER 10

For the third start in a row, the Red Sox staked Pedro Martinez to a 3-0 lead in the first inning. And for the second start in a row, Pedro dominated. This time he went eight shutout innings, allowing only three hits while striking out nine. Of his 117 pitches, 79 were strikes. In the 14 innings covering his last two starts, Pedro has struck out 18 and allowed just one run.

Baltimore's Melvin Mora called him "nasty," adding, "That's the best pitcher in the world right there."

I think he might be right—right now.

The Red Sox went 7-2 on their four-city road trip, during which they faced three teams likely to be in the playoffs. They certainly hit better than they frequently have on the road this year, scoring 66 runs. But it was the starting pitching that made the difference. Check it out:

At Philadelphia—Jeff Suppan: 6 IP, 5 ER (no-decision)
At Chicago—John Burkett: 6 IP, 1 ER (win)
At Chicago—Derek Lowe: 7 IP, 3 ER (no-decision)
At New York—Pedro Martinez: 6 IP, 1 ER (win)
At New York—Tim Wakefield: 7 IP, 0 ER (win)
At New York—Jeff Suppan: 7 IP, 2 ER (loss)
At Baltimore—John Burkett: 5.1 IP, 5 ER (no-decision)
At Baltimore—Derek Lowe: 6 IP, 1 ER (win)
At Baltimore—Pedro Martinez: 8 IP, 0 ER (win)

That's seven quality starts and an earned run average of 2.78. If this staff can pitch even remotely like that the rest of the way, the wild-card race won't even be close. Right now the Sox still hold a two-game lead over Seattle, but they just finished the toughest part of their schedule, a 26-game stretch against the best of the West—the Yankees, White Sox, and Phillies.

During that stretch they had to deal with two bouts of pharyngitis and the benching of their clean-up hitter, and still they went 17-9.

"I feel great about this team," Kevin Millar said. "Right now, we control our own destiny. We just have to keep winning baseball games."

One other big development on the trip was the re-emergence of Bill Mueller in the batting race. He went to Baltimore with a .322 average, but after going 9-for-11 in the series, including home runs in the final two games in Baltimore, Mueller is up to .333. That's eight points ahead of Manny Ramirez and Derek Jeter. Nomar Garciaparra remains in the top 10, but after going just 7-for-40 on the road trip, he's down to .313. He did manage to homer twice and drive in six runs in the nine games, but he's really looked bad at times recently.

SEPTEMBER 11

It's been two years since the attack on the World Trade Center. Today Roger Clemens listened to young children read aloud the names of 2,792 victims, and then went out and won his 307th game.

"That's difficult, when you have to hear a young kid...do that," Clemens said.

During the seventh inning stretch, more than 31,000 people at Yankee Stadium joined in the singing of "God Bless America." The time was 9:11 p.m.

The Red Sox were off today, and now trail the Yankees by five games.

SEPTEMBER 12

Friday night at Fenway was just another walk in the park—"walk" being the operative word. Chicago White Sox pitchers issued 12 walks tonight. So, while Nomar, Manny, Ortiz, and Millar combined to go 0-for-13, the Red Sox still won easily, 7-4.

The Red Sox only had five hits, the fewest they've had at Fenway Park this season. But three of their walks came with the bases loaded. Five of the walks came around to score. And Jeff Suppan pitched a second straight "better than average" game. He gave up three runs in six innings, and it's starting to look like all five of the Red Sox starters can be counted on now.

However, everybody wins! The Red Sox, Yankees, A's, and Mariners all won tonight—giving them winning streaks of three, four, six, and three, respectively. So, despite winning eight of their last 10 games, the Red Sox only lead the Mariners by 1 1/2 games in the wild-card race, and trail the Yankees by four games.

SEPTEMBER 13

You just knew somebody was going to snap eventually. Unfortunately, it was the Red Sox. While the M's, A's, and Yanks all extended their winning streaks, the Red Sox modest streak was snapped. So, the wild-card lead is down to a measly half game. That's far too close for comfort with 15 games to play.

For the second straight night, the Red Sox only managed five hits, but this time they were facing Bartolo Colon for a full nine innings. Colon only gave two free passes. The Sox lost, 3-1.

Colon was the story of the game, throwing his third complete game in a row and firing gas up around 97 miles-per-hour late in the game. But Tim Wakefield gave the hose of a different color another quality start. He went seven, giving up three.

The other major story line is Nomar Garciaparra's continuing struggle. It's been a season of peaks and valleys for him. After hitting .273 in April, he turned things around and hit .339 in May. Then it was .398 in June, but .269 in July. He batted .325 in August, but his September has been a putrid .149. That's 7-for-47! And while he did drive in the only Sox run tonight with a sacrifice fly, he also stranded runners at first and second in the sixth. And with the Sox trailing 3-1 in the eighth, Nomar stepped up to the plate with runners on second and third. A base hit would have tied the game, but he popped up to second.

Nomar's a rock. He plays hard. He plays hurt. He plays to win. And he usually plays well. Just not lately.

SEPTEMBER 14

The Red Sox were strutting around like peacocks when their offense was exploding during their recent road trip, but that giant, colorful tail might be between their legs after scoring just three runs on the weekend. The wrong Sox won again. This time it was left-hander Mark Buehrle scattering seven hits over seven innings and picking up his 13th win of the year, 7-2.

SEPTEMBER 15

When the Red Sox make it to the postseason, opposing teams will have to deal with an emerging one-two punch that could be the best in baseball. "One" is obviously Pedro Martinez, and the "two" is an increasingly impressive Derek Lowe. He's back, baby!

Lowe is 5-0 in his last seven starts, while posting a 2.58 ERA. Tonight, he improved to 16-6 by giving up just four hits and two runs in eight innings. Of those 24 outs, 17 came on grounders, six on strikeouts, and only one was a fly ball out.

"When you're a sinkerball guy, you get in a good rhythm and you like your chances," Lowe said.

And I like the Red Sox chances with Lowe, Pedro, Suppan, and Wakefield. That could be a Fearsome Foursome in the postseason. That's no disrespect to John Burkett, but if it were up to me, he'd be the odd man out when they switch to a four-man rotation in the playoffs.

The Red Sox won 8-2 with home runs from Manny Ramirez and David Ortiz. For Ortiz, it was his 11th homer in 23 games.

All this, and the Mariners lost, once again falling 1 1/2 games behind the Red Sox. Meanwhile, the Yankees are undoubtedly feeling pretty good about themselves these days and thinking they've turned everything around. Since the Red Sox got to within 1 1/2 games of them on September 6, the Yankees have won eight of their last nine games and gotten their lead over the Red Sox back to 5 1/2 games. But all they're doing is what they've done all year, and that is beating up on the bad teams. No disrespect intended, because if the Red Sox were able to do it as well as the Yankees, they'd be in first place. But the Yankees can, and probably will, close out this season on some incredible hot streak while playing Detroit, Tampa Bay, and Baltimore. The fact remains, though, that they've lost six of eight series against winning teams since the All-Star break. They simply won't know if they've turned things around until they get into the postseason. And by then, it may be too late.

SEPTEMBER 16

They sure do make him work for it. Tonight, Pedro Martinez was as untouchable as a frigid black belt. But once again the Red Sox gave him very little breathing room. It gave an otherwise mundane Tuesday night game against Tampa Bay a playoff atmosphere. Fans were apprehensive about every pitch. When an obviously rejuvenated Pedro is facing a bad team like the D-Rays, there is a customary level of confidence, but that was absent tonight, because the Red Sox couldn't figure out Jeremi Gonzalez—who had lost four straight starts coming in. Suddenly, Gonzalez is the second coming of Bob Feller, and the Sox only pushed one run across through the first seven innings.

Pedro was making that run stand up, but not without some anxious moments. For instance, in the sixth, Pedro left Tampa Bay catcher Toby Hall stranded at second base after a leadoff double, but the real challenge was stranding Aubrey Huff at third base after a leadoff *triple* in the seventh. And he made it look so easy. Two quick pop-ups, then three quick strikes to Damian Rolls, and no blood.

Tampa Bay finally got to Pedro in the eighth, tying the game at 1-1, and it looked like Pedro might end up with another well-pitched no-decision. But Nomar Garciaparra, batting second in the order in an effort to get him hitting better, swung at the first pitch as he so often does, and roped a double down the left-field line. Todd Walker grounded out to the right side, sending Nomar to third, and Manny Ramirez was intentionally walked for the 26th time this year. That's the Red Sox team record for a right-handed hitter. The overall team record is 33, set by Ted Williams in 1957.

The walk to Manny left it up to David Ortiz, who promptly singled hard to right, making him 6-for-10 with nine RBI when following an intentional walk to Manny. Bill Mueller added what proved to be an important insurance run with a sacrifice fly. It was important, because Pedro came out to pitch his third complete game of the year, and Tampa Bay blooped a couple of singles over the infield and scored another run. But Pedro was not to be denied. He finished what he started, and the Red Sox won, 3-2. It was the Red Sox 22nd victory in their last at bat, and they're now 24-15 in one-run games.

The Devil Rays' two runs were the first earned runs they've scored against Pedro in 30 innings this year. Pedro picked up his 100th win in a Red Sox uniform, his 13th this year against four losses. He also lowered his league-leading ERA to 2.34.

For all the negative energy I claim he's brought to the team this year, I'm still glad Pedro's on the Red Sox. After all, he just helped Boston take a 2 1/2 game lead in the wild-card race. Seattle is dropping like a stone.

The Red Sox announced that playoff tickets go on sale tomorrow!

SEPTEMBER 17

The Red Sox, who have stayed remarkably injury free this year, were without Trot Nixon, Johnny Damon, and Kevin Millar tonight. Nixon is still bothered by a strained calf, Damon has an abdominal strain, and Kevin Millar missed his second straight game due to food poisoning. The absence of these three from the lineup may have contributed to the Red Sox being shut out for the first time at home this year, 7-0. But c'mon, it was the Devil Rays.

Other than a Todd Walker double that broke the major-league team record for extra base hits in a season (608), nothing was good about this one. We move on, 1 1/2 games ahead of the Mariners, who beat Texas behind Jamie Moyer's 19th win.

SEPTEMBER 18

Excitement and enthusiasm always need to be tempered somewhat when the Red Sox play the Devil Rays, but Tim Wakefield is a crunch-time performer. Here we are late in the season, and he is consistently coming up with his best efforts. In his last three starts, including tonight's, Wakefield has given up six runs in 22 1/3 innings. Tonight, he left to a standing ovation, with one out in the ninth and runners on first and second. Byung-Hyun Kim got the final two outs—allowing one of the inherited runners to score—and the Red Sox won, 4-3. Manny Ramirez hit his third home run in five games.

With the Mariners' 10th-inning loss to the Rangers, the Sox have a 2 1/2 game lead in the wild-card race, and Seattle flies to Oakland while the Sox hit the road for three in Cleveland. The A's have won 26 more games than the Indians this year.

While Johnny Damon and Trot Nixon were out of the lineup once again, Millar returned, but Bill Mueller left with back spasms. These all appear to be minor nuisances which should heal in time for the playoffs.

SEPTEMBER 19

This was a watershed moment—one that brings us full circle. This season began with the controversial "closer by committee" theory, which failed miserably. Things in the bullpen stabilized somewhat when Byung-Hyun Kim was officially made the closer, but his struggles in August (5.74

ERA and only three saves) combined with Grady Little's reluctance to use him against the Yankees, and then what happened tonight, have made it clear that Kim is no longer the unquestioned closer. We're 153 games into the regular season, and the Red Sox still don't know who their closer is. It looks like the committee has reconvened.

Kim was awesome in July, picking up two wins and six saves while posting a 0.96 ERA. But August was an abomination, and Kim has become as trustworthy with a lead as Jayson Blair (the *New York Times* reporter who fabricated stories about the Washington sniper and others in 2003). It's quite possibly a case of perception being reality, however. Because in truth, Kim has made eight appearances this month, pitching a total of nine innings—without giving up an *earned* run. (His unforgettable performance against Baltimore on the eighth of this month resulted in four unearned runs.) Yet he's obviously lost his manager's confidence, and quite possibly his job.

Tonight against Cleveland, the Sox only managed a sacrifice fly from Todd Walker and a homer from Nomar Garciaparra, giving John Burkett two runs to work with. Burkett was especially sharp for seven innings but ran into a bit of trouble in the eighth following an error and a walk. Mike Timlin extricated the Sox from the jam with a couple of strikeouts and a failed sacrifice. So the ball was handed to Kim in the ninth to protect a 2-0 lead.

Kim retired the first two Indians on groundouts. Then he hit the next two batters and was immediately pulled from the game. The fact that Little had Alan Embree warming up in the bullpen, just in case, tells you something.

"We're in a situation now where we don't have time to wait for someone to get it together," Little said. Then he added something that sounded very similar to his springtime thoughts. "I'm going to go with the hot hand. If the hot hand is on the mound, he'll stay there. If not, someone else will get the ball."

Hello, committee!

Embree got the final out for a nice, easy, two-pitch save. Red Sox win, 2-0. But where do they go from here? They've won 90 games this year, and their save leader has 14. Who knows if he'll be given another chance to get to 15?

Personally, I'd give Timlin another chance to close. He's been the most consistent man in the pen all year. He throws strikes—only eight walks in 81 winnings. And while he's also given up 11 home runs, only four have come since the All-Star break. He had a couple of rough outings earlier this month, but 22 of his last 27 appearances have been scoreless. He's not perfect, but he's 37 years old, and he's got 116 career saves. I think he can handle the pressure, and his ability stacks up to anyone's in the Red Sox pen. Some will lobby for Scott Williamson to get a chance in the final week, but he's been terrible since his arrival. Yes, he saved 27 games for the Reds before the trade, but he's been unreliable ever since. Maybe he's one of those guys who doesn't pitch well unless it's a save situation. But the Red Sox need wins in order to get to the postseason. This is not the best time to be experimenting.

Fortunately, the starting pitching has come on strong of late and is going deeper into games, which diminishes the bullpen's role and limits the damage it can do. The Red Sox have won seven of their last 10 games, all of the wins going to the starters, who have combined for a 2.67 ERA during that stretch.

Meanwhile, Seattle beat Oakland's Tim Hudson tonight. The lead stands at 2 1/2 games.

SEPTEMBER 20

Teams that are steamrolling toward the playoffs are not supposed to get flattened like this. On September 8, the Red Sox threw up that throw-up-inducing clunker against the Orioles. Three days ago, they were blanked by the lowly Devil Rays at home. And tonight, they gave up seven runs in the seventh inning against the Indians. That's three awful losses in 13 days to truly awful teams. In between, the Red Sox have played pretty good baseball and put themselves in a position to clinch a playoff berth.

But it's disheartening to see them play down to their competition's level.

This game was well in hand as Derek Lowe entered the seventh inning with a 4-1 lead. Trot Nixon returned to the lineup and blasted his 27th home run. Kevin Millar added a clutch two-out RBI single in the sixth. And the Sox got two more in the top of the seventh.

But Lowe gave up a leadoff home run to Josh Bard, and by the time the Cleveland catcher batted for the second time in the same inning, Damian Jackson had made a costly error, Lowe had thrown a wild pitch with the bases loaded, Scott Sauerbeck had walked two batters and hit another, and the Indians had taken the lead, 8-4. Then, Scott Williamson couldn't get out of the eighth until he was rescued by an increasingly annoyed Grady Little.

Williamson threw a pair of wild pitches, walked two hitters, and gave up five runs. It looked like Little was going to just leave him out there to embarrass himself, but he finally, mercifully, pulled the plug. Sauerbeck's ERA rose to 7.24 while Williamson's jumped to 7.00. They've been about as useful as those things you don't usually find on a bull.

And wouldn't you know, Seattle pounded the A's for a second straight win in Oakland. The wild-card lead is down to 1 1/2 games. And Andy Pettitte picked up his 20th win of the year for New York. The Yankees clinched a playoff berth with a 7-1 win over Tampa Bay.

At least Pedro goes tomorrow. So you can probably write down a "W" for the Red Sox. Though you'd better write it in pencil—one with an eraser—just in case.

SEPTEMBER 21

I woke up this morning and said my own little prayer. You want to know what it was? I told the man upstairs that I didn't feel like I deserved any more help from Him than the other team did. But whatever He did, don't give me any less. Amen. Then I got dressed and came to the park.

—Red Sox manager Grady Little

Grady Little's prayers were answered by Pedro Martinez, who threw another seven shutout innings—making him 4-0 with a 0.90 ERA in September. Considering Toronto's Roy Halladay and New York's Andy Pettitte are already 20-game winners, and Seattle's Jamie Moyer will probably get there, Pedro has virtually no shot at this year's Cy Young Award. But he should get some consideration.

The award is supposed to go to the best pitcher in each league, and Pedro leads the American League in ERA, Ks, WHIP, and winning percentage. His ERA is nearly a run better than Halladay's and Mike Mussina's, more than a run better than Moyer's, and nearly two runs better than Pettitte's. Pettitte has 20 wins, with an ERA over 4.00, because he receives nearly seven runs of support per game (second in the league behind Derek Lowe). Meanwhile, Pedro only has 14 wins, in part because of 10 no-decisions. He's allowed three runs or fewer in 24 of his 28 starts. Halladay has given up *more* than three runs in a game 10 times this year. Pedro has 17 more strikeouts than Halladay in 69 fewer innings.

Still, Halladay would be a worthy recipient. He's got 21 wins already and should make two more starts. His ERA is an impressive 3.18, and his 252 innings pitched prove he's a real workhorse. It's a shame Pedro got hurt and had all those no-decisions. Give him three or four more wins, and the Cy Young race would be extraordinarily intriguing.

Meanwhile, Kim's the closer again. Case closed? Not likely. But after Pedro escaped a bases-loaded jam in the seventh inning with his 11th strikeout, and Mike Timlin skated through the eighth, the Red Sox held a 2-0 lead heading for the bottom of the ninth. The call went out to Byung-Hyun Kim.

"B.K. was a welcome sight," Little said. "It was a big step for him, very important. We need these guys to pitch good."

And Kim pitched very well. Three up, three down. Eleven pitches, nine strikes. Fifteen saves in 18 opportunities. But I don't think the committee is dead.

Assuming the Red Sox make the playoffs, and leaping to the conclusion that they get past Oakland with Kim as their closer, what happens if they face the Yankees in the Championship Series? Little has already expressed strong reservations about using Kim against the Yankees. So, to whom does he go in the ninth inning? And does he call on Kim earlier in the game? Or does he just never use him? And if that's the case, why put him on the ALCS roster? And wouldn't it be an incredibly gutsy call to leave your closer *off* the roster? Just a few things to think about.

And think about this while you're at it. The Red Sox have scored three runs or fewer eight times in September—the same number of times they were held to that limit in August. But the big difference is that they were 0-8 in such games in August, but they're 4-4 in those games this month.

Today's 2-0 win over Cleveland was the third time this month the Red Sox have won when scoring just two runs. And that's only happened two other times all year. It's just more evidence that the pitching is getting much better.

Other notes from today's game: Manny Ramirez drove in his 100th run of the season, tying him for the team lead with Nomar Garciaparra, who got his 100th during last night's debacle. It's the sixth year in a row Manny has hit the century mark, and the eighth time in the last nine years. In fact, since 1995, only Sammy Sosa and Rafael Palmeiro have driven in more runs than Manny.

Johnny Damon was back in the lineup after missing four games with an abdominal strain, and Bill Mueller returned after sitting out two games with back spasms.

The wild-card lead is back up to 2 1/2 games! Oakland finally came through with a 12-0 win over Seattle.

SEPTEMBER 22

I kind of put myself in the frame of mind like we do on an airplane when we are getting ready to take off, and they say, "Buckle your seatbelts," and there might be a little turbulence. But tonight we had a safe landing, and that is all we can ask. It was a big win for the ball club.

—Red Sox manager Grady Little

Two days in a row I find myself beginning the diary entry with the "Potent Quotable," Grady Little. But he deftly extended his metaphor and made it work. The Red Sox got solo home runs from Manny Ramirez, Trot Nixon, and David Ortiz. Plus, Jeff Suppan pitched six strong innings and left the game with a 6-2 lead. But because of the season's "never-ending story," also known as the bullpen, the game wasn't completely secure until Byung-Hyun Kim retired the side in order in the ninth. The Red Sox won, 7-5. The "turbulence" provided by Todd Jones, Alan Embree, and Mike Timlin turned out to be a non-factor.

The Red Sox magic number dropped to four.

SEPTEMBER 23

There haven't been too many scenes like the one that took place at home plate tonight. And I'll tell you something else. This Red Sox team has spent a lot of time in recent weeks trying to convince anyone with a microphone or a notebook that this team "loves each other," and that they have "wonderful chemistry." They've been saying all the right things, but because they had to say it, I wondered if it were true. Tonight, in my mind at least, they proved it. This is a team. They pull for one another. And when they win, or lose, they know they did it as a team. And I doubt there's ever been a *championship* team that wasn't a "team" first.

Here's how the magic unfolded tonight. Tim Wakefield gave up a three-run homer to Luis Matos in the second inning, and it looked like that was going to hold up for the Orioles. The Red Sox scratched out single runs in the second and fifth innings, but they only managed three hits through the first seven innings against the unheralded duo of Eric DuBose and John Parrish. In the eighth, Manny Ramirez led off with a single and was pinch-run for by Adrian Brown. Brown stole second *and* third, but was left stranded.

It looked like the game was over when the Orioles padded their lead with two runs in the ninth inning. The game's most frustrating moment came with two outs. Bronson Arroyo was on the hill and put runners on first and second. With Alan Embree loose in the pen, and the left-handed hitting Jay Gibbons stepping to the plate, the basic question was: who is more likely to get Gibbons out, Arroyo or Embree? Keep in mind this is the most important out of the game. I think you have to go with the lefty against lefty, but Little stuck with Arroyo. Bad move. Gibbons singled to right, where Gabe Kapler bobbled the ball long enough for *both* runners to score. The Orioles now had a 5-2 lead. What chance did the Red Sox have to come back now?

The difference between a one-run deficit and a three-run deficit feels like a lot more than two runs. That's because when Jason Varitek delivered a one-out single, there was still no hope in the air. If the Red Sox had trailed by just one run, I would have been on the edge of my seat. And when Varitek got to second on a passed ball, the game would have taken on a whole new meaning. Instead, when Johnny Damon grounded out to second, moving Varitek to third, I barely noticed that without the preceding passed ball, that would have been a game-ending double play. Now Varitek was on third, and it didn't seem to matter. Why the heck didn't Embree pitch to Gibbons?

Nomar Garciaparra, still batting second, drew a walk. Now the tying run was coming up to the plate, but it was Todd Walker. No offense, but he's not your typical home-run threat. And remember, Manny is no longer hitting behind him, because he was taken out of the game for a pinch runner in the eighth. So, it was Adrian Brown in the on-deck circle. With two outs, the Red Sox were going to need to string together two or three more hits to bring home the tying run.

There was some hope making its way into the ballpark. Orioles closer Jorge Julio was obviously laboring. He entered the game with one out in the eighth, and now with Walker at the plate, he just didn't seem to have command. The count went to 3-2. Then Walker dropped the head of the bat on a pitch low and inside and golfed it toward right field. The ball was hit hard, but height was the issue. Walker spoke to the ball while heading down the first base line. "Get up! Get up!" he said.

In fact, everybody get up! Todd Walker just tied the game with a three-run homer! The ball just barely cleared the right-field bullpen, and Walker gave three emphatic fist pumps as he rounded the first base bag. What chance did the Red Sox have to come back from three runs down in the ninth inning? As it turned out, a pretty good one!

"It was awesome," Walker said. "Being here in Boston, and these fans and how much they love baseball and everything you hear about. And we're fighting for a playoff spot. All things considered, that was just awesome."

Byung-Hyun Kim took care of the O's in the 10th. And it seemed like just a matter of time before the Red Sox would win this thing. Red Sox fans didn't have to wait long, because David Ortiz led off the home half of the 10th with a home run into the Monster seats. Game over. Sox win, 6-5.

"I think both the home run and the game were by far the biggest thrills of my life to this point," Walker said. "Just the way it happened and the circumstance. I think a win like that can carry us a long way."

I could listen to Walker talk all night.

And I'll never forget the scene at home plate following the home run by Ortiz. As soon as bat hit ball, Ortiz turned to the dugout as if to say, "Let's go home, guys!" The ball soared, and the crowd roared. By the time Ortiz rounded third, the entire team had surrounded home plate and was waiting to slap him on the back. Ortiz did a little slide step before stomping on home plate with both feet, and his circle of friends began jumping in unison. It was a jubilant sea of red sweatshirts and jackets bobbing, bouncing, and laughing together—as a team. It was a contagious kind of joy—a beautiful thing.

Meanwhile, the Mariners just don't have the requisite magic. While the Red Sox were rallying back to win in dramatic fashion once again, the Mariners lost to the Angels when Tim Salmon homered off Shigetoshi Hasegawa in the 11th inning. The Mariners have been swimming upstream ever since the Red Sox swept them at Fenway Park, and Salmon's home run left them "dead in the water." The Mariners have gone 38-43 since June 27, blowing an eight-game lead over the A's in the process.

The Red Sox magic number is two. Get ready for Octoberfest! The Red Sox are going to the postseason.

SEPTEMBER 24

If I told you the Red Sox bullpen threw 8 2/3 innings tonight, you would probably assume one of three things. First, the game went into extra innings. Second, there was an injury to the starting pitcher. Or third, that John Burkett got pounded like a tenderized piece of meat.

If you picked option three, you're right.

Burkett only retired one batter before he was the one retired for the night. By the time the Red Sox came to bat in the first inning, they were already in a seven-run hole. Six of those runs were charged to Burkett, whose chance of starting a postseason game was greatly reduced.

The Red Sox only got three of those runs back, while the bullpen shut down the Orioles the rest of the way. The Mariners had lost earlier in the day, so there had been a chance the Red Sox could clinch the wild card, but that celebration will have to wait.

The Red Sox, who established a single-season record for total bases with 2,749, will play their final home game tomorrow, and it sure would be nice to clinch in front of the home crowd.

SEPTEMBER 25

I've been a bridesmaid before. I want to be a bride.
—Red Sox relief pitcher Alan Embree

A team that set so many offensive records *should* clinch like this. Two runs in the first. Five in the second, including a solo shot from Jason Varitek and a three-run blast from Nomar Garciaparra. Two more runs in the third. And a three-run homer from Kevin Millar in the fourth. And all the while, Derek Lowe was tossing a no-hitter for 4 1/3. The night turned into a New Year's Rockin' Eve bash with 34,000 people waiting for the ball to drop (not the other shoe). Everybody knew midnight was going to come, but the celebration couldn't start until the final out. Ramiro Mendoza, called upon to pitch with an 11-run lead, got Brian Roberts on a called third strike, and it was time to party!

Players rushed out onto the field, coming together at the pitcher's mound, where they traded hugs and congratulatory pats on the back. On cue, the stadium speakers blared The Standells' hit, "Dirty Water." Champagne bottles opened, and the customary dousing began.

Manny Ramirez suddenly became "Mister Talkative." Surrounded by a group of reporters at home plate, he said, "I've been to the playoffs like four times. And this time I want to win it all. To win it here for these fans would be unbelievable."

Back on the mound, David Ortiz and Kevin Millar were working up a little dance number. Derek Lowe sprayed fans behind the first base dugout. Trot Nixon spoke on one fan's cell phone. Even Scott Sauerbeck received high fives and group hugs from fans along the base lines.

"This is the reason why a player chooses Boston, the way they support you," center fielder Johnny Damon said. "We're definitely going to do it this year."

Nomar Garciaparra seemed to enjoy celebrating with the fans more than with his teammates, though he did that as well. But his first priority seemed to be to let the fans know how much he appreciated their support. He did a victory lap around the outfield, carrying postseason hats and T-shirts with him and tossing them into the crowd.

"This is a great night for them. And this is really for them. But we know we have a lot left to do," Garciaparra said.

Even with the smell of victory cigars emanating throughout the clubhouse, and Manny Ramirez spraying everyone in his path with a water hose, and Todd Jones pouring champagne on an appreciative John Henry, the team seemed to appropriately temper its jubilance with thoughts about wanting to accomplish so much more.

Jason Varitek explained that unsatisfied feeling this way, "I like this team, and this is really great. But I think I'll like our next celebrations a little better."

Meanwhile, *this* celebration continued for a couple of hours. John Burkett, savvy veteran that he is, wore goggles in the locker room—explaining that it gave him a decided advantage in the champagne wars. Grady Little had champagne poured over his head while I interviewed him, and I asked if that ever got annoying. He said "No," and offered to pour some on my head as well. Truth be told, I wanted to share in the celebration, but I declined his offer. I regret that.

The celebration spilled into the streets when Kevin Millar, Derek Lowe, Todd Walker, Lou Merloni, and Gabe Kapler ran down Yawkey Way with some 500 people right on their heels. It was a scene reminiscent of Rocky Balboa running through the streets of Philadelphia. The fans chanted "Bring on Oakland," and players ducked into a local bar where they passed out free drinks to several customers.

This was a great night! But it's only phase one in a four-phase process. Make the playoffs. Beat the A's. Win the ALCS. And bring home the first World Series championship since 1918.

It's a new century. A new Red Sox team. And there is cause for new hope!

By the way, the Yankees clinched the division title two days earlier, meaning that for the sixth year in a row the American League East finished in this order: New York, Boston, Toronto, Baltimore, and Tampa Bay.

SEPTEMBER 26

On their magical mystery tour to the postseason, the Red Sox received their fair share—and occasionally not-so-fair share—of criticism. Grady Little heard plenty of it. Manny, Nomar, Pedro, and most emphatically, the bullpen got two ears full. But the bloodsport of criticism may have gone a bit too far when people began judging and condemning the Red Sox for being too happy. That's what happened around Boston following the team's uncommonly jubilant wild-card celebration. Was it overdone? Did they celebrate too much? Not a chance.

Champagne, cigars, and congratulations are standard operating procedure after clinching a playoff berth of any kind. Where the Red Sox took it to the next level was their inclusion of the fans. Running around the base paths and in the streets, dancing on the pitcher's mound, and passing out wild-card T-shirts and hats were done for the fans. If the players wanted to tone down their public celebration, they could have quickly disappeared into the clubhouse, gotten drunk, and boarded the bus for the airport. Instead, they prolonged the celebration in order to share it with the thousands of fans who stuck around to see it.

And in case anybody missed it, the Yankees uncorked six cases of champagne when they clinched the Eastern Division title. They poured it all over each other. They drank a lot of beer. They whooped and hollered. They had a shaving cream fight. And they passed out T-shirts that read, "Six in a Row Eastern Division Champions." Now, are we supposed to believe there's a difference between winning the division and winning the wild card? All the Yankees did, like the Red Sox, was get into the playoffs, something they've done nine years in a row. And nobody tried to deny them their moment of happiness. The fact that they clinched in Detroit may also be the reason their celebration wasn't of a greater magnitude. The Red Sox celebration was certainly more on the wild side, but how much wilder was it really? And what's with all the derision toward a team that merely smiled too much, or hugged a little too long?

Grady Little said, "I heard a lot of talk today that maybe we celebrated too much. That's the most ridiculous thing I've ever heard. That's probably from somebody who's never been in that situation before. Or else it's somebody who just really didn't want us to win. That's what it boils down to. It's somebody that's mad that the Red Sox won and they're getting ready to play in October."

I don't disagree. There are far too many people who call themselves Red Sox fans, but they're so angry with the team due to years of frustration, that they really don't want the team to win. Their relationship with the team is: the team loses, and they complain about it. When that doesn't happen, these so-called fans don't know how to react. And if anybody thought that looked like a World Series celebration, they should wait a few weeks to see how one of those really looks in Boston.

Regarding tonight's game, the Red Sox got themselves ready for the playoffs with a 7-2 win over the Devil Rays. It was their 95th win—the first time the Red Sox have won that many games since advancing to the World Series in 1986.

Pedro Martinez threw three shutout innings—51 pitches, two K's. He's ready. The three innings were all about the work. Pedro had thrown 353 pitches in his previous three starts. So, a short night should go a long way when he opens the series against Oakland on Wednesday. Pedro finished the season with an American League-leading ERA of 2.22.

John Burkett, who only got to pitch to eight batters two nights ago, also got some work in. Three innings, two runs allowed, while picking up his 12th win of the year. It'll be interesting to see if he gets a postseason start.

SEPTEMBER 27

The Red Sox are in Florida playing games that don't matter, in front of small crowds, using guys who spend most of their time on the bench.

Sounds a lot like spring training. But the Sox aren't getting ready for opening day. It's *closing time* on the regular season. And it's a good thing this game didn't count, because the Red Sox lost on what would have been a controversial call—if anybody really cared.

With the Sox trailing 5-4 in the ninth, David McCarty sent a shot to deep left-center field. The ball was caught—but not by a Tampa Bay outfielder. Instead, a fan hauled it in. I've seen at least five different replays, and it's impossible to tell if the fan reached over the fence, or if the ball would have cleared the fence anyway. But second base umpire Joe West, who was at least 150 feet away, called it fan interference. Now, the rule states that if the ball isn't catchable, the umpire can put the runner where he thinks the runner would have ended up. Or, if he thinks the outfielder would have caught the ball, he can call the batter out. West determined from his disadvantaged vantage point that Carl Crawford would have caught the ball. Instead of a game-tying home run, McCarty was out, and the game ended one batter later.

The fence at Tropicana Field is 11 feet 5 inches high, and Crawford wasn't even close to the fan's glove. But the only person in the ballpark who was genuinely upset about the call seemed to be Sox catcher Doug Mirabelli. He was ejected for shouting from the dugout.

I'm convinced that West wouldn't have made the same call if the game mattered. But in the ninth inning of game 162, he made a call that prevented extra innings. That's just what I think.

In New York, Roger Clemens finished his regular-season career with his 310th win. Clemens gave up two runs in six innings and returned to the hill for the start of the seventh. But before he threw his first pitch of the inning, Joe Torre went out to get him. That way, Clemens was able to leave to a standing ovation. A nice move by Torre! Clemens finished with a career record of 310-160 with a 3.19 ERA. He's one of the best ever.

The Red Sox announced today that Tim Wakefield will start Game Two against the A's. The primary reason for the move is the disparity between Derek Lowe's record at home and on the road. Lowe was 11-2 with a 3.21 ERA at Fenway Park—where he'll start Game Three. On the road, he was 6-5 with a 6.11 ERA.

"I've had all kinds of numbers in front of me the last three or four days, and I'm sure I'll have a lot more between now and Wednesday," Grady Little said. "One of the most important factors was infield pop outs, fair or foul. Wakefield's had 75 this year, and Derek Lowe's had 12."

Now, that's research!

SEPTEMBER 28

There was a bottle of champagne waiting for Bill Mueller after today's game, a gift from Tim Wakefield on behalf of the team.

"We have a great group of people here," said Mueller. "It just goes to show what type of people they are. Everyone in here has had a great year."

But no one else in the American League has had as high a batting average. Mueller went 0-for-1 today. Manny Ramirez did not play. And the Yankees' Derek Jeter went 0-for-3 in his game. So, the batting race finished this way: Mueller, .326, Ramirez .325, and Jeter .324.

Mueller's batting average is the lowest for an American League champion since Minnesota's Rod Carew hit .318 in 1972.

Back in New York, Roger Clemens got to be "manager for a day," and David Wells won his 200th game. As manager, it was Clemens's job to pull Wells in the eighth inning. The Rocket signaled to the bullpen, then gave Wells a hug. Boomer left to a standing ovation, and finished the season with 15 wins and only 20 walks in 213 innings.

The Yankees finished with 101 victories, tying the Braves for the most in baseball, and bettering the Red Sox by six games. The Yankees went 16-5 down the stretch. But again, the only teams they played in September with a winning record were Boston and Chicago. And they lost both of those series.

The Yankees and their first-round opponents—the Twins—had similar finishes. Minnesota went 19-7 in September, but they played 13 games against Cleveland and Detroit. In fact, other than seven games against Chicago, they hadn't faced a team with a winning record since July 22. So, while it's true the Twins went 46-23 in the second half—going from five games under .500 at the break to the Central Division champions—it's hard to tell if they can stand up to the Yankees. Especially when you consider the Yankees have won 13 straight against the Twins over the past two years.

SEPTEMBER 30

Sports fans are big-game hunters. We think we're sitting in front of a television with a bowl of trail mix balanced precariously on our midsections, but we're really driving around with a deer on the hood. We tell ourselves that we're keeping track of scores around the league, but we're really tracking bighorn sheep and pronghorn antelope. We think it's a remote control in our hands, but it's really a Browning Gold Hunter, or a Remington 870 Magnum. We're hunting big game! Only the best will do. Let Elmer Fudd hunt rabbits. We're after caribou, mule deer, and something called javelina. (Obviously, I looked all this stuff up. The only thing I've ever shot is skeet—and in order to be as politically correct as possible, we ate it and made clothes from it.) Anyway, it turns out a javelina is just another name for a collared peccary, which is another name for a tayaussa, which is another name for a musk hog. Basically, it's a pig. So, I don't even know why it was on the page that listed big game. It doesn't look like anything you'd have to shoot. It's so ugly, I think it would want to die.

Anyway—it's big game we're after! And the biggest is the "Cougar Game." No predator species exhibits more intelligence, furtiveness, and eagle vision than the big cats (that was on the same page as the javelina information). Now that the baseball playoffs have begun, every game is a Cougar Game.

The Minnesota Twins waltzed right into that lion's den known as Yankee Stadium, and lived to tell about it. That's because the Yankees uncharacteristically played like a team that had never been to the postseason. They were sloppy and uninspired. But more importantly, they were without magic. It appears the bloom is off their rose, and the shine is off whatever it is that shines, because this was one of those games the Yankees usually win.

The Yankees had won 13 straight against Minnesota, and New York's Game One starter, Mike Mussina, has a 20-2 lifetime record against the Twins. So, the decided advantage heading into the game belonged to New York.

Then of course, after Twins' starter, Johan Santana, had thrown four shutout innings, he was forced to leave the game with tightness in his right hamstring. Santana was overpowering the Yankees, so naturally the baseball gods conspired to get him out of the game.

"The phone rang and we were like, 'Oh, my God,'" said Twins reliever LaTroy Hawkins.

But the Twins bullpen threw four more shutout innings, giving the Twins a 3-0 lead heading into the bottom of the ninth inning.

Bernie Williams led off with a single. Here comes the Yankees rally!

Hideki Matsui hit a long drive to the left-field corner. It looked like it might have enough to go the distance, but Twins leftfielder Shannon Stewart leaped and snared the ball just as it was about to hit the top of the wall. That's a double in most Yankees games, but today it was a crucial out.

"At first I was like, 'Whew,'" said Twins catcher A. J. Pierzynski, "and then I was thinking, 'Thank God, not Jeffrey Maier'" a reference to the boy who reached over the fence to catch Derek Jeter's home run in the 1996 playoffs. But the Yankees wouldn't be so lucky this time.

Aaron Boone was up next, and he *did* double to left, moving Williams to third. It sure looked as if the Yankees were going to produce another miracle comeback.

Ruben Sierra flied to shallow right—no advance for the runners. Now there were two outs, but the potential tying run was at the plate.

Alfonso Soriano hit a slow roller to second and beat it out for an infield single. That was a little bit of magic! Runners were on the corners for Nick Johnson, with the Yankees trailing, 3-1. Johnson grounded out to end it.

The Yankees not only failed in the clutch, they gave the game away. In the sixth inning, Torii Hunter hit a low line drive to right-center field. Bernie Williams misread how hard the ball had been hit, and it skipped past him to the wall, allowing Matthew LeCroy to score from first base. Soriano took the relay throw in the outfield, and fired the ball well over Boone's head at third base trying to get Hunter. Instead, Hunter trotted home to give the Twins their 3-0 lead.

I'll tell you, if I were a Yankees fan, not only would I have thrown up in my mouth, I would be rather upset over Mussina's postgame assessment.

"I'm OK with the way I pitched," Mussina said. "I got out of a jam early and a bases-loaded one after that. It's playoff baseball, so you know the games are low scoring and you just want to get a few runs. We couldn't do it."

He also said, "When the game gets sloppy and the ball gets thrown around a little bit that makes it tough."

In both statements, he subtly laid the blame on his teammates. Allow me to paraphrase: they were sloppy, and they didn't score enough runs. Otherwise, we might have won, because I pitched pretty well.

Is that how a champion talks? Shouldn't he have said something more along the lines of, "I made a few too many mistakes and the Twins were able to capitalize on them. If I hadn't made those mistakes, we probably would have won that game."

Hear me now and listen to me later, Pedro Martinez. I don't want to hear you saying anything "Moose"-like after Game One against the A's tomorrow. Even if you give up an unearned run in a 1-0 loss, I don't want to hear you say that you're "OK with the way (you) pitched." Just win, baby!

That's right, tomorrow is October, and the Red Sox are still playing baseball. The first three playoff games today finished with scores of 3-1, 2-0 (Giants over Marlins), and 4-2 (Cubs over Braves). Pitching has been the story so far, and that should certainly continue with Pedro facing Tim Hudson. Martinez has only made four appearances in the postseason, and he's 3-0 with a 1.13 ERA. And Hudson, of course, is the guy who fired a two-hit shutout at the Red Sox on August 11. This one has "instant classic" written all over it.

12

Octoberfest

OCTOBER 1

Why should the playoffs be any different than the regular season? Pedro Martinez went seven innings. The offense rallied back with a clutch home run. And the bullpen couldn't close it out. It was one of the greatest playoff games ever, but it was also the same old song and dance.

It all began well enough. When Todd Walker took Tim Hudson deep in the first inning, I shouted, "He hit it high. He hit it deep. He hit it gone! Game over!" It may have been a bit premature to declare the game over with only one out in the first inning, but that's the kind of confidence I had in Pedro tonight. I truly believed he would paint his masterpiece.

Instead, after Manny Ramirez bounced to second with the bases loaded in the third inning, the A's responded by taking a 3-1 lead in the home half of the inning. It became increasingly obvious that Pedro just didn't have a strikeout pitch tonight. Batters weren't swinging and missing. Certainly Erubiel Durazo didn't miss when he stroked a two-run double. And Miguel Tejada didn't miss when he shot a line drive back through the middle with two outs. The Red Sox suddenly trailed, but they were hitting Hudson (five hits through the first three innings). So there was reason to believe.

In the fifth, Jason Varitek lifted a one-out homer to the seats in the right-field bleachers. That made it 3-2, Oakland. But with runners on the corners and two away, Ramirez bounced out to short to end the inning. If you're counting, that's five men stranded by Ramirez. He went 0-for-5 dropping his postseason batting average to .249 and his Division Series batting average to .182.

Meanwhile, the highly anticipated classic pitching matchup wasn't materializing. Both starters labored to keep the game close. Pedro allowed three runs in the third, threw a runner out at the plate in the fifth, and loaded the bases in the seventh. And for Hudson's part, it became evident in the fifth inning that he was pitching in some discomfort due to tightness in his right forearm and thumb caused by dehydration.

Hudson finally left the game with two outs and a runner on in the seventh. Todd Walker, who was 3-for-3 with a home run against him, was the next batter. So, the A's brought in their best lefty in the pen, Ricardo Rincon. Gone!

Todd Walker blasted his second home run of the game, and I couldn't help but mutter, "This truly is a team of destiny." However, the Sox lead was only 4-3, and it was obvious that Pedro's pitch count would preclude him from going beyond the seventh inning, unless it was an especially quick inning. It wasn't.

The inning began with a single to left by Ramon Hernandez. Then on a "custom made" double play ball, Walker threw the ball into the dugout. He's forgiven. But instead of two outs and nobody on, there was one out, and the tying run was at second.

An out and a walk later, Pedro was looking at another confrontation with Durazo. It turned into an 11-pitch at bat, with Durazo fouling off fastball after fastball. Finally, Pedro threw the deuce, and Durazo chased it in the dirt. But he was able to check his swing for ball four, and the bases were loaded for Eric Chavez. That turned into a one-pitch at bat, with Chavez popping up to third. It was Pedro's 130th pitch, a season high, and he was done for the night. He had battled like the warrior he is. But if he were truly on top of his game, 130 pitches would have been a complete game. But Pedro was not at his very best. He finished with more walks (four) than strikeouts (three).

The Red Sox stranded more runners in the eighth. Bill Mueller doubled Ortiz to third with one out, and when David McCarty was sent up to pinch hit for Trot Nixon against Rincon, A's skipper Ken Macha called on his underhand throwing righty, Chad Bradford. Grady Little did the double switch, and sent his only left-hander on the bench, Adrian Brown, up to face Bradford. Again, the choices were Nixon against Rincon, McCarty against Bradford, or Brown against Bradford. All the Red Sox needed was contact. Nixon, having missed 13 of the final 18 games with a calf strain, looked awful in his first three at bats, so I don't quarrel with pinch hitting for him against the lefty. But McCarty has been swinging a hot bat off the bench—hitting .340 in 24 games with the Red Sox. Brown was just 3-for-15 with four strikeouts since being called up from

Pawtucket. However, in their big-league careers, Brown has struck out once every 7.2 at bats, and McCarty strikes out once every four at bats. So, if it's contact you want, maybe you go with the left-handed-hitting guy who strikes out a lot less. Brown struck out.

After Varitek was intentionally walked to load the bases, Johnny Damon chopped to third to end the inning.

Mike Timlin pitched a 1-2-3 eighth inning. And A's closer extraordinaire Keith Foulke pitched a scoreless eighth and ninth, setting the stage for Byung-Hyun Kim to try to close out a 4-3 game in the ninth. And he couldn't do it. And it's the *way* he couldn't do it that is so maddening!

With one out, he walked light-hitting Billy McMillon on four pitches. Throw a strike! Then he hit the also light-hitting Chris Singleton. Throw a strike! Then he struck out Mark Ellis. Thank you.

But with the left-handed swinging Durazo coming up, Little made the same move he had on September 19 against Cleveland. He brought in Alan Embree. I can't argue with the move. Embree isn't exactly deadly against left-handers, but when Kim is obviously struggling, he has to be taken out.

Durazo singled to left to tie the game, and the game was almost lost when Eric Chavez grounded to short. The game-winning run was on third, and Nomar Garciaparra uncorked a high throw that pulled Kevin Millar off the bag. Fortunately, Millar was able to get back to the bag in time for the third out. We headed into extra innings.

Foulke stayed in the game through the 10th, finishing up with three shutout innings. Scott Williamson pitched the 10th for the Red Sox. And then, in yet another show of complete lack of faith in his bullpen, Little brought in Derek Lowe to pitch the 11th. Lowe, of course, is scheduled to start Game Three back in Boston, but his arm is resilient enough to go about two innings tonight. But who expected to see him trotting out to the bullpen tonight? Not me.

Lowe, acting as a Red Sox reliever should, walked the first batter he faced. But he escaped the 11th inning without a problem. In the 12th, though, there were problems—first, with the Red Sox offense. Manny led off with a walk and moved to second on a wild pitch by Rich Harden. So, the go-ahead run was on second with nobody out. Ortiz and Millar both made outs, and Manny was still loitering at second. Bill Mueller was intentionally walked, which brought up Gabe Kapler. Kapler hit a rope down the third base line that Eric Chavez made some kind of Brooks Robinson-ian play on to keep the ball from turning into a two-run double. Instead, Chavez hopped off his belly and raced Manny to the third base bag. Chavez got there first, and the inning was over. Too many squandered opportunities for the Red Sox in this one. They left 13 men on base, seven in scoring position.

Again, Lowe gave up a leadoff walk to start the 12th. But that shouldn't have been a problem, because Chavez hit a sharp two-hopper to second. Double play? No. The Sox can't turn it—just too slow around the second base bag between Damian Jackson (a defensive replacement) and Nomar. Then with Chavez running, Tejada grounded to third. Two outs and a man on second. A's first baseman Scott Hatteburg walked as Chavez was stealing third. The winning run was 90 feet away. The first pitch to Terrance Long was a strike, and Hatteburg advanced to second on the ever-popular defensive indifference. Now, with first base open, Little orders Long walked. The A's had successfully loaded the bases without ever getting the ball out of the infield. And then they won the game with a ball that traveled about 30 feet up the third base line.

It was a beautiful squeeze bunt by the A's slow-footed catcher Ramon Hernandez. Mueller came charging in from deep third, and pretty much took a big bite out of the ball as Chavez crossed home plate. The A's squeezed by the Red Sox in a tension-filled 12-inning classic! Damn!

"It was the biggest hit in my career," said Hernandez. "When you're playing a team like the Red Sox that's got good pitching and good hitting, you've got to try whatever you can to win."

It took four hours and 37 minutes to refill my heart with anger and angst, and my head with doubts.

OCTOBER 2

It was the Day of the Lefty. Barry Zito threw his "twelve-six" curveball all day, and Andy Pettitte won his 11th postseason game, passing Whitey Ford (another lefty) on the Yankees' all-time list. The A's took a commanding 2-0 lead in their series against the Red Sox with a 5-1 win, while the Yankees beat the Twins 4-1, evening that series at one game apiece.

Zito was what a defending Cy Young Award winner is supposed to be—the winning pitcher. He went seven innings, striking out nine batters and allowing just one run. His job was made a bit easier by the fact that the teams took batting practice about 10 hours after last night's game ended. It's a strange schedule that had the Sox and A's playing late on Wednesday and then again Thursday afternoon. But Sox starter Tim Wakefield had the same advantage against the A's hitters. And while Wakefield was effective (six innings, seven Ks), he wasn't nearly as sharp as Zito and his curve.

"Zito pitched a great game," Nomar Garciaparra said. "He put us against the wall, but we've been there before."

Yes, they have. The Red Sox are one of only three American League teams to come back from a 2-0 hole in the best-of-five Division Series. In 1999, Boston lost the first two to Cleveland and came roaring back to win three straight—only to be eliminated by the Yankees in the championship series in five games.

Also, the A's have been here before, too. They took the first two games of the 2001 Division Series against the Yankees, only to drop the next three.

"Anyone who was around in 2001 knows we can't take anything for granted," said Eric Byrnes. "I guarantee that nobody in here has thought beyond today's game."

Still, if the Red Sox are going to mount a comeback, they're going to need a lot more from the heart of their order. Manny Ramirez, David Ortiz, and Kevin Millar are a combined 3-for-27 in the first two games, and they're still looking for their first RBI.

All in all, not a good day. But what would you expect on the 25th anniversary of Bucky Dent's home run that beat the Red Sox in a one-game playoff against the Yankees?

OCTOBER 3

Flying home from Oakland, the Red Sox remained predictably confident that they'd be flying back to Oakland for a Game Five. Nothing seems to shake this team. They win. They play hard. They lose. They play hard. And they always seem to be worry free. I wish their confidence was just a little bit more contagious. Personally, I feel very confident the Sox will win Game Three, and extremely confident about Game Five. But it's that Game Four I'm worried about. That's when John Burkett starts against Tim Hudson. There hasn't been a mismatch that bad since Julia Roberts married Lyle Lovett. And obviously, without winning Game Four the Red Sox can't take Game Five.

Here's how it's shaping up. Derek Lowe goes up against Oakland lefty Ted Lilly. And the numbers are on the Lowe side. Lowe is 20-6 with a 2.68 ERA at Fenway Park over the past two seasons. He was 11-2 there this year. And while it's true that Lilly won six of his final seven starts, it's equally true that the Red Sox knocked him around on August 20 to the tune of 10 hits and six runs in just 3 1/2 innings. That's a nice tune.

There's some concern that because Lowe pitched two innings of relief in the first game, his effectiveness and durability will be affected in tomorrow's start, but Lowe says the relief appearance actually helped him.

"As crazy as it sounds," he said. "My last start was last Thursday, so I was looking at nine days' worth of rest and, for a starting pitcher, that's a long time not to get in the game. I felt a little rusty two days ago and hopefully the rust has worn off. As far as the number of pitches goes, that won't affect me this time of year. You could pitch significantly more pitches and still be ready for Saturday. Saturday night, the crowd is going to be electric. If anything, the crowd will push you through it."

No doubt the Red Sox fans will be doing their part to "cowboy up." That's the phrase Sox players have adopted as their rallying cry. Fitting. It's a term used by rodeo riders who get thrown, but get right back on the horse. Mike Timlin got it started when he made "Cowboy Up" T-shirts for his teammates a few months ago, but Kevin Millar made it popular.

"I think for this team it's perfect," Millar said. "Me and Trot Nixon have used that saying since we were playing winter ball in Mexico back in '95. A cowboy is just like your tough guy, the guy that falls off the horse, broken arms and all that kind of stuff."

And now it's time for the Red Sox to pick themselves up, dust themselves off, and start all over again with a three-game winning streak. Or else they will have not lived up to their destiny.

OCTOBER 4

A gift this big probably needs to be reported to the IRS. The A's did everything they could to blow this game, but it took a blow from Trot Nixon in the 11th inning to finally keep hope alive for the Red Sox.

With the Red Sox desperately needing to get their offense jump-started, it looked as if they were ready to jump on Ted Lilly in the first inning. Johnny Damon led off with a double, and Nomar Garciaparra followed with a walk. I was thinking, "Here we go!" And then the momentum was gone. Bill Mueller, Manny Ramirez, and David Ortiz all struck out.

So, the Sox tried again in the second. Kevin Millar started with an infield single. Jason Varitek hit a potential double-play ball to short, but Miguel Tejada bobbled it. Everybody's safe. Gabe Kapler grounded to third, where Eric Chavez scooped it up, stepped on third for the out, and then threw the ball away. Runners were on the corners. Then, Damian Jackson grounded to third, and Varitek got caught in a rundown. But on his way back to third, Chavez got in his way. Interference was called, and Varitek was allowed to score. By the time the inning was over, the A's had committed three errors, and the Sox had scored only one run.

Then it got weird.

With the Red Sox clinging to a 1-0 lead in the sixth inning, Oakland's Eric Byrnes stood on third base with one out. Tejada tapped back to the pitcher. Lowe had no chance to get Byrnes, who was running on contact, but he threw home anyway. Byrnes slid into Jason Varitek's left leg and bounced around in a cloud of dust. The ball skipped to the backstop, and while Byrnes began to limp off the field, Varitek ran back to get the ball and tagged Byrnes. The home plate umpire signaled that Byrnes was out, because he had never touched the plate! Replays showed the call was correct. Varitek had successfully blocked home plate, and Byrnes was apparently unaware he had failed to do the most basic thing. Of course, Varitek had actually tagged Byrnes with his glove while the ball was in his bare hand. But nobody seemed to notice, or they just didn't care.

Still in the sixth, Oakland managed to load the bases, and Ramon Hernandez hit a chopper to Nomar Garciaparra's right. Nomar tried to backhand a tough in-between hop, but the ball snuck under his glove. The runner from third scored easily, but Tejada bumped into Mueller on his way around third base. The umpire immediately indicated that interference had occurred, and Tejada stopped running in between third base and home plate. Manny Ramirez's throw came in, and Varitek tagged out a motionless Tejada, who thought he would be allowed to score because of the interference call. But that's not so.

As we learned in rule 7.06 (b), the umpire has the discretion to award an extra base to an obstructed runner.

"The runner is in peril to be put out," said Steve Palermo, a baseball umpire supervisor. "(Third base umpire) Bill Welke determined that Miguel Tejada would not have scored if there had not been obstruction."

But the only reason Welke made that determination is that Tejada stopped running and was out by 15 feet. If Tejada had continued to go full speed, he might have been safe. And even if he had been out by a few feet, Welke could have reasonably assumed that he would have been safe if it weren't for the interference at third. Tejada blew it by not running hard, and by not knowing the rule.

It was a blunder nearly equivalent to Fred "Bonehead" Merkle's in 1908. The New York Giants first baseman failed to touch second base on an apparent game-winning hit against the Cubs. The game ultimately ended in a 1-1 tie, and the teams finished the season with identical records. Chicago won both the makeup game and the pennant, and Merkle became infamous. Now we have Bonehead Tejada.

Remember though, the A's did score one run on the play, so the score was tied 1-1 after six innings. In the seventh, Oakland loaded the bases with one out, but failed to score when Billy McMillon lined to second and Durazo lined to center. Meanwhile, the Red Sox hadn't gotten a hit off Lilly since the second inning.

Both starters left after the seventh, so it was going to be a battle of the bullpens. That's a battle the Red Sox don't often win, but they were perfect on this night. Mike Timlin, who routinely went two innings early in the season, but hadn't been asked to get more than five outs in a game since the middle of June, put down nine A's in a row. He was immense! Three perfect innings!

But guess who was warming up in the bullpen in the ninth inning? It was none other than Pedro Martinez. Grady Little said after the game that Pedro would have only been used for one inning if the Red Sox had had the lead in the ninth. That didn't happen, but it was nice to see him up, considering he's scheduled to start Game Five in two days.

Three innings were all the Red Sox could ask for from Timlin. So, Little went to Scott Williamson in the top of the 11th inning. Williamson added to the perfection with a 1-2-3 inning, including a pair of strikeouts.

Oakland manager Ken Macha called upon rookie flamethrower Rich Harden to face the Red Sox, who had scored just five runs in 31 innings up to this point. Harden only got to throw nine pitches, the first two to Kevin Millar, who popped up. Doug Mirabelli singled on the third pitch he saw. Then Trot Nixon, called upon to pinch hit, stroked a 1-1 pitch into the center field bleachers. Game over! Sox win, 3-1.

Nixon pumped his fist in the air as he rounded first base, and by the time he came around to score, the entire Red Sox team was there waiting to pounce on him in celebration. Nixon, who had been playing whiffleball in the Red Sox weight room to help his eye-hand coordination just minutes before the home run, called it the biggest hit of his life.

"He was waiting for that pitch, I guess," Harden said. "I give him credit."

All of Red Sox Nation was waiting for that pitch, and it turned into one of the biggest home runs in Red Sox history. Some will compare it to Bernie Carbo's eighth inning home run off Rawley Eastwick in Game Six of the 1975 World Series, because Carbo was also pinch hitting, and the balls traveled to the same general area, some 400 feet away in straightaway center. But Carbo's home run only tied the game, and was merely a prelude to Carlton Fisk's game winner in the 12th. Still, it was the World Series and not the wild-card round, so both of those homers would be of greater magnitude than Nixon's blast. But this one felt pretty darn good, too.

Carbo, by the way, only had three hits in seven at bats during the 1975 World Series, and two of the hits were pinch-hit home runs. When he rounded the bases in the eighth inning of Game Six, he shouted toward Cincinnati Reds third baseman Pete Rose, "Don't you wish you were this strong? Don't you wish you were this strong?" And Rose yelled back, "Isn't this a great game? Isn't this fun?"

It *was* fun until the Red Sox blew a 3-0 lead in Game Seven, finally losing 4-3 on a ninth-inning single by Joe Morgan. The Red Sox really have been SOOOO close!

And they're getting close again after one of the most bizarre and glorious baseball games ever.

"I have never seen two obstruction plays in the same game, never," said former Major League Baseball umpire Steve Palermo. "You might not see one obstruction play in a month, two months, or even an entire season. It's not a play that happens very often."

And you think this stuff just happens? It's fate, I tell you. The A's should be celebrating right now, except that they committed four errors and made two huge baserunning gaffes. And isn't it a strange rule that doesn't allow Tejada to score, but when Varitek was interfered with on his way *back* to third base, he was turned around and sent home? Strange but true—just like the Red Sox season.

High praise should be passed around to Derek Lowe, Mike Timlin, and of course Trot Nixon, but it should also be noted that there's no meat in either of these lineups. Manny Ramirez and David Ortiz are a combined 1-for-25. And Tejada and Eric Chavez are 1-for-29 so far.

Finally, Byung-Hyun Kim flipped off the crowd during pregame introductions. The crowd booed him, so he responded by subtly raising his hand toward his cap while simultaneously raising his middle finger. Kim may have thrown his last pitch for the Red Sox.

OCTOBER 5

David Ortiz was in an 0-for-16 slump during the postseason. Going back to the regular season, Ortiz was also in a 1-for-31 slump against Oakland pitching. He was facing Keith Foulke, who led the American League with 43 saves. And he admitted later, he couldn't really see the ball, because of an extremely tough sun. So, of course, Ortiz hit a game-winning two-out, two-run double on a 3-2 pitch in the eighth inning! I mean, what would you expect him to do?

Ortiz was second in the American League with 16 game-winning runs batted in during the regular season. Twenty-four times his hits gave the Red Sox a lead, and he had 42 two-out RBI. It was another last-at-bat victory for the Red

Sox—their second in a row and the 25th time they've done it this year.

"I don't think I was struggling," said Ortiz. "I'm just not hitting the ball where I want it. Everybody knows this is the best pitching in the American League. If I was struggling, I don't think I would have hit the ball to win the game. Don't give up on me, people. Come on."

Who could give up on this team now? With their 5-4 win today, the Red Sox have evened the series at two games apiece and will have Pedro Martinez starting the fifth and deciding game in Oakland tomorrow. If there's such a thing as day-to-day momentum in baseball, the Red Sox have it. And if, as they say, momentum is only as good as the next day's starting pitcher, the Red Sox have that, too. The Red Sox are in perfect position to complete the comeback.

"My heart is racing," Sox starter John Burkett said. "I can barely talk. It's unbelievable. I've never felt like this."

Burkett deserves a lot of credit for keeping the Red Sox in the game, but he was long gone by the time Ortiz banged a one-hopper off the wall in right. And so was Oakland starter Tim Hudson. The Red Sox first break of the day came when Hudson, pitching on three days' rest, couldn't start the second inning. He had a strained oblique muscle in his left side. So, after retiring the side in order in the first, his day was done.

The Red Sox couldn't really take advantage of their good fortune, though. Knuckleballer Steve Sparks came in and gave the A's four solid innings, allowing just a two-run homer to Johnny Damon. Burkett had a 2-1 lead going into the sixth inning, and Grady Little may have left him in for one batter too many. That batter was Jermaine Dye, who ripped a three-run homer into the Monster seats in left. Oakland led 4-2 and needed just 12 more outs to finish the Red Sox season.

But Ricardo Rincon relieved Sparks in the Red Sox sixth, and for the second time in the series, Todd Walker took him deep. That made it a one-run game and set the stage for Ortiz's heroics in the eighth.

Ken Macha pulled Rincon and handed the ball over to Foulke for the final six outs. But Foulke is not your typical closer. He's effective, but not dominant, and his best pitch is a change-up. After throwing 51 pitches during three scoreless innings in Game One, Foulke came back and threw 20 more pitches while picking up the save in Game Two. That's a lot of work for a closer, and it served as an opportunity for the Red Sox to begin to figure him out.

Nomar Garciaparra stroked a one-out double to deep center, and one out later, Manny Ramirez hit a sharp single to left. Combined, Nomar and Manny were 4-for-26 against Foulke. Still, against all odds, runners were on the corners with two down as David Ortiz stepped to the plate looking for his first hit of the series. Inexplicably, Ortiz never saw Foulke's signature pitch—the change-up. In fact, he barely saw any of Foulke's pitches.

"I was talking about it with somebody," Ortiz said later. "I told them all you see is a black point coming right at me."

But seeing the ball is so overrated! And Ortiz put a good swing on a 3-2 pitch and lifted the ball deep toward the warning track in right field. The ball hung in the air for an inordinately long time—almost too long—as Dye raced over to try to snare it.

"When it was first hit, I saw it, then it went into the sun," Dye said. "This field is not good for the sun late in the game. It was hit so hard, in my mind I just wanted it to stay in the ballpark."

It did, and the Red Sox caught another break. Instead of bouncing over the wall for a ground-rule double that would have tied the game and stopped Manny at third, the ball caromed off the wall, giving Manny a chance to race all the way home. He was running on the 3-2 pitch and scored easily. Ortiz clapped his hands hard as he stood on second base, and the Red Sox had a 5-4 lead.

Still, there remained the little matter of closing out the game. Scott Williamson, who had pitched a perfect eighth inning, was sent out to get the three most important outs of the season. He started by striking out Eric Byrnes and Mark Ellis, and Erubiel Durazo popped to third. It's only taken 166 games, but it looks like the Red Sox have found themselves a closer.

"Today was, beyond a doubt, the best he's thrown the ball," said Boston catcher Jason Varitek. "It's confidence."

And it's concentration. Admittedly, Williamson had had trouble focusing when he was first traded to the Red Sox. At that time, his wife had just given birth to the couple's first baby—a boy. Both mother and son remained hospitalized with complications. And with his mind on more important things, Williamson had struggled on the mound. Wife and child are fine now, and daddy is getting the job done. The guy who compiled an ERA of 6.20 during the regular season with the Red Sox has pitched in every game of the series, striking out eight and throwing five scoreless innings. He's picked up the win in each of the past two games, and emerged as the team's closer—and perhaps savior.

"It's all right. I'll take Barry Zito over Pedro Martinez any day," Tim Hudson said, referring to the next night's pitching matchup.

Well, good luck with that. The A's can speak with all the confident bravado they want. The fact remains that they've lost eight straight elimination games—the worst streak in major-league history. This is a team that can't close the deal, and Hudson thinks they'll do it against Pedro? Puh-leeeze!

First of all, pitchers working on three days' rest in the playoffs are 5-14 since 1998. It's a desperate strategy employed by panicky managers. And it just doesn't work. Secondly, Martinez is 7-2 with a 2.34 ERA in 10 career starts against the A's. He's never lost in the postseason. And he's 4-1 in seven starts at Network Associates Coliseum.

If you need more, the A's best hitters, Eric Chavez and Miguel Tejada, are now 2-for-37 in the series. They're pressing. And tomorrow, Pedro will be *de*-pressing them.

As for Byung-Hyun Kim's obscene gesture yesterday, he made a public apology and will not be fined by the team. He apparently won't be *used* by the team either. Kim warmed up during extra innings last night, but when he felt tightness in his shoulder, he said he was unavailable to pitch. Let me get this straight. He blew Game One, flipped off the crowd in Game Three, and then complains of a little stiffness and can't pitch with the season on the line. Great! And to think I made a case for this guy as the team's regular-season MVP.

I'm not always that bright.

Meanwhile, the Yankees closed out the Twins in four games. They won the last three games, 4-1, 3-1, and 8-1. It's going to be great when the Red Sox close out the A's tomorrow night and then start a seven-game series with the Yankees in New York on Wednesday night! Add to that, the possibility of a Red Sox–Cubs World Series. Chicago closed out the Braves tonight with a 5-1 victory in the fifth game. The Cubs will face the Marlins in the NLCS.

OCTOBER 6

Watching the last 15 minutes of tonight's game was like having a man with a chainsaw trying to get into your house, before finally running out of gas and just going home. It was that scary, and that big a relief when it was over. It may only be the first-round divisional series, but it still has to rank among the best playoff series ever. There were three final at-bat victories, and the bases were loaded when the final out was made.

The pitching matchup began as expected. Pedro blinked first when he gave up a run in the fourth inning, but there were indications the game would soon turn in the Red Sox favor. Zito was throwing his big, slow curveball for first- and second-pitch strikes in the early innings, but by the fifth, the ball had started bouncing in the dirt, and he was falling behind in counts. When he lost his control, the Red Sox finally took control.

Jason Varitek led off the sixth inning with a home run, tying the game at 1-1. Then Johnny Damon walked, and Todd Walker was hit by a pitch. That put runners on first and second for Manny Ramirez, who was just 3-for-18 in the series and was still looking for his first RBI. The 2-2 pitch was a fat fastball on the inner half of the plate, and Manny just drilled it. It was one of those "no doubt about it" shots to left field, and Manny stood in the batter's box long enough to admire it. As the ball sailed over the fence, he pointed to his teammates in the dugout and began to circle the bases. Some will call it showboating, but it's not poor sportsmanship to take pride in an accomplishment. It's called being a poor loser when you complain about it, which the A's later did.

And to be sure, the Red Sox had just accomplished something. They had given Pedro Martinez a 4-1 lead in the sixth inning. That should have been enough to turn on the cruise control. But it wasn't.

Oakland came right back with doubles from Erubiel Durazo and Miguel Tejada to make it a 4-2 game in the bottom of the sixth. The A's didn't score in the seventh, but it was a costly inning nonetheless. Damian Jackson, who had entered the game as a defensive replacement for Todd Walker at second base, sprinted toward shallow center field in search of a pop fly. Johnny Damon also streaked in toward the ball. Both players were going full speed when they collided. Jackson's forehead smashed into Damon's right cheek, and both players flopped limply to the turf. Nomar Garciaparra got there an instant later, and stepped over and between the bodies in search of the baseball. He found it lying on the ground. Quickly and alertly, he picked up the ball, turned, and fired it toward second base. Bill Mueller had moved from his position at third base and was covering the middle of the diamond. Garciaparra's throw was perfect, and Mueller applied the tag on Jermaine Dye, who had been trying to turn the mishap into a double. It was a fantastic play on behalf of both Nomar and Mueller. The play ended the inning, and apprehensive attention to Damon began.

Jackson got up relatively quickly and ultimately stayed in the game. Damon, however, was unconscious for a few minutes, and was lifted on a stretcher into an ambulance that had made its way onto the field. Damon waved to the crowd before the ambulance doors closed. He was signaling to the crowd that he was all right, but it was apparent that he wasn't. There was no word immediately following the game about his status or the extent of his injuries.

It was a troubling moment for the Red Sox, and trouble reared its ugly head again in the eighth. Chris Singleton doubled to right and was quickly brought home on a base hit by Billy McMillon. This was not exactly Murderer's Row that Pedro was dealing with, but after his 130-pitch effort in Game One, he was clearly tiring. Now it was suddenly a one-run game. How long would Grady

Little stick with Pedro? When would he turn this game over to the bullpen? How about now?

Little made the right, albeit a surprising move. Instead of showing a misguided and stubborn allegiance to his ace, he bounced out of the dugout and called for Alan Embree to face left-handers Durazo and Eric Chavez. Embree got them both on fly balls, then yielded to Mike Timlin, who got Tejada on a grounder to short. Inning over. And when the Red Sox threatened but failed to add any insurance runs in the ninth, the game was handed over to Scott Williamson—who dropped it.

The newly anointed closer and savior was pitching in his fifth straight game, which may explain why he just didn't have it. Williamson threw pitch after pitch up high out of the strike zone and ultimately walked the first two batters, Scott Hatteburg and Jose Guillen. This was unbelievable! The Red Sox were clinging to their destiny and a one-run lead, but the game was slipping through their fingertips. They had no one else to turn to—except Derek Lowe. Another decisive and proactive move from Little. He yanked Williamson and brought in Lowe just two days after he threw seven innings. Lowe can handle the workload, and he was the best option at that moment.

The A's went with the sacrifice bunt, and Ramon Hernandez laid it down perfectly, moving the runners over to second and third. It was the second time in this series Hernandez did his job with a bunt against Derek Lowe. The winning run was in scoring position with one out, and you had to expect the A's to at least push across the tying run. Lowe is not a strikeout pitcher—only 110 strikeouts in 213 innings this year. If he's on top of his game, the hitters will be on top of the ball hitting grounders. And with the infield drawn in, the Red Sox were hoping for a hot shot right at someone in order to cut the tying run down at the plate.

A's manager Ken Macha sent backup catcher Adam Melhuse up to pinch hit for Jermaine Dye. Dye only hit .172 in limited action during the season, but he had three hits in his last seven at bats during the series. Melhuse, a left-handed hitter, batted .299 during the season. It seemed like a good move until Melhuse struck out looking on what Lowe called a "lock-up sinker." Now there were two outs, and the tying run was still 90 feet away.

Chris Singleton ran the count to 2-and-2, but refused to chase Lowe's next two pitches, which were out of the strike zone. The bases were loaded, and it was Terrance Long against Derek Lowe. This battle would decide the season for two teams.

Lowe didn't waste any time. He went right after Long, and then he gambled. Jason Varitek had gone out to the mound and asked Lowe if he was willing to throw inside. Lowe was ready to do whatever it took. So, on a 1-2 pitch, Lowe went back to the "lock-up sinker," which starts at the hitter and tails back over the plate. If it starts on the plate, of course, it will tail into the heart of the zone and become a meatball. The pitch really needs to be perfect. And it was. It locked up Long, who couldn't get the bat off his shoulder. Strike three looking! The Red Sox had completed another amazing comeback!

"It's not like anything I've ever felt before," Lowe said. "It's a win for Boston, for the Red Sox Nation."

Grady Little added, "It feels pretty good, to tell you the truth. Every single game in this series was outstanding. I think it was nothing short of what people expected, and it was all brought about by some outstanding pitching by both teams."

It's only the fourth time since their 1918 World Series victory that the Red Sox have won a playoff series, and it sets them up for a date with the Yankees in the ALCS. Both teams have an enormous amount of talent, but the Red Sox seem to have a little bit of magic working for them. And that could make all the difference. The Red Sox have become this year's Cinderella story. You know, if Cinderella had had a $105 million budget.

OCTOBER 7

My s--- doesn't work in the playoffs. My job is to get us to the playoffs. What happens after that is the ----ing luck.
—Oakland A's GM Billy Beane in *Moneyball*

But of course, luck is the residue of design, and no matter how well designed or built the A's were, they just ran into bad luck. It was their misfortune that Mark Mulder's season ended in mid-August because of a stress fracture in his right femur. It certainly didn't help their cause when Tim Hudson left Game Four early on Sunday. However, that unfortunate situation may have been helped along by poor judgment.

Hudson has now confirmed published reports that he was involved in an altercation at a Boston bar, known as the Q, on Friday night.

"It had nothing to do with that," Hudson said. "It was just a small verbal altercation that resulted in some finger-pointing and a couple shoves, that's about it."

That's his story and he's sticking to it. But the *San Francisco Chronicle* quoted an unidentified member of Q's security staff who said Hudson was "throwing haymakers."

Pushing, shoving, and throwing punches are three good ways to strain an oblique muscle or, at the very least, contribute to the injury, but whether the bar incident had anything to do with Hudson's injury doesn't really matter. Fact is, two of their "big three" pitchers were unable to perform either at all, or up to their usual level. That's bad luck. Meanwhile, hitting a "black point" while mired in an 0-for-16 slump is good luck.

So bring on the Yankees!

And leave Byung-Hyun Kim behind! In a not-so-surprising move, the Red Sox opted to keep Kim off the playoff roster for the ALCS. Now that Kim has lost his job as closer, and with his struggles against the Yankees well documented, there really wouldn't be any good time to use him. The Red Sox maintain that Kim has some shoulder stiffness, and they couldn't risk putting someone on the roster who might not be available. But Kim could have been 100 percent healthy, and he still would have been 100 percent *not* on the team. Adrian Brown was also omitted from the series roster, as the Red Sox opted for both Todd Jones and Jeff Suppan. Johnny Damon was placed on the roster, which means the Red Sox expect him to come back from his concussion sooner rather than later.

13

Destiny Derailed

OCTOBER 8: GAME ONE

> I want to thank the good Lord for making me a Yankee.
>
> —Joe DiMaggio

That quote is everywhere at Yankee Stadium. There's no way to avoid it. It's engraved in large letters high atop the stadium. It's written on a sign where fans enter. It's in the media room. And it's in the Yankees' clubhouse. Didn't Joltin' Joe ever say anything else?

Meanwhile, call it a throng, or call it a hoard. Either way, there were a whole bunch of media representatives taking up space behind home plate and in front of both dugouts several hours before Game One. Jason Varitek, looking for some room to stretch out, shooed them away as if they were a flock of geese pooping on his lawn. It ruffled a few feathers, but the mood remained electric. The show was about to begin.

The pitching matchup for Game One pitted Tim Wakefield against Mike Mussina—the Red Sox number three starter against the Yankees ace. The Yankees clearly had the edge. Heading into the postseason, Mussina's playoff ERA was 2.93, while Wakefield's was 7.11. But Wakefield beat the Yankees twice during the regular season, including most recently on September 6, when he shut them out through seven innings. Mussina had three no-decisions against the Red Sox this year, despite pitching into the eighth inning in all three starts.

There was no score through three innings, and the Red Sox only had one hit before Manny Ramirez led off with a single that deflected off Mussina's glove. David Ortiz was up next, and his stats were at war with one another. Against the Yankees this year, Ortiz had six home runs and 14 RBI in 15 games, but lifetime against Mussina he was 0-for-20 with 13 strikeouts. Gone! The good stats conquered the bad, and Ortiz hit a two-run bomb into the front row of the right-field upper deck! Mussina responded by striking out the side, but the Red Sox had a 2-0 lead.

Todd Walker led off the fifth with a shot down the right-field line. There was no question the ball had more than enough air under it to carry it the required 314 feet to the foul pole. But would it stay fair? Remember, for the postseason there are six umpires on the field, and Angel Hernandez was straddling the foul line in perfect position to make the call. With his back to home plate, he waved his arms toward the stands. It was a foul ball.

But wait! The umpires huddled, and after a short conference, home plate umpire Tim McClelland made a circling motion with his right forefinger raised over his head, which told the crowd he had overruled the original call. It was a home run after all. Replays showed that McClelland was right, and that a fan had actually reached in front of the pole, attempting to catch the ball. That fan, 18-year-old Josh Mandelbaum of Fair Lawn, New Jersey, was an unabashed Yankees fan who said later, "It would have been foul, clearly." Well, clearly, it wasn't. And clearly, he should move to Foul Lawn, New Jersey.

The end result was that Walker, who hit just 13 home runs in 587 at bats during the regular season, had just hit his fourth home run in 18 at bats in the postseason.

"I don't think I can explain, and I don't think I want to," Walker said.

The Red Sox had a 3-0 lead. Two outs after Walker's homer, Ramirez shot a lazy fly ball to the right side that had just enough carry on it to get over the wall. The Red Sox only had six hits, but three of them were home runs, and they had a 4-0 lead.

And Wakefield was doing the rest. From the second through the sixth inning, he retired 14 Yankees in a row. He was throwing first-pitch strikes with his knuckleball, and the Yankees were flailing away at them. Mike Timlin later said, "It's like trying to hit a butterfly with a boat paddle."

"It's tough because you don't really have a game plan," Derek Jeter said. "It's not like you can say, 'Well, let me wait for this pitch if it goes in this direction,' because he doesn't even know where it's going."

After the Red Sox added another run in the seventh on a Kevin Millar single, Wakefield started the bottom half of the inning by hitting Jason Giambi and walking Bernie Williams. Though tossing a two-hit shutout, Wakefield's night was over. It seemed like an awfully quick hook, but Grady Little had newfound confidence in at least three guys in his bullpen. And he was handing the game over to them.

Alan Embree got the first call, which seemed like a solid move, because it forced Jorge Posada to hit from the right side, thus keeping him away from the short porch in right. Posada doubled to right-center field, but Gabe Kapler made a great sliding play to cut the ball off, momentarily saving a run. Hideki Matsui followed with a sacrifice fly to left, and Aaron Boone ended the inning with a pop-up to center. The Yankees had chipped away, but the Red Sox still had a 5-2 lead after seven.

The eighth inning belonged to Mike Timlin, who retired the side in order. And so it was up to the Red Sox new closer, Scott Williamson, to put the wraps on this one, with more than 55,000 people rooting for him to fail. Williamson struck out Jason Giambi and then got Bernie Williams to ground out to first. The Red Sox were one out away. Posada stood in the box, and as soon as Jason Varitek had strike three securely in his glove, Posada walked away. He knew. He knew it was a strike. And he knew the Red Sox now had a closer to be reckoned with. The Red Sox bullpen, a glaring weakness during the regular season, had just extended its postseason scoreless streak to 14 2/3 innings. Timlin hasn't so much as given up a hit in his 5 1/3 playoff innings.

The Red Sox took Game One, 5-2, and it didn't really seem that hard. They were undaunted by the surroundings and unaffected by their emotional wins against Oakland. In very businesslike fashion, they homered, pitched, and closed the deal.

Also, Johnny Damon spoke to reporters before the game and expressed hope that he could return by Game Three on Saturday. His right eye remains puffy, but his overall progress has been swift. "I had no idea what was going on for the next four or five hours," he said. "I was in really bad shape. I do remember waving my hands to the crowd, but at that moment I actually thought I was walking off the field. I thought I was on my feet and didn't realize I was on a stretcher."

OCTOBER 9: GAME TWO

The Red Sox had Andy Pettitte on the ropes. They were about to deliver the knockout blow. And then it was like his mouthpiece came out or something, so time was called. That gave him time to recover. And then the fight was on.

"We had a chance to get Pettitte," said first baseman Kevin Millar, "and we didn't."

Gabe Kapler began the night with an infield single. Then Bill Mueller worked the count full. Kapler broke for second base on the payoff pitch, but Mueller took a called strike three, and Kapler was thrown out by five feet. Nomar and Manny followed with back-to-back singles, and David Ortiz walked to load the bases. So, the Red Sox had three hits and a walk with no runs. Then Kevin Millar popped up to end the inning.

In the second, Pettitte found himself in trouble once again. This time, Jason Varitek led off with a double, and Trot Nixon singled him over to third. Damian Jackson soft-served a single to center, scoring Varitek. At this point in the game, the Red Sox had sent nine men to the plate. Six had base hits, one walked, and two had been retired, but the Red Sox still only had one run.

Yankees pitching coach Mel Stottlemyre went out to try to calm Pettitte down. Perhaps he told Pettitte to throw an inside fastball to Gabe Kapler so he'd smash the ball hard to Derek Jeter, who could then step on second and throw to first for a double play. Because that's exactly what happened.

"If the ball goes to either side of him, we've got a huge inning," Jason Varitek said after the game.

Instead, the inning ended when Mueller dribbled a ball down the third base line. Aaron Boone bare-handed it and threw to first just in time for the final out.

In the Yankees second, Nick Johnson blasted a two-run homer off Derek Lowe to give the Yankees a 2-1 lead. It was New York's first hit of the game. Missed opportunities.

The Yankees had escaped and now went on the attack. In the third, Derek Jeter's major-league-best 108th postseason hit was followed by singles from Jason Giambi and Bernie Williams to make the game 3-1. With runners on first and second, Jorge Posada hit a low line drive to Jackson at second base. If he had caught it, it would have been an inning-ending double play. Instead, he dropped it and the bases were loaded. Lowe got out of the trouble when Hideki Matsui grounded to first, and Millar threw home to get the force-out there. Then Johnson grounded to short.

The Yankees added another run in the fifth inning on a Matsui single that scored Williams. By then, Pettitte had settled down, and the Red Sox were unable to mount another threat. In the fifth, Nomar singled with two outs, and Manny flied to the warning track. Nothing. In the sixth, Varitek hit a two-out solo home run to left. His third home run of the postseason cut the

Yankees lead to 4-2. Something. But not enough.

Pettitte and Lowe each pitched 6 2/3 innings. Pettitte gave up nine hits, Lowe seven. But Pettitte only gave up two runs, while Lowe was charged with *six*. The last two runs came home in the seventh when Scott Sauerbeck relieved Lowe and gave up a two-run double to Posada. I don't care if I never see Sauerbeck in a game again.

The Yankees evened the series with a 6-2 win, but it could have been a very different story if the Red Sox had gotten one or two more key hits in the first two innings. They let a good fighter off the ropes, and it cost them.

Here's something to think about, heading into the huge Game Three matchup between Pedro Martinez and Roger Clemens at Fenway Park. Both guys are known for "protecting" their hitters when opposing pitchers throw too far inside. Well, after Jose Contreras fired a fastball past David Ortiz's upper lip in the eighth inning, Sox pitcher Bronson Arroyo drilled Alfonso Soriano in the shoulder. Soriano lingered a moment at the plate as he stared back at Arroyo.

Keep in mind that bad blood between these teams started earlier in the year when Pedro hit both Soriano and Jeter in back-to-back at bats on July 7. Soriano actually struck out on the pitch that hit him. But a lot of people think the inside pitches by Pedro were a response to Kevin Millar's getting plunked by Clemens two days earlier. You never know what can happen when foolish macho pride is involved.

Quote of the day: Grady Little was asked in the pregame press conference what this season has taught him. Without hesitation he said, "I want to have a closer."

OCTOBER 10: TRAVEL DAY

The city that never sleeps rested a little easier last night, with the Yankees taking the second game of the series. But the Big Apple's worries aren't over. Effectively, this is now a five-game series with the first three games at Fenway Park, and Pedro Martinez is set to start the first and last games. Both of those games will be against Roger Clemens.

This reminds me of the end of the first *Rocky* movie when Apollo Creed said, "Ain't gonna be no rematch." Well, there was. And there will be a "Rocky II" for Pedro and Rocket. Two of baseball's heavyweights will answer the bell again tomorrow in a rematch of their 1999 battle, which Pedro won by a knockout. Clemens gave up five runs on six hits in two-plus innings, while Pedro threw seven shutout innings, allowing just two hits and striking out 12. The 13-1 final was the Yankees' most lopsided loss in postseason history, and it dropped Clemens's postseason record at the time to 2-3 in 11 career starts.

But that was the only game the Red Sox won in that series. The Sox already have a win in this series, so now they're looking for Pedro to take control. He got the win in the final game of the Oakland series, but it took a lot of help from four different relievers to get it done. He needs to be better tomorrow.

And we're reminded that in his last 10 starts against the Yankees, Pedro is 2-3, and the Red Sox are 3-7. If you want to go further back, Pedro's only won three of his last 16 starts against New York, and the Red Sox are 4-12 in those games. It's all about Pedro now.

OCTOBER 11: GAME THREE

We knew it was going to be quite a battle. We knew it was going to be very emotional, a lot of intensity. But I think we've upgraded from a battle to a war.

—Red Sox manager Grady Little

There will be many images from this season flashing through the minds of Red Sox fans. Some happy, some sad. But none will be more vivid than the sight of Pedro Martinez grabbing the face of 72-year-old Yankees coach Don Zimmer with both hands and tossing him to the ground. As it happened in real time, or more like surreal time, you couldn't believe your eyes. Only an onslaught of replays could confirm what the rational mind was convinced could not be true.

But that's what happened when both benches cleared in the fourth inning. It all started in the top half of the inning, when the Yankees scored twice and took a 4-2 lead. Pedro had given up a walk to Jorge Posada and a single to Nick Johnson. Then Hideki Matsui hit a long double that bounced into the right-field stands. With runners on second and third, Sox catcher Jason Varitek went out to the mound and engaged in a lengthy discussion with his ace. Varitek returned behind the plate, and the next pitch whizzed past Karim Garcia's head. The ball nicked Garcia's shoulder as he attempted to duck out of the way.

"There's no question in my mind that Pedro hit him on purpose. He can thread a needle any time he wants," Joe Torre said. "You know what kind of respect I have for Pedro's ability to pitch, but I didn't care for that."

Nor did any of the other Yankees. Several of them jumped to the top step of the visitor's dugout and began shouting at Pedro, especially Posada. Pedro, in return, pointed at his own temple and appeared to say to the Yankees catcher, "I'll hit you in the head."

Now, several times I've heard Pedro defend his willingness to throw inside by saying, "*If* I want to hit a guy in the head, I'll hit a guy in the head," which is his way of saying that he puts the ball where he wants to. This time, he apparently wanted to put the ball about neck high behind Garcia.

"He had great control, then he comes at my head with his first pitch? If he hits me in the shoulder, I would have taken my base without a problem," Garcia said.

Two things about that: First, the ball *did* hit him in the shoulder, or rather, grazed him. Second, does Garcia have any idea how close a person's shoulder is to his head?

Anyway, that pitch set the stage for an overdose of testosterone in the Red Sox half of the inning. Roger Clemens ran the count to 1-2 before throwing a fastball head high, but on the inside corner of the plate. It was the perfect "purpose" pitch. The home plate umpire, Alfonso Marquez, warned both benches when tempers flared in the top half of the inning. So, there was no way Clemens could hit anyone with a pitch without getting tossed from the game. So, he threw the pitch as close to Ramirez as he could without getting in trouble for it.

"If I wanted it near him, he'd know it," Clemens said, sounding a lot like Pedro has on many occasions.

And even though the pitch wasn't that close, it was too close for comfort as far as Ramirez was concerned. He started barking at Clemens and walking toward the mound—still holding his bat. Players and coaches from both sides sauntered onto the field. It didn't seem like anyone was really looking for a fight, but they were duty bound by baseball's code of ethics to make their way out to where the action was. Suddenly (which is an odd adverb to use to describe anything done by a 72-year-old, but that's how it appeared), Zimmer made his way over to where Pedro was standing and lunged at him in an obvious effort to land a left hook. Pedro reached out, put both hands around "Jaba the Gerbil's" jowls and tossed him to the ground. It's too bad Pedro couldn't handle the Yankees lineup just as easily.

Zimmer rolled over on his back, then onto his stomach again. Seeing him on the ground like that, potentially hurt, seemed to restore sanity to the situation. Though not everyone knew who it was at first.

"I saw a bald head on the ground and I wasn't sure if it was Zim or

Boomer," Clemens said, referring to portly left-hander David Wells. And what does that say about Wells that he could be mistaken for a round-bodied septuagenarian?

Some would like to have seen Pedro devise another way of handling the situation with Zimmer that didn't include a World Wrestling move. But, in truth, he handled his attacker as gently as he could.

"I could never hit him. I would never do it," Martinez said. "I was just trying to dodge him and push him away, and too bad his body fell. I hope he's fine."

Zimmer was fine, except for a small cut on the bridge of his nose. And while he was later taken by ambulance to Beth Israel Deaconess Medical Center, the trip was purely precautionary.

Despite a 10-minute delay due to the skirmish and the attention paid to Zimmer, there were no ejections. And Manny Ramirez struck out on the next pitch, swinging feebly at a fastball on the outside part of the plate.

Lost in all the hysteria was the fact that Pedro had given up four runs and six hits in four innings, and that the Red Sox were trailing 4-2. The incidents in both halves of the fourth inning evidently put the hitters back on their heels a bit. Pedro retired the final 11 Yankees he faced, and the Red Sox only managed two more hits the rest of the way. The Red Sox scored in the seventh inning when Trot Nixon bounced into a double play with runners on the corners, but Mariano Rivera closed it out by retiring all six batters he faced in the eighth and ninth innings. The Red Sox lost, 4-3. Once again, Pedro let them down.

This was a pivotal game in the series, and he was outpitched and outclassed by Roger Clemens. Clemens, the fiery kid with the eyeblack who was tossed out of a 1995 Red Sox playoff game for cursing at and trying to attack home plate umpire Terry Cooney, turns out to be the one who can keep his head while those around him were losing theirs.

"You're a great pitcher," Clemens said of Martinez. "Be great. Just because you're being hit around doesn't mean you get to stick one behind somebody's head."

While that makes Clemens the "pot" and Pedro the "kettle," the point remains the same. Pedro didn't have his best stuff on a night when he and his team needed it most. So, he resorted to intimidation tactics. And while it worked, it was also too late. And he lost some respect tonight.

"To me, this whole thing started over one pitch," Torre said. "I don't think that we have any anger for the whole team. It's that one incident that bothers me and just the one person involved."

It's tough when the villain is on your team. My own inclination would be to defend Pedro and maintain that if pitches "up and in" are part of the game, then all he did was play some hard-nosed hardball. But Pedro took a hard, round weapon and fired it at someone's head at 90 miles per hour. Indefensible.

But wait! There's more. There was also a skirmish in the Yankees bullpen in the middle of the ninth inning. As if seeing Don Zimmer thrown around like a floppy-cheeked rag doll wasn't bizarre enough, we also had a member of the Red Sox ground crew getting pummeled by a couple of Yankees. This story is still developing, but it appears that 24-year-old Paul Williams, who teaches special-needs children when he's not working in the Fenway bullpen, waved a towel toward the crowd after the Yankees hit into an inning-ending double play in the ninth. Yankees reliever Jeff Nelson took offense. And this is where the story becomes unclear. Williams maintains that Nelson sucker-punched him, and that while the two of them were rolling around on the ground, several other Yankees, including Garcia, started hitting and kicking him. There's a possibility that Nelson and Garcia could be arrested or charged with assault.

When it was over, Garcia had to leave the game, because he was unable to stop the bleeding from the knuckles on his left hand. Garcia got into the fray when he was going out to his position in right field and noticed the skirmish going on over the wall in the bullpen. Williams was taken to the hospital where he was treated for, among other things, cleat marks on his back.

He probably feels a lot like the Red Sox do right now. This is the sixth time the Yankees have held a 2-1 lead in a seven-game Championship Series, and they've won the other five series in either five or six games.

Meanwhile, the Cubs are holding up their end of the bargain for a Cubs–Red Sox World Series. They took a 3-1 lead over the Marlins tonight.

OCTOBER 12: RAIN OUT

Rain is good. It gives us water to drink. It helps the flowers grow. And it allows the Red Sox to skip John Burkett in the rotation. Today's game was rained out, so both managers will return to their Game One starters in Game Four tomorrow. In jeopardy of falling into a 3-1 hole, the Red Sox have to like their chances with Wakefield going up against Mussina again instead of Burkett against David Wells. Burkett has 166 career wins, and exactly none of them are against the Yankees, though he does have that one postseason victory when he was pitching for the Rangers. In the regular season, though, he's 0-6, and the Yankees have averaged nearly nine runs a game against him. The rain definitely helps the Red Sox.

The rainout also allows Derek Lowe to pitch in Game Five at home, where he's much more effective. Then Burkett will end up facing Andy Pettitte in a Game Six back at Yankee Stadium. That's not an advantageous matchup, but at least it's Game Six. And the Red Sox could be up 3-2 by then.

Fines from Game Three were passed down today by Major League Baseball. And the vice president in charge of discipline, Bob Watson, apparently believes Pedro Martinez intentionally threw at Karim Garcia. Why else would Pedro get a $50,000 fine for actions committed during a game in which he wasn't even ejected? Manny Ramirez was fined $25,000 for overreacting. Garcia was fined $10,000 because he was the most aggressive player on the field when the benches cleared. And poor old Don Zimmer was fined $5,000 for putting his head in Pedro's hands and rolling on the ground.

Zimmer was the only involved party to apologize, and he did so briefly and emotionally. Sitting in front of the microphone in the interview room, Zimmer fought back tears, saying, "I'm embarrassed for what happened last night. I'm embarrassed for the Yankees, the Red Sox, the fans, the umpires, and my family."

Boston owner John Henry said, "I wouldn't mind seeing the same thing coming from our side."

But it never happened.

The Marlins staved off elimination when Josh Becket fired a two-hitter at the Cubs. Florida won 4-0, but still trails that NLCS, 3-2.

OCTOBER 13: GAME FOUR

There remains a "field of dreams" atmosphere at Fenway Park, especially when the Red Sox and Yankees face each other in the playoffs. You look out over the field with a dozen or so men standing on it, and it could be 1920, or 1970, or right now. Only the inordinate number of cell phones being used around you betrays the fantasy.

The pregame ceremonies included Ryan Reynolds singing his original song, "Cowboy Up," and Michael Bolton forgetting the words to the national anthem. Bolton was booed. Reynolds probably should have been.

The Wakefield-Mussina rematch began as the first game did—goose eggs for three innings, and the Red Sox getting on the board in the fourth. The Yankees, in very un-Yankee-like fashion, squandered good opportunities in the first and third innings. The game began with a walk to Soriano and a single by Jeter; then Jason Giambi lined a hard shot to first base. Kevin Millar snared it easily and stepped on first for the double play. Then, in the third, David Dellucci was hit by a pitch and stole second. Both Soriano and Jeter flied to shallow center, leaving it up to Giambi. A passed ball put Dellucci on third, but Giambi flied to left. Giambi was now 2-for-12 in the ALCS without an RBI, and 6-for-28 in the postseason, with two RBI and no home runs. The Yankees were 0-for-5 with runners in scoring position in the first three innings.

In the fourth, Todd Walker put his name in the Red Sox record books. Now, when people ask which Red Sox player hit the most home runs in one postseason, others will guess Ted Williams, Carlton Fisk, Jim Rice, or Mo Vaughn. But the answer will be Todd Walker. He stroked a 2-2 pitch off Mike Mussina deep to right for his fifth home run of the 2003 playoffs, breaking the Red Sox record of four established by Nomar Garciaparra and John Valentin in 1999. It was also the Red Sox fifth home run of the ALCS, and their fourth off Mussina.

"I'm getting some good pitches to hit," Walker said. "I'm getting some good counts. I can't explain the home runs, but I'm trying to hit the ball hard, and I'm trying to square it up as much as I can."

The Yankees got that run back in the top half of the fifth when Derek Jeter bounced a double off the third base bag, scoring Dellucci and moving Soriano to third. Surprisingly, when Giambi hit a fly ball to shallow center field with one out, third base coach Willie Randolph told Soriano to hold. Johnny Damon doesn't have a very strong arm, and I would have expected the Yankees to test him every chance they got. Damon's throw was fairly strong, but slightly up the third base line. It's hard to say if Soriano would have scored, but he ultimately didn't. Bernie Williams walked, and Jorge Posada lined out to left to end the threat.

"He would have been out if he went," Joe Torre said. "We know that Damon doesn't have a very strong arm, but the throw he made, I don't think he would have been safe. I didn't think that was a bad play."

In the Red Sox fifth inning, Mike Mussina threw 11 pitches, 10 for strikes. The first three pitches were enough to strike out Kevin Millar. Mussina's next pitch was a home run by Trot Nixon, a blast to center field reminiscent of his game-winning home run against the A's. Then Mussina struck out Bill Mueller on three pitches, and retired Doug Mirabelli on four.

Wakefield's knuckler continued to dance, and Mussina held the Red Sox scoreless in the sixth. But in the seventh, Mussina found himself in a jam.

With one out, he walked Millar on four straight pitches. With left-hander Felix Heredia warmed in the bullpen, Torre opted to let Mussina pitch to Trot Nixon, who had already homered off Mussina tonight. Nixon promptly doubled off the left-field wall. I've heard a fair amount of praise heaped on Hideki Matsui, who pretended Nixon's ball was catchable. Leftfielders at Fenway frequently attempt to fool runners by acting as if they can catch the ball, then simply turning around and playing it off the wall. Those who think Matsui deked well suggest that's why Millar stopped at third. But it's safe to say there aren't too many Red Sox players who score from first base on a wall-ball double—especially with one out. Millar wasn't going anywhere.

After Mussina intentionally walked Bill Mueller, who was only hitting .182 in the postseason, it was Jason Varitek to the rescue!

Varitek doesn't start when Wakefield pitches, so he had gone to the bullpen to help warm up the relievers. But with the bases loaded and one out in the seventh, Grady Little made a rare call to the bullpen. He was looking for a pinch hitter.

Varitek grabbed his catcher's gear and sprinted in from right field. It was an adrenaline rush for Varitek and the entire crowd. This could be the game breaker and a chance to even the series at two games apiece. But was this a good move by Little, considering that Varitek was 2-for-36 with 17 strikeouts in his career against Mussina?

"I figured he was due," Little said. "He has struggled against Moose in his career, as a lot of hitters have. But he's been big for us in a lot of situations just like that throughout the season."

Varitek wasn't exactly big this time, but, as always, his heart was. Varitek ripped a shot to the left side. It was a hard-hit ball, tailor-made for a 6-4-3 double play. Jeter fielded it cleanly and snapped a throw to Soriano covering second. Soriano stepped off the bag back toward left field and got off a quick throw to first. Safe!

Varitek spread his arms out in a safe sign as he crossed the first base bag, and the umpire did the same. By hustling all the way down the first base line, Varitek had managed to beat it out as the third Red Sox run crossed the plate.

"Over the last few years, I've hit the ball well (against Mussina) and just have not had a whole lot of success," Varitek said. "I knew he was throwing a lot of splits, and I ended up hitting a split."

Varitek's hustle made each and every Red Sox fan so happy that no one seemed to mind when he got picked off first base to end the inning with Nixon standing over at third base.

Wakefield started the eighth inning, but was quickly removed after he walked Giambi. Mike Timlin came in, and his first pitch to Williams was driven deep to center field. The ball floated long enough for Damon to make a nice running catch as he got to the warning track. Timlin then easily retired Posada and Matsui on a ground ball to first and an inning-ending strikeout.

The Red Sox failed to score in the eighth. So, the game was now in the hands of Scott Williamson. I sat in the stands thinking, "Scott, don't hurt me!"

With two strikes on Nick Johnson, Williamson threw a hard slider in on his hands. Strike three.

Ruben Sierra, pinch hitting for Aaron Boone, drove a fastball into the Red Sox bullpen. "Please, Scott, don't hurt me!"

Dellucci struck out. So, it was up to Soriano, who had hit 38 home runs during the regular season. With the score 3-2, the crowd began waving complimentary Red Sox towels over their head. The count quickly went to no balls and two strikes. The crowd, anticipating the final punchout, reached its loudest roar of the night. Ball one. Undeterred, the fans spun those towels from the left-field grandstand to the center field bleachers and over to the seats deep in right field. Strike three! Williamson had struck out the side and preserved the victory. The series was now tied 2-2.

This was no easy accomplishment. It's the kind of game the Yankees almost always win. In fact, in 20 playoff games decided by one run since their most recent amazing run began in 1996, the Yankees have won 17 and lost three. And they haven't lost a one-run ALCS game since Game Two in 1980.

The Red Sox have two wins in the series, and Tim Wakefield has them both. Mike Mussina, by the way, has both losses for the Yankees. Mussina is 0-4 with a 4.98 ERA in his last six postseason starts. He's now 0-3 this postseason and is 1-3 in six career ALCS starts. He pitched well—6 2/3 innings pitched, six hits, three runs, 10 strikeouts. But Wakefield pitched better—seven innings pitched, one run, five hits, eight strikeouts.

The crowd stayed to sing, "Joy to the World" (the "Jeremiah was a Bullfrog" version, not the Christmas carol). But when Journey's "Don't Stop Believing" came blasting out of the loudspeakers, the exit aisles started getting crowded. I don't think it was the sentiment that got people walking, just the music.

Out in the street, it was easier to see the windows in the Prudential Building that spelled out "Go Sox." Shirtless fans sprinted down to Kenmore Square. I saw a man hold out a dollar to a beggar and demand that he say "Yankees suck" before he would hand over the money. The beggar enthusiastically obliged and received his "one buck for one suck." I overheard another man say, "Move over, Reggie Jackson. Todd Walker is the real 'Mr.

October' now."

This was a genuine celebration, because the fans knew the difference between being down 3-1 and being knotted at two games each. Hope could have died today. Instead, it is born again.

OCTOBER 14: GAME FIVE

Four hours before game time, Grady Little was sitting alone in the stands, Section 15, comfortably positioned with his right ankle perched on his left knee. He was talking on a cell phone and seemed perfectly relaxed. It helped me to relax.

Seven hours later, I feel rather differently. Being a Red Sox fan is like going home every night expecting to find your wife in bed with another man. Tonight's game felt as if I pulled up to my house and there was another car in the driveway.

After retiring the first four Yankees he faced, Derek Lowe walked Jorge Posada with one out in the second. The Yankees stayed out of the double play by starting Posada from first as Hideki Matsui grounded to third. Posada moved up to second, and Matsui was retired at first. Now there were two outs and a man on second.

Lowe fell behind, 3-0, to Nick Johnson, so with first base open, the Sox intentionally walked Johnson. To me, that's a little too much respect for a guy who was hitting .143 in the postseason, and who hit only 14 home runs during the regular season. It's only the second inning, for crying out loud!

Anyway, the walk gave Lowe a chance to pitch to the right-handed-hitting Aaron Boone. Boone was 0-for-9 in the series, including 0-for-3 with two strikeouts against Lowe in Game Two. So, it wasn't a crazy move to walk Johnson, just unnecessary.

Boone bounced a ball down the third base line that Bill Mueller backed up on and then fumbled. Boone was credited with an infield single, and the Yankees had loaded the bases without hitting the ball out of the infield. Karim Garcia and Alfonso Soriano followed with clean base hits, and the Yankees had a 3-0 lead. Compare that to the Red Sox who had six hits off Andy Pettitte in two innings in Game Two, but only had one run. This is how ball games are won and lost.

Trot Nixon was hit by a David Wells pitch to lead off the third, and Varitek followed with a single. Johnny Damon's ground ball to the right moved runners to second and third with one out. But Wells got Todd Walker, a.k.a. "Mr. October," to hit a short fly ball to left. That left it up to Nomar

Garciaparra. Nomar had hit .300 in the Oakland series, but he didn't drive in a run during those five games, and he only scored twice. Granted, his one-out double in the eighth inning of Game Four helped set the stage for David Ortiz's dramatics, but Nomar has made very little contribution other than that. He was 2-for-17 in the first four games against the Yankees, and this was a golden opportunity for him to break out of his slump in a big way—at home, against a lefty, with runners in scoring position. Here we go!

Nomar took the first pitch. I like that, even though it was a strike. Ball one. Strike two. Nomar was in the hole, but Wells tried to get too fine with him. Hoping Nomar would chase something, Wells threw the next two pitches out of the strike zone. Nomar didn't bite. The count was full. The crowd was alive! Wells, never known as a power pitcher, reared back and gave it everything he had. Everything he has is a 90-mile-per-hour fastball. It was up around the letters, but right down the heart of the plate. Nomar swung. And the crowd fell silent. Wells walked off the mound pumping his fist. Nomar stood in the batter's box long enough to remove his helmet and his batting gloves. He had struck out. That pitch was such a meatball, there must have been tomato sauce in Jorge Posada's glove. In July, Nomar would have crushed that pitch. But this is not the July Nomar we're seeing. This is a continuation of the September Nomar who hit just .170 and watched his batting average drop 21 points to .301.

Manny Ramirez led off the fourth inning with a home run to left, making the score 3-1 Yankees. David Ortiz followed with a sharp single, and it looked as if this might finally be the moment the Red Sox would begin pummeling the portly left-hander. Wells, after all, spent a good portion of the season in Joe Torre's doghouse. He was nearly pulled from the starting rotation in August when he gave up 22 runs in 22 2/3 innings. Perfect, he's not. Overweight, he is. But he's 9-2 in the postseason, and he seemed focused out there tonight.

Kevin Millar grounded into a 4-6-3 double play, and Bill Mueller struck out. Wells escaped without any further damage, and the Red Sox continued to trail, 3-1. Mueller has been an even greater disappointment than Nomar. At least Nomar's pathetic September provided an indication that he might struggle in October. But Mueller batted .333 in September, which enabled him to hold on and win the batting title. But he went into the tank faster than Shamu. He's 2-for-17 in this series, and in the last three games, he's 0-for-8 with four strikeouts.

The Red Sox had another chance to light up Wells in the fifth, but failed once again. With Johnny Damon on first and two outs, Walker singled, and

Nomar walked, loading the bases for Manny Ramirez. As Manny walked up to the plate, Yankees pitching coach Mel Stottlemyre made his way out to the mound. Wells was visibly upset about home-plate umpire Joe West's strike zone. Sottlemyre went to the hill with only one thing in mind: get Wells to calm down. Mission accomplished. Manny hit a ground ball to third, and the inning was over.

"Boomer showed me nothing that surprised me out there tonight," said Grady Little. "He has the ability to make pitches when he needs to."

Meanwhile, after that troublesome second inning that could have ended if Mueller had made the play on Boone's ground ball, Lowe was nearly unhittable. He gave up one legitimate hit to Jason Giambi in the fifth, one infield single (again to Boone), and one walk, and two Yankees reached on errors. Lowe was never in trouble—until the eighth. He began by walking Giambi, and then Posada delivered a one-out single. Alan Embree was called upon to pitch to the Yankees' back-to-back lefties, Matsui and Johnson. Embree got Matsui to bounce back to the mound, but a run scored on the play. And Johnson flied to left to end the inning with the Yankees up, 4-1.

A three-run lead after seven innings is just about a mortal lock for the Yankees. It's Mariano Rivera time, especially in the postseason. Rivera had two two-inning saves in the Division Series against Minnesota, and another two-inning save in Game Three against Boston. And Torre called for him to get six more outs tonight. But on Rivera's second pitch, Walker ripped a shot into right field and legged it out for a leadoff triple. That enabled Nomar to get his first RBI of the postseason. It was a weak ground ball to first, but Walker scored without a throw.

Was it possible the Red Sox could come back from three runs down against Rivera? Remember, the Red Sox had gotten to him for three runs and seven hits in back-to-back games in May. Rivera only gave up 61 hits in 70 innings all year, but he gave up 16 hits in 10 innings against the Red Sox. Rivera is the best closer ever, but he was a little less flawless against the Red Sox.

Well, it didn't happen. Rivera got out of the eighth without any further damage and retired the side in order in the ninth. The Yankees won, 4-2. They'll head back to New York looking to close out the series in six games.

Once again, the Red Sox will hand the ball to John Burkett in an elimination game. Ten days after giving up nine hits in 5 1/3 innings against Oakland, Burkett will stand on the mound at Yankee Stadium in front of 55,000 people and attempt to outduel Andy Pettitte. Pettitte is 2-0 with a 1.98 ERA this postseason. Burkett is…well, Burkett is a concern.

OCTOBER 15: GAME SIX

Here we are back at Yankee Stadium. It's like the Roman Coliseum with a state-of-the-art scoreboard. The Yankees are the lions, with a 100-year history of devouring their opponents. And the fans here are the same ones who cheered for the lions. No doubt, they are all direct descendants of the fans who rooted for Goliath. Yankees fans still believe they've earned a special seat at the social table simply because they were geographically blessed at birth and landed in the tri-state area, or they were agile enough to jump on a bandwagon right around 1996. They happen to root for the best team in baseball; what's so special about that? Why should that raise their self-esteem?

Really, one of the best and worst parts of being a sports fan is when your team is the underdog. The Yankees are always the alpha dog. So, when they do what they're expected to do, where's the thrill? It's like giving a person a standing ovation for breathing.

But Yankees fans were at the stadium this afternoon just waiting for the inevitable. They were prepared to take what was rightfully theirs: a victory from the Boston Red Sox. With winds gusting between 20 and 45 miles per hour, the first pitch was thrown at 4:19 p.m. The crowd's first major eruption occurred at 4:32 p.m. That's when Jason Giambi homered off John Burkett. Uh-oh!

Burkett almost made it out of the first inning without any trouble. But after retiring Soriano and Jeter, the first pitch he threw to Giambi was smacked deep to right. Giambi's first home run of the postseason, a span of 32 at bats, gave the Yankees a 1-0 lead.

In the third inning, Andy Pettitte lost control of the strike zone. It began when he left a pitch over the heart of the plate that Jason Varitek hit on a line over the wall in left, tying the game 1-1. Johnny Damon walked, Todd Walker singled, and Nomar Garciaparra did what he's done all postseason long. He grounded to short. Derek Jeter flipped the ball to third, getting the lead runner there. Runners were still at first and second. It was hard to tell if Pettitte simply wanted no part of Manny Ramirez in that situation, or if it was further evidence that he didn't have command of his pitches. Anyway, he walked Ramirez on four pitches, loading the bases for David Ortiz.

After Ortiz brought home the winning runs in Game Four against Oakland, he went right back into his funk. He's been 4-for-20 since then, and batting just .135 in the postseason. But the only stat that matters for Ortiz, it seems, is clutch base hits. And he came up with another one.

Ortiz let the bat fly on the first offering from Pettitte. It wasn't quite the stroke he was looking for, but it was effective. The soft fly landed safely in left-center field, scoring two runs and giving the Red Sox a 3-1 lead. Kevin Millar followed with a base hit up the middle, and the Red Sox had a 4-1 lead. What could have been a huge inning ended abruptly, however, when Bill Mueller grounded into a double play. You know it's bad when you start rooting for a player to strike out just so he won't hurt the team too badly.

The Red Sox four-run inning quieted the crowd, but the Yankees' four-run inning revved them right back up. This is where I have a significant problem with Grady Little. I have to assume that, like most of us, Little entered this game afraid of the big inning. Burkett had a wonderfully consistent season for the Red Sox this year. He was the classic wily old veteran. His only problem was that he frequently fell victim to the big inning. Oftentimes it was the first inning. Other times the implosion would come much later, in the fifth or sixth. But almost always it was there. Knowing this, Little had to be prepared to have a quicker hook than a Vaudeville act. His top priority tonight was to make sure Burkett didn't get rocked. And in that effort, he failed.

In the fourth, Posada and Matsui hit one-out singles. Time to worry. Nick Johnson pounded a double to the right-field corner. The ball bounced off a fan's hands, which held Matsui at third, but Posada scored. Now was the time to go out and get Burkett. But Little left him in to pitch to Aaron Boone. This guy has been awful! And he was again, grounding out to short as the Yankees' third run of the game came across.

Now there were two outs, and Nick Johnson was on second base. It looked as if Little might get away with leaving Burkett out there. This was, after all, the "Geezer Series." Thirty-seven-year-old Tim Wakefield had two wins. Forty-one-year-old Roger Clemens and 40-year-old David Wells each had victories for the Yankees. Why couldn't 38-year-old John Burkett come up big today?

Nomar Garciaparra's error certainly didn't help. Karim Garcia hit an easy ground ball to short. As rough a time as Nomar's had at the plate in the postseason, his fielding had been excellent—until now. As Nomar rolled to his left, he hunched over and put his glove down almost on the ground. The ball jumped up, landing half-in and half-out of his glove, and the half-out part won the battle. The ball fell to the dirt, and the inning continued. Alfonso Soriano drove the very next pitch into the left-center-field gap, and the Yankees had taken a 5-4 lead. Now Little came out to get Burkett.

Bronson Arroyo came in and threw four balls out of the strike zone, walking Derek Jeter. Runners were now on first and second with Giambi coming up. A blast would put the game out of reach. A left-handed reliever might have been more effective here, but Arroyo was left alone on the hill. Giambi worked the count full, and then Arroyo got him swinging. That was a big out, the kind that's often forgotten once everybody's gone home, but in this case, it kept the Red Sox within striking distance.

The Sox had a similar situation in the fifth. Mueller was up again with runners on first and second. A base hit would have tied the game, but Mueller's struggles continued. He struck out.

Primarily because of that four-run third inning, Pettitte's pitch count was rather high (92) after five innings. As mentioned, Torre only needs to play seven-inning games in the postseason, because he knows that Mariano Rivera will take care of the rest. So, when Jorge Posada homered to left off Arroyo in the fifth inning to make it a 6-4 Yankees lead, Torre decided to go to his bullpen. The plan was to get two innings out of Jose Contreras and the final two from Rivera.

Contreras had already made three appearances in this series, going 3 1/3 innings without allowing a run, and striking out four. There was reason for Torre to be confident. And the move seemed to work when Contreras came in, firing off a bunch of nasty splitters, and struck out the side in the sixth. Doesn't this just make all the sense in the world? The guy the Red Sox lost out on to the Yankees during the winter is about to be the guy who shuts them down in the ALCS. Son of a gun!

The Yankees looked to extend their lead in the sixth inning against the third Red Sox pitcher of the afternoon, Todd Jones. Jones struck out Garcia, but then Soriano and Jeter reached on a single and a walk, respectively. The door to the Red Sox bullpen opened again, and this time Alan Embree walked through.

The Red Sox were using a severe shift in the infield against Giambi. Mueller moved into the shortstop position, while Garciaparra went to the first base side of second, and Walker played on the outfield grass. This appeared to make it easy for a runner to steal third base, because he'd probably be able to beat Mueller to the bag. The Yankees had had other opportunities in the series to take advantage of that defense, but hadn't done so. They probably didn't want to risk taking the bat out of Giambi's hands, but he's struggled so much, Torre probably wouldn't mind if someone else swung the bat. So, on the first pitch, the runners took off. Neither drew a throw. Runners were on second and third now, so if the Sox wanted to walk Giambi, first base was open. But with the switch-hitting Bernie Williams on deck, Embree continued to pitch to Giambi. Embree struck him out and got Williams to ground to third. Inning over. The Yankees still led, 6-4, but they had blown a good chance to put this one away.

With Contreras looking dominant yet again, and Rivera waiting in the wings, a two-run deficit felt insurmountable. The Red Sox hadn't been able to get anything going offensively since the third inning. And the crowd at Yankee Stadium made it very difficult to remain optimistic. Then Nomar led off the seventh with a deep drive to center field. Those gusty winds that continued to blow since before the game carried his ball to the base of the wall. It caromed hard past Williams, but Matsui was backing up the play and quickly scooped up the ball. He wheeled and fired in the general direction of third base, but this was a clear-cut case of ineffective hustle. Matsui never stopped to look at third base, opting to throw based on his memory of where the base would be. Garciaparra was going into third base standing up when he noticed Matsui's throw had missed its mark by a good 30 feet and bounced into the left-field stands. Garciaparra was awarded home plate on the triple and the error. The crowd barely reacted, but a moment or two later I thought to myself, "Hey, idiot! It's a one-run game in the seventh inning. Get back into this thing!"

I was an idiot. Not the good kind, though, like a happy idiot. I had become a doubting, pessimistic idiot. But I snapped out of it in time to see Manny Ramirez drive a ball to about the same area Nomar's had gone. He coasted into second base with a double, then moved to third on a wild pitch. Contreras had only thrown three pitches in the inning. Two of them went to the wall; the other went to the backstop. And the tying run was 90 feet away, with nobody out.

There are a whole bunch of ways to bring a man home from third base with nobody out. Ortiz chose to bounce the ball off the first base bag for a rare infield single. The game was tied, and the inning continued.

After Kevin Millar flied out, Mueller contributed (finally) with a base hit up the middle. Torre came out to get a dejected Contreras and brought in his left-hander, Felix Heredia, to face Trot Nixon. Nixon would eventually strike out, but the 2-1 pitch to him was another wild one, and the runners advanced to second and third. So, with Nixon out of the way, Heredia was told to intentionally walk Varitek. This would load the bases, but it would also allow Heredia to face another left-handed hitter, Johnny Damon. But Damon never got to hit. No, Little didn't bring in a right-handed bat like Gabe Kapler or David McCarty. Damon didn't get to hit, because Heredia never threw him a strike. Four straight balls forced in the go-ahead run. The Red Sox led, 7-6.

Todd Walker struck out to end the inning, but the Red Sox had batted around. Torre had tried to shrink the game from nine to seven to five innings, but it hadn't worked, because Contreras hadn't gotten the job done. Torre also intentionally loaded the bases, leaving Heredia with no room for error. That's the same Heredia who had thrown a wild pitch earlier in the inning, and who walked 33 batters in 87 innings during the regular season.

Since Burkett had only lasted 3 1/3 innings, this game was going to be left up to the Red Sox bullpen. That really meant Embree, Mike Timlin, and Scott Williamson. Embree took care of the seventh. In the eighth, the Yankees got a runner to second against Timlin, but he got Jeter to ground out to third. Mueller bobbled the ball momentarily, but threw a hard strike to first *just* in time to get Jeter.

The Red Sox made it a little easier on Williamson by getting two insurance runs in the top of the ninth. After Mueller doubled off Jeff Nelson, Torre went to the pen for another lefty to face Nixon. Nixon quickly fell behind, 0-2, but after watching a pitch out off the plate, Nixon blasted the next one deep to right. It was a bomb! And it took the life out of the Yankees.

"They took our game," said Posada. "Coming into the ninth inning, we had a good feeling about it. But they took that feeling away."

In the ninth, Williamson struck out Giambi and induced two fly balls to center field. The Red Sox won, 9-6, and evened the series at three games apiece.

Little added, "I've never been around a club quite like this."

And it's true. To come back and win three in a row against Oakland, and then go to New York, fall behind, and come back to win a fourth straight elimination game says something very special about this Red Sox team.

"I guess it was supposed to come down to Game Seven," Torre said. Millar concurred, "The gods of baseball wanted to see this happen."

And the gods must *not* be crazy. Because this is the best of what baseball has to offer. Game Seven between the Yankees and the Red Sox with Pedro Martinez going against Roger Clemens. What more needs to be said? All you can do is watch it unfold before your eyes, smiling all the while, and trying to remember every moment of it.

With one out to go, several fans in my section began chanting, "We want Pedro!" And then one man, quite unabashedly considering there was a police officer standing only a few feet away, said, "Yeah, and he better be wearing a helmet."

The lingering effects of Game Three's extracurricular activities are very much alive in the minds of Yankees fans. Let's hope cooler heads prevail tomorrow, so that one of baseball's best and most historical events can go off without any security issues. The fans and players really need to control themselves.

OCTOBER 16: GAME SEVEN

No one has tasted champagne in the visitor's dugout at Yankee Stadium since the Dodgers in 1981. Tonight, the Red Sox get their chance. It would be payback for Yankees celebrations at Fenway Park in 1978 and 1999, and it would bring them to their first World Series since 1986.

"In Pedro We Trust." That's what this all boils down to. This will be his defining moment, more so than his relief appearance against the Indians in 1999, or the duel that never really materialized against Clemens in those same playoffs. This is Game Seven, baby! They don't get any bigger than this. If Pedro can carry the Red Sox past the Yankees and into the World Series, he will be immortalized. If he fails, he will be remembered first and foremost for that failure. He knows this, which is why I believe he'll come up big. He is a man of destiny on a team that goes by the same name. He knows he needs to come up much bigger than he did in his first three starts this postseason—21 innings, 10 runs, 19 hits, six walks, and only 15 K's. That's a 4.29 ERA, or just over two runs *more* than his regular season ERA. Pedro has been pedestrian. Tonight, he needs to spread his wings and fly.

The first indication of change around the ballpark occurred in the media room, where there was an uncommon fervor to the more common rumblings. The name "Giambi" leaped out of conversations as I walked through the interview room to get a soda. I happened to glance at the chalkboard where the lineups were posted. Scanning quickly down the Yankees names, it was easy to notice a lineup shakeup. Jason Giambi had been dropped to number seven in the order. Giambi had struck out three times yesterday and five times in his last 15 at bats against Red Sox pitching, but he was still the most feared hitter in the Yankees lineup. With 41 home runs during the regular season, Giambi had become the first Yankee since Mickey Mantle to have back-to-back 40-home-run seasons.

The Giambi drop took some attention away from the night's pitching matchup. Pedro and the Rocket would meet for the third time in the postseason. The first game went to Pedro in 1999, and the second one went to Clemens five days ago. This would be like Ali versus Frasier! They fought three times, each match living up to its hype. And no matter what happened under the bright lights of the city tonight, this game will certainly be remembered and talked about for a long, long time.

Clemens came out shaky. That was obvious when he got two strikes on Todd Walker but couldn't finish him off. After 10 pitches, Walker finally laced a single to center. It's always a sign of trouble when a power pitcher, or a strikeout pitcher, can't find a pitch to punch a guy out. Despite Walker's being stranded at second, I felt good.

Pedro came out and struck out Alfonso Soriano on four pitches. His second pitch to Nick Johnson (batting second in the revised lineup) was a bit inside and about neck high. That elicited a fair number of boos, but it looked identical to the kind of message pitch that Clemens had thrown Manny Ramirez in Game Three. Just "up" enough, and just "in" enough, to let the hitters know that he wasn't about to change his pitching style, but not too far up or in to get in trouble with the home plate umpire.

Johnson walked, and Bernie Williams rapped a two-out single. That brought Hideki Matsui to the plate with runners on first and second. With the count full, Matsui flied harmlessly to center field.

Further evidence that Clemens just didn't have all the right stuff for this one came in the second inning, when Trot Nixon hit a line drive to right-center field. The ball was hit too hard to come down too soon. The ball sailed over the wall for Nixon's third home run in four games, and his fourth of the postseason. It was a two-run homer, and the Red Sox led, 2-0. I thought for a moment, "Will that be enough?"

The question was no longer pertinent after the Red Sox tacked on another run. Jason Varitek doubled with two outs. Then Johnny Damon hit a ground ball to third. Enrique Wilson gloved it, but instead of throwing immediately to first to get Damon, he attempted to tag Varitek going from second to third. Varitek avoided the tag, so Wilson had to hurry his throw. It went wide of first base, and Varitek came around to score. The Red Sox were on top, 3-0. Sometimes that's all they need when Pedro is on the hill.

Clemens retired the Red Sox in order in the third, but his very first pitch of the fourth inning was given a nice, long ride by Kevin Millar. It was a high fly ball down the left-field line, clearing the fence just to the right of the foul pole. (By the way, can we put a stop to the nonsense about whether it's a foul pole or a fair pole? It's the only pole out there. So, can't we just drop the adjective and call them the left- and right-field poles?)

Not satisfied with their newfound 4-0 lead, the Red Sox went after more. Clemens walked Nixon as Mike Mussina started warming up in the bullpen. Mussina, of course, had just pitched three days ago, but he was the best pitcher available—and there's no tomorrow for the losing team. The Red Sox executed a perfect hit and run, with Bill Mueller doing the hitting and Nixon running to third on the base hit. Runners were on the corners with nobody out, and the Yankees were already down four runs. Their season was evaporating. One or two more hits could just about put this away!

Torre made the move for Mussina. Clemens left to a standing ovation. No one knew if the last strikeout he ever recorded was against Bill Mueller, or if the last base hit he ever surrendered was to Bill Mueller. Clemens left with a line of three innings pitched, four runs, three earned runs, and six hits. And people wondered, "Is that it for Clemens?"

This time Mussina got Varitek to strike out. And this is where I was hoping Grady Little might go slightly unconventional. Johnny Damon, a man who can handle the bat, was up, with runners on first and third. The Red Sox weren't playing for a big inning. They were playing to extend their lead. If they could just push a run across here and a run across there, the lead would eventually become insurmountable against Pedro. So, why not have Damon squeeze? Nixon would score, and Mueller would advance to second. There would still be a runner in scoring position, and the Red Sox would have a five-run lead. I liked the idea when I thought of it, but figured that Little was banking on Damon being fast enough to stay out of the double play, so he'd let him swing away. Damon hit the ball right at Derek Jeter, who stepped on second and threw to first for the inning-ending double play. It was a simply magnificent job by Mussina to get out of that inning without any further damage.

The Red Sox had another chance to pad their lead in the fifth. Nomar and Manny had one-out singles, putting runners on first and second for David Ortiz. But Ortiz struck out swinging, and Kevin Millar grounded to short, ending the threat.

Meanwhile, Pedro was making quick work of the Yankees. He had a two-hit shutout through four innings, but the first pitch he threw in the fifth was one that Giambi liked very much. Giambi lifted it high, deep, and gone to right center, and the score was 4-1. All three hits against Pedro had been by left-handed batters.

Mussina was immense for the New Yorkers. He got them through the middle innings, allowing just two hits in three innings. Now, instead of being ruined by a starting pitcher who only goes three innings, the Yankees had made it through six innings and only trailed by three runs. Mussina had given them hope. And Pedro gave them a little more when he gave up a two-out home run to Giambi in the seventh inning. It was a 2-2 pitch. Pedro was one strike away from retiring the side in order. Instead, it was 4-2, and the tension was building.

Enrique Wilson followed the Giambi blast with a high chopper to first. Millar gloved it while moving to his left into foul ground. An easy flip to Pedro covering first would have ended the inning, but Millar felt he could get to the bag himself—until he inexplicably slipped and fell. Can you believe that?

Karim Garcia followed with a sharply hit ball into right field, putting runners on first and second and bringing the go-ahead run to the plate. If Pedro was feeling the pressure, he wasn't showing it. His face was flat and emotionless as Soriano came to bat. Pedro was determined not to let his defining moment end in failure. He reared back and fired his 100th pitch of the night for *strike three* past Soriano. Pedro looked to the heavens with his right hand on his heart, and then pointed skyward. He received several congratulatory hugs from his teammates in the dugout. The Red Sox were six outs away from a trip to the World Series.

In the eighth, things got even brighter when Joe Torre may have been guilty of overmanaging just a bit. With one out, he brought in David Wells to pitch to Ortiz. Wells is 40 years old and likes to think he's been blessed with a rubber arm, but he pitched seven innings just two days ago. Ortiz homered on the first pitch he saw from Wells. That felt like the final nail.

But to the surprise of many, Pedro returned to the hill for the eighth inning. The game seemed perfectly set up for the new and vastly improved Red Sox bullpen. Once as untrustworthy as a kleptomaniac at a yard sale, the Sox bullpen had become a strength during the playoffs. Since the second game of the Oakland series, the bullpen had only allowed two runs in its last 25 innings.

But Little chose to go with his ace, and that decision left an indelible imprint on this historic series. Primarily, because it didn't work.

Pedro began the inning by getting Nick Johnson to pop to short. After two quick strikes to Jeter, the Yankees shortstop drove a ball deep to right. Nixon barely missed it as it one-hopped the wall, and Jeter stood on second. Again Pedro got two strikes on the hitter, but Bernie Williams was able to rap a single to center field, scoring Jeter with the Yankees' third run.

Five of the last seven Yankees batters had gotten a hit, and Pedro's pitch count stood at 115. He was still throwing in the low 90's, but like Clemens earlier in the game, he wasn't able to finish off the hitters. Alan Embree was loose in the bullpen and waiting for Little to touch his left arm on his way out to the mound. This was the time to take Pedro out and let Embree pitch to

Hideki Matsui. But Little never emerged from the dugout.

Matsui looked at the first two pitches, both strikes. Then Pedro threw him one on the inner half of the plate, and Matsui turned on it and rifled it down the right-field line. It one-hopped into the stands along the foul line for a ground rule double. The tying run was now at second base with one out.

Now, Little came out of the dugout—jogging, actually. But he was facing a dilemma. Posada, a switch-hitter, was the next batter. (Personally, I'm not a big fan of bringing Embree in to face Posada on the right side.) So the choice was either stay with Pedro, or bring Mike Timlin in, with Posada batting from the left. Keep in mind, the right-field porch is only 314 feet away at Yankee Stadium, and a home run would put the Yankees ahead. As well as Timlin has pitched in the postseason (*zero* runs, and only one hit in 9 2/3 innings), he did give up 11 home runs in 72 innings during the regular season. Perhaps that was something to consider. Still, Pedro's pitch count was rising and at the time stood at 118. So, should Little stick with his ace, or go to his newly reliable setup man? Moments like these on the mound are the stuff of legend.

"He asked me if I had enough bullets in my tank to get him out and I said yes; I would never say no," Martinez said. "I tried hard. I did whatever was possible to win the ball game."

Little had asked Pedro if he had enough to get out of the jam, and Pedro had said he did. So Little left his tiring and struggling ace out there to stare into the belly of the beast alone. With a double pat on Pedro's right shoulder, Little hustled off the mound.

"Pedro Martinez has been our man all year long and in situations like that, he's the one we want on the mound over anybody we can bring out of the bullpen," said Little. "He had enough left in his tank to finish off Posada. He made some good pitches to him, and (Posada) squeezed his ball over the infield and there's nothing we can do about it now."

That's exactly right. Posada lofted a 2-2 pitch into shallow center field. Damon, Nomar, and Walker were converging like an ever- shrinking isosceles triangle, but the ball landed equidistant from each of them. If the ball had carried 15 feet further, Damon would have had it; 15 feet left or right, and one of the infielders would have tracked it down. Had that happened, there would have been two outs with runners on second and third. So many "ifs," but two runs scored on the broken-bat blooper, and the game was tied at 5-5. Pedro gave up hits to seven of the last nine Yankees he faced. All four hits in the eighth inning came with two strikes. The second-guessing was immediate concerning Little's decision to leave Pedro in the game. But Pedro should have been out there, and he should have been able to get the job done.

Clearly, there was reason to believe that the best pitcher on the planet could get three more outs without giving up three more runs.

"I wouldn't put Grady on the spot whatsoever," he said. "I am the ace of the team. You have to trust me. I wasn't really thinking about pitch counts. This is no time to say I'm tired. There is no reason to blame Grady. He doesn't play the game. We do. I do."

And there was plenty more game to be played. In fact, there was plenty more happening in the eighth inning. Pedro was finally lifted after the Posada hit. Posada, by the way, made it all the way to second base. He was there as Embree came in to get Giambi on a fly ball to center field. Timlin came in to pitch to Wilson, but Torre sent up his left-handed pinch hitter, Ruben Sierra, instead. So, Timlin intentionally walked him in order to pitch to Karim Garcia. But Timlin was unusually careful with Garcia and walked him on four pitches. Suddenly, the bases were loaded for Soriano.

He shot one back through the box. The ball hit the pitching rubber and deflected to Walker, who got the force out at second base to end the inning. The Red Sox had been five outs away from the World Series, but now they had to try to regroup and rally after a shocking turn in the eighth inning.

But that's an especially difficult thing to do against Mariano Rivera. Torre didn't waste any time going to "Mr. Automatic." Rivera started the ninth having given up only eight runs in 89 postseason innings. During the Yankees' remarkable run since 1996, Rivera has 25 saves, a record of 6-1, and a 0.79 ERA in the playoffs. So far this postseason, he's had four two-inning saves. And he was being called upon to buy the Yankees enough time to win their 39th American League pennant. And he did.

Timlin pitched the ninth, and Tim Wakefield pitched a 1-2-3 10th. Wakefield was the wild card as the game went into extra innings. Rivera's time was limited to two, maybe three, innings, but Wakefield could go on forever. At some point, this game would turn in the Red Sox favor, because the Yankees bullpen was full of ineffective relievers. If Wakefield could outlast Rivera, the Red Sox could still trust in Williamson. I still believed this was a team of destiny, but nothing comes easily for these guys. Remember all those late-inning losses during the regular season? Remember the Oakland series? Remember, they came to New York needing to win two games. So, Pedro's collapse couldn't take the fight out of these guys. It was a stunningly disappointing development, but going into extra innings, the Red Sox had the advantage—as soon as Rivera couldn't go anymore.

But Rivera kept on pitching. He made his first three-inning appearance since September of 1996. His 48th pitch got Doug Mirabelli to strike out looking to end the 11th inning. The Yankees, who got only three sub-par innings from Clemens when this game started, had worked their way through the 11th with three outstanding innings apiece from Mussina and Rivera.

And then it ended!

It was so fast, so furious!

The first pitch of the home half of the 11th inning was a knuckleball down and in that went up and out in a hurry. Aaron Boone turned on it, and some 55,000 pairs of eyes turned to watch it sail high and far down the left-field line. Tim Wakefield's eyes were not among those who watched. He glanced quickly over his shoulder, then turned and headed for the dugout long before the ball ended up in the hands of Rick Peterson, a 47-year-old Yankees fan from Manhattan. The Yankees had taken Game Seven of the ALCS from the Red Sox, 6-5, in 11 innings.

It was the biggest home run in New York since Bobby Thompson's "shot heard round the world" in 1951. And something tells me Aaron Boone may soon be getting a new middle name—the same one given to Bucky Dent 25 years ago.

Many of these Yankees already own four World Series championship rings, yet they claimed that beating the Red Sox in this seven-game series was bigger and sweeter than anything else they've accomplished.

Rivera, who ran out to the mound and collapsed in a bowing gesture during Boone's home run trot, said, "We were down by four runs. Buddy, you can't forget that!"

And Torre added this perspective, "To play them 26 times and beat our rival like we did, it couldn't be more satisfying. This has to be the sweetest taste of all for me."

That tells you all you need to know about this rivalry and the intensity of this series.

From the Red Sox we heard:

There was a lot of joy to remember this season. I think Red Sox Nation will be proud, and is proud of this team, and will remember it for a long time.
—Red Sox president Larry Lucchino.

I think this team is terrific. I don't think there was a better team in baseball than this team, to be honest with you. We ran out of chances and opportunities to show what we were made of. This team, they were really mature in the way that they handled it. They were hurting and disappointed, but they also held their heads high and supported one another in really tough times.

—Red Sox GM Theo Epstein.

It hurts. All I have to say is, 'I'm sorry.' It's disappointing to come in here knowing that we're going home tomorrow. I feel like I let everyone down.

—Tim Wakefield.

I'm just proud of these guys. I'm proud to be a Boston Red Sox. We just fell short.

—Jason Varitek.

The Red Sox, who pulled out 25 victories in their final at bat this year, including the postseason, were victimized by similar dramatics. In the end, Boone, who didn't even start the game because he was swinging the bat so poorly, was the fundamental instrument that did the baseball gods' bidding. As they had in 1949 and in 1978, the Yankees ended the Red Sox season with their own hands, but this one hurt the most. This one came in extra innings, at Yankee Stadium, and it prevented the Red Sox from getting to the World Series. Dent's home run was in the seventh inning, and it kept the Red Sox from going to the playoffs. Boone's blast was a walk-off homer in a Game Seven. Time will heal this wound. But it's going to take a long, long time.

But anyone heaping all the blame on Little didn't pay attention when Pettitte was let off the hook in Game Two, or when Nomar (one RBI in the postseason) and Manny batted with runners in scoring position against David Wells in Game Five, or when Pedro was outpitched by Roger in Game Three. A hit here, or a hit there, or Pedro's coming out in Game Three like he was supposed to, and this series never would have gone seven games. This entire Red Sox team contributed to a wonderful season. They all contributed to the wins, and they all played their part in the losses, Little included. But to blame one person would be an ignorant oversimplification.

OCTOBER 17

Fenway Park—the day after it all came crashing down. There were a few players straggling in to finish cleaning out their lockers, picking up whatever they had left behind when they arrived early in the morning from New York. Red Sox GM Theo Epstein walked briskly past a small gathering of reporters, and blurted that he would be available to talk in about an hour. The field was empty, though a green tarp covered the section behind home plate that had been painted the day before with the 2003 World Series emblem. The paint crews were ready for the World Series to open at Fenway. The fans were ready to overstuff the place. The Red Sox were ready to take on the underdog Florida Marlins. Aaron Boone was not ready.

In the early afternoon, Nomar Garciaparra and his fiancée, soccer star Mia Hamm, arrived with a soccer ball inside a backpack. After all, what do two athletic celebrities do when their seasons are over? They kick the soccer ball around the Fenway Park outfield, that's what. Ah, young love!

Nomar and Mia provided the only discernable energy at the ballpark. Everyone else moved in a slow-motion trance. That included team president and CEO Larry Lucchino, who couldn't mask his disappointment, but spoke glowingly of a wonderful team and a wonderful season.

"Oh, it even hurts a little bit more in the light of day," Lucchino said. "When you wake up the next morning, and you realize just how close we came, it's a rough feeling. I am focusing on the pride and thrill and the excitement and the likeability and appeal of this team. And I'm determined to remember that.

"This was a remarkable group of baseball players. They cared about each other. They truly felt like a band of brothers. I hope we're able to succeed in reassembling a team that has the same personality and character of this one.

"A lot of people will remember it for years. There will be debates and discussions about it for years. There will be this near miss—this miracle on 161st Street—that almost happened if we had gone in there and won the last two games of that series. I hope people will remember more than just the series. They'll remember a tight and tense series and a few plays and decisions to be sure. But I hope they remember more than that. This team brought a lot of joy to a lot of people.

"Our ultimate goal is to win the World Series, and we came extraordinarily close to that this year. But in a few days, people will look back on this season and the thrilling postseason, look at the come-from-behind wins during the year, look at the personalities on this team, and I think they'll remember it with enormous pride."

Neither Lucchino nor Epstein was willing to involve himself in the second-guessing surrounding Grady Little's decision to stay with Pedro Martinez in the eighth inning. To say the least, it was not a popular decision in New England, and Little is not a particularly popular person at this time. The Red Sox have an option on Little's contract for next year, but they never opted to pick it up. It was a two-year audition for Little, and with 93 and 95 wins, and a trip to the ALCS, you might think he passed the audition. But the Red Sox never really threw him their support, and his miscalculated choice to leave Pedro in the game may have cost him his job. In fact, the Red Sox continued silence about his job status speaks volumes. Very few people expect Little to return for 2004. The wound is just too deep, and forgiveness will not come easily.

I asked Epstein if "what happened in the eighth inning would be a factor when deciding what to do with Grady, or if it was too small a snapshot on which to judge him," and he simply said, "I'm not going to answer that question today."

In my mind, that answered the question.

"It was a very, very disappointing game," Epstein went on. "Thought we had the game when David hit that home run. I was thinking about the '49 Red Sox, Ted Williams, Johnny Pesky, Bobby Doerr, the 1978 team, and all the other great Red Sox teams that couldn't beat the Yankees. We were going to do this for them.

"It was a successful regular season. But the postseason was an incredible ride; just thrill after thrill. But we didn't win our last game. That's what we didn't do. We didn't beat the Yankees and we didn't win the World Series, and that was our ultimate goal. But in life you don't always get the result you're looking for. It hurts. But some time later, you can look back and really enjoy the journey.

"I think our team is good enough to win the World Series, but it didn't happen this year. That's why you need to create an organization that can sustain success year after year. Looking back on it, that might be our greatest accomplishment. Management changed the tone and substance of the organization. And we need to get in there every single year, so that someday we'll win it.

"Give us a couple of years; that's all we're going to need. This was my first year, and I'm proud of what we accomplished. Just give us a couple more years."

Sure, what's a couple more years on top of 85 anyway?

OCTOBER 18

The heat is on! But Grady Little refuses to feel the burn. There is now a "Killer B's" lineage connecting Red Sox heartache. Call it Bucky, Buckner, and Boone. But a disproportionate number of Red Sox fans would prefer to talk about the "G-Force"—Grady. After the seventh game, it's time to play the blame game. And Grady Little is the winner for being the loser. But Little remains unfazed by the criticism, and intractable about his decision.

"Pedro was throwing as well in that seventh and eighth inning as he had the whole game," Little said. "We don't have instant radar readings, but we do have what we're seeing, and we saw a guy who had a lot of life in his arm and he wanted to be out there. There wasn't a lot of conference between us at that time, but my decision to leave him in there was not much different than in the two years I've been here with Pedro. When he gets into a jam, he's the one I want out there to get out of that jam more than anyone else. If people want to judge Grady Little on the results of a decision I made in that last game the other day, so be it. In my heart, I know we had a great season here."

Grady's right, of course. But he was wrong to leave Pedro in the game—at least it turned out to be the wrong decision. But perhaps enough time has passed to allow cooler heads to calmly sort through the evidence and reach a conclusion objectively, instead of emotionally. Yes, as it turned out, Grady Little made the wrong move. In all probability, he may have made the wrong move as many as four times (letting Pedro Martinez start the eighth inning, then leaving him in after each of the three straight hits). But Grady Little, as he likes to call himself, did not make the "worst managerial decision" of all time. He did not "cost the Red Sox a trip to the World Series." And he is not dumber than you, or you, or you, or you, or you, or me.

First, if you simply divide the number of Pedro's pitches thrown by the number of his starts, you'll see that Pedro averaged 98 pitches. So, the obvious question would be, why would you throw Pedro out there for the eighth inning when he had already thrown 100 pitches, more than his average? Well, by definition, average means there were starts in which Pedro threw more than 98 pitches and starts in which he threw fewer.

For example, there was the shelling against Baltimore in which Pedro only lasted 4 1/3 innings. He was pulled after five ineffective innings against Minnesota, and that was followed by a six-inning start in which the Red Sox were pounding the Rangers 12-3. Then when he returned from injury, he went just three and five innings in his first two starts back. And of course, there was his bout with "pharyngitis fatigue" and his three-inning tuneup on the final weekend of the season against Tampa Bay. So, yes, Pedro averaged 98 pitches per start this year, but if you take out the short outings due to injury, sickness, ineffectiveness, or the final tuneup, then he averaged 106 pitches per start. And I would argue that Game Seven of the League Championship Series is not an "average" start. We were looking for an above-average performance.

And look more closely at the end of the year. In Pedro's last three starts (excluding the tune-up), he threw 116, 122, and 115 pitches. It's clear that the Red Sox babied him all year in an attempt to build him up so that he would be rested, yet strong, for the postseason. He, not Grady, let them down. Pedro threw 130 pitches in Game One against Oakland, getting himself out of a bases-loaded jam in the seventh. Yes, it was the seventh inning as opposed to the eighth, but you should be counting pitches, not innings. Pitches make a pitcher tired, not the number of times he goes and sits on the bench between innings.

Pedro followed up that 130-pitch effort with games of 100 and 98 pitches, so he should have been fully recovered from any residual effects of that start. Also consider that Pedro's postseason ERA going into Game Seven was 4.29. He was a *huge* disappointment. But for seven innings on the biggest stage, he was finally at least resembling the Pedro who had led the American League in ERA.

So there were two ways for Grady to assess the situation. Either Pedro had been underachieving throughout the postseason, and he got hit a little bit there in the seventh (two legit hits, and a bouncer to first that Millar tripped into a hit), so he better take him out. Or, he was finally pitching like Pedro, and he'd only thrown 100 pitches, so let's keep it going. Little's decision looks bad because of the results, but to suggest it was the move of an idiot is the suggestion of an idiot who wasn't paying attention all season long.

To send the best pitcher in baseball to the hill and expect him to hold a three-run lead is not lunacy. Only the lunatic fringe would argue otherwise. It should be clear to all that Grady at least had a reason. In fact, he had several reasons. And therefore, what he did was reasonable. But to fire him for one move that didn't work out, no matter how big the stage, would be unreasonable.

One statistic that has been thrown around, but not delved into, is that opposing batters hit .230 against Pedro on pitches 85 to 100, but from 101 to 120, they hit .370. This is intended to prove that Pedro was either incapable of getting the job done in the eighth, or unlikely to do so. But if Pedro had given up two hits and gotten three batters out in the eighth, the Yankees would have gone two-for-five for a batting average of .400, and Pedro would have gotten out of the inning without any trouble. Instead, the Yankees went four-for-five, for a batting average of .800. Was Grady supposed to have foreseen that kind of John Burkett-like collapse?

Twice against the Yankees during the regular season, Pedro went well up over 100 pitches. He threw 115 on July 7, and 128 on July 25. And in his 128-pitch complete game against Anaheim on August 6, he struck out the side in the eighth; his last pitch that inning was his 108th. Every hit against Pedro in the eighth inning of Game Seven came with two strikes. His fastball was cruising in at 92 to 95 miles per hour. He still had command of the strike zone, and he hadn't lost his velocity. So, Grady stuck with him. While that turned out to be the wrong move, it wasn't stupid.

Little had asked Pedro if he still had "enough bullets in the tank." And despite the mixed metaphor, Pedro assured his manager he could get the job done. Many people grumble, "What is he supposed to say?" as if there's a place for false bravado in the field of competition. If an athlete believes his performance will hurt the team, he's supposed to say so. It's not cowardice to ask out if it's in the team's best interest. Anything else is foolish pride.

If Pedro wanted to stay in to protect his reputation or image, but knew he didn't have anything left, then his pride cost the Red Sox a trip to the World Series. And if he truly believed he could get the Yankees in the eighth, then it was merely the Yankees' abilities and clutch performances that bit the Red Sox in the rear. And that's not only easier to swallow, it makes Little's decision a bit more defensible. The best pitcher in the game said, "Give me the ball." Little could have taken it from him, but he believed in his ace as much as his ace believed in himself. It just didn't work out.

Would a call to the bullpen have worked? Probably. Should Pedro Martinez have been able to get three more outs before three more runs scored? Definitely. I like to think the Yankees won that game with great performances from Mike Mussina, Mariano Rivera, and Jason Giambi. The Killer B's didn't slay the Red Sox through the years. One- and seven-game playoffs are much bigger than one individual. Baseball is too complex to break a game down to a singular moment and assess blame. But there's little doubt that Little's done as manager of the Red Sox.

Earlier in these pages, I wrote, "I don't criticize the Red Sox for feeling they have to baby their fragile superstar. What bothers me is that Pedro allows it. What scares me is that Pedro has become so obsessed with his own health that he won't put himself at risk—*ever*. Here's the nightmare: Game Seven of the World Series. Pedro's pitching a beauty. But with all his strikeouts and a couple of early-inning jams, he's thrown 121 pitches through seven innings. There's still no score in the game. Pedro doesn't come out for the eighth inning."

In my hypothetical, I was afraid that the Red Sox and Pedro would co-conspire to continue to baby their ace, and leave the game in someone else's hands. And in that nightmare, Pedro's pitch count was at 121. The reality was he had thrown only 100 pitches. I wanted Pedro to come out for the eighth inning. And I remain convinced that he should have been able to hold the lead. I'm disappointed in the results, but at least I know the Yankees won that game by beating the best. That's the game, and that's when superstars are asked to rise to the challenge. Grady Little asked Pedro to rise. But the Red Sox fell.

I began this diary believing the Red Sox were a team of destiny—destined to win the World Series for the first time in 85 years. But that destiny was derailed. This *was* a team of destiny. But they were merely destined to entertain, to inspire, to galvanize a region, and to be remembered.

I don't know how history will remember this Red Sox team. I only hope it will be kind. This was a special group of players who were carried warmly in the hearts of those who watched them, cheered for them, and ultimately cried with them. I don't really know the character of the 1978 Red Sox, nor do I remember all the special moments that lifted the 1986 Red Sox into the World Series. History only reminds me of Bucky Dent and Bill Buckner. Those are tales that are both sad and incomplete. And I fear that history will remain equally unkind to Grady Little. For History is a convincing soul. The story she tells grows stronger as she grows older. Details fade, leaving only general truths to remain self-evident. Only time will be able to tell us what history chooses to remember about the 2003 Boston Red Sox. I hope the memories are sweet—right up to the bitter end.

Aaaarrggh! We were so close!

Damn, it hurts. But it's nice to know my chances of living past the age of 44 have increased dramatically—if you believe in that sort of thing.